ARRESTED DEVELOPMENT

A VETERAN POLICE CHIEF SOUNDS OFF
ABOUT PROTEST, RACISM, CORRUPTION
AND THE SEVEN STEPS NECESSARY TO
IMPROVE OUR NATION'S POLICE

DAVID C. COUPER

D1528463

ISBN 13: 9798781963997

DEDICATION

For Sabine

police officer partner unsurpassed
friend colleague
love of my life

For Christine

nurse
in whom I found
unsurpassed
love and purpose
once again

"Every valuable human being must be a radical and a rebel, for what he must aim at is to make things better than they are."

Niels Bohr (1885-1962), Danish physicist

"Our nation's critics make our country a better place to live tomorrow. It is precisely those who stand up and define an existing social problem or condition who pave the way to the ultimate solution of a problem or condition."

Police Chief David Couper
West High School Graduation Madison, WI.
June 1973

Contents

Introductions

The Third Edition

Much has transpired in American policing since the first publication of this book in 2012. There was the Occupy Movement (during the book's final stages in 2011), the killing of Michael Brown in 2014, and then our nation (and a good part of the world) raised its collective conscience after watching George Floyd's death in 2020. This focus on Floyd's death continued to conviction of Minneapolis Police Officer Derek Chauvin the following year.

If American policing should have learned anything during this decade of police uses of force is that the way things are being done are not producing their intended result: using force to quell an assembly of relatively peaceful protesters does not work and killing an inordinate number of Black youths does not bring about their compliance (let alone their trust and support).

A style of policing that depends on the threat of deadly force is not one that should exist in a free and democratic political system; especially one that is becoming more and more diverse and less and less white.

What I have proposed to improve, even transform, policing is a style that is harmonious with the national values we proclaim as "we the people."

We developed this system of policing in Madison, Wisconsin through the early 1970s and into the 1990s. It is a system of delivering democratic, community-oriented police services in a city of a quarter of a million residents in which, where approximately 10 percent of the population are citizens of color. Nearby, 40,000 students attend the University of Wisconsin.

Madison was and is a progressive city which considers itself quite liberal. Yet a recent study of Madison and Dane County, called "Race to Equity,"[1] revealed that all is not well in Mad City. Instead, the report uncovered

> *...the pervasiveness and the extremity of the county's black-white disparities, which are generally more extreme than those found in most other jurisdictions across the state and nation. There is not a single indicator that we analyzed in which African American well-being is on par with that of whites. In many ways, of course, this should not be unexpected. The hard truth is that African Americans fare worse than whites on virtually all status indicators in virtually every part of the nation. What is extraordinary about Dane County's numbers, however, is the sheer magnitude of the disparities that we found in many of the most fundamental status indicators.*

To many who lived and worked in Madison and Dane County, this was a wake-up call that soon dissipated. The overall community attitude was one of "Yes, things might be difficult for people of color in our city, but we are certainly better than other cities!" This turned out not to be true.

In light of this information and what we are learning about Alexander Hamilton, "redlining," the sheer number of lynchings throughout the country (from Selma to Duluth), the Tulsa massacre, and other race-biased actions is that we live in a racist society that is both historical and present.

It is precisely within that system that our nation's police must operate and must understand and acknowledge how bias (much of it unconscious)

---

1. https://racetoequity.net/wp-content/uploads/2016/11/WCCF-R2E-Report.pdf

affects those of us who call ourselves white and benefit from a racial privilege.

It is possible to cease the bondage in which we put our police who must work in this system and liberate them so they become more effective and supported. Whether we like it or not, police are in a position in our society to either undermine or reinforce the dominate values we profess as a nation: "truth, justice and the American way!" (Which, incidentally, comes from my boyhood and Superman comics!) Nevertheless, the origins of these values are found in our Declaration of Independence and our Constitution. We Americans do believe we are the "good guys" in the world, that our system of government is the best: a "government of the people, by the people and for the people." We can accentuate these values by improving our police.

This has always been my dream. From that spring day in 1960 when a young Marine came off active duty, took an oath of honor, became a police officer, and continued to be one for the next 33 years. We can make our dreams come true. But in order to do that, we must strongly believe in them and persist in making them become real.

The Second Edition – 2017

A LOT HAS HAPPENED IN American policing since 2011 when the first edition of this book was published. It was three years before Michael Brown, Jr. died after being shot by a police officer in Ferguson, Missouri. Many Americans saw an image of his body lying in the street where he bled and died. We saw the yellow tape separating grieving family members and angry neighborhood residents from police casually standing near the crime scene. No cover appears on his body. No officers are seen conversing with area residents. Brown was too long lying on that street. Later we would learn from the Department of Justice how Ferguson policed their many citizens who were of African American descent. I remember reading that they found the basically white police department came to see African

Americans as "sources of revenue," not as a people to be protected and served.[2]

Ferguson became a turning point in American policing as the county SWAT team rolled into Ferguson looking more like an occupying military force with their armored vehicle, automatic rifles, rooftop snipers, and camouflaged uniforms.

Civil disorder, property damage, and arrests followed for many nights. Suddenly cellphone videos flooded YouTube as people all over the country began to record and post what they believed to be improper behavior by police in their cities. Soon, thousands of videos appeared there and on other social media sites; many of them were viewed hundreds of thousands of times within hours of their posting.

During the past two years, we have had a presidential task force that provided America with 59 recommendations for police improvement.[3] Additionally, America's leading police chiefs, members of the Police Executive Research Forum (PERF), issued thirty guidelines on use of force.[4] Any citizen or police officer can access these reports and find within them a way forward for police to build or rebuild trust and support in their communities.

The Four Obstacles described in this book continue to challenge police: Anti-intellectualism, Violence, Corruption, and Disrespect. They apply today as much as they did five years ago when the first edition was published. The same is true for the Seven Steps I describe later in this book. They will help police to continuously and sustainably improve. Anyone in business, industry, or government who stays in place today will soon fall behind. Staying in place is no longer an option. It is unacceptable and, quite frankly, un-American.

2. https://www.justice.gov/sites/default/files/opa/press-releases/attachments/2015/03/04/ferguson_police_department_report.pdf. July 27, 2017; 1020 hrs.

3. http://www.cops.usdoj.gov/pdf/taskforce/taskforce_finalreport.pdf. July 27, 1030 hrs.

4. http://www.policeforum.org/assets/30%20guiding%20principles.pdf. July 27, 1035

The First Edition – 2012

I NEVER THOUGHT I WOULD become a chief of police. I was born in Minnesota in 1938, the eldest of two children. I was raised in the Minneapolis-St. Paul metro area. My father was a car salesman who worked only on commission. My mother, like most mothers at that time, was a stay-at-home mom. I would say that given the swings in our family finances, we were lower than middle class. I remember things like refrigerators and cars being repossessed, late rent payments, and my parents being hounded by bill collectors. We never owned a home.

When I was a kid, I had a drive to organize things and work to improve them. This drive never left me. In middle school, I organized an animal hospital and set up a system for feeding neighborhood stray dogs and cats. Then there was my neighborhood football team. I got local merchants to sponsor us, had numbered jerseys made, and set up a schedule to play other teams. It sounds strange today, but we didn't have a coach, and no parent ever came to one of our games.

I was more a jock than a scholar when I attended University High School in Minneapolis. I played football as a defensive end and wrestled as a light heavyweight. In my senior year, I joined the 4th Infantry Battalion, a local Marine Corps reserve unit. It happened after I saw the 1943 film, *Gung Ho.* It was about the 2nd Marine Raider Battalion in World War II.

The battalion was led by Lt. Col. Evans Carlson (played by Randolph Scott). I'll never forget the speech he gave to his men. It was about the concept of "gung ho." Carlson saw the idea work when he served in China during the 1930s. The Chinese characters "gung" and "ho" mean *work together-work in harmony.*[5]

After graduation in 1956, I went on active duty for four years. I spent

---

5.   Carlson explained in a 1943 interview: "I was trying to build up the same sort of working spirit I had in China where all the soldiers dedicated themselves to one idea and worked together to put that idea over. I told the boys about it again and again. I told them of the motto of the Chinese Cooperatives, Gung Ho. It means Work Together-Work in Harmony." See the 1943 *Life Magazine* article at: http://books.google.com/books December 7, 2011; 0758 hrs.).

two years as a member of the Marine detachment aboard the aircraft carrier *U.S.S. Boxer* in the South Pacific during the hydrogen bomb tests. What I remember most about my sea duty was leading my first amphibious landing. Our sailors on the *Boxer* had been given liberty ashore on nearby Kwajalein Island. I was aboard the carrier as sergeant of the guard when I was called out to break up a fight between our sailors and those from another ship from our battle group. I assembled my guard detachment, outfitted them with batons, and headed to shore in a landing craft.

Landing on the beach, we found most of the fighting over. The only police action was giving first aid to a few of the remaining combatants. It was this amphibious landing that gave me my first taste of police work.

I loved the Marines and wanted more responsibility. I wanted to be an officer, but to be an officer in the Marines, you needed to have a college degree. So I went back home and enrolled in the University of Minnesota.

By this time, I was married with a child and I needed a job. It was obvious to me that with my military background, policing was the answer. What other skills could I possibly need?

That's how I became a cop. I went to school during the day and worked on the beat at night. Like many of my colleagues who joined the police, I had also stumbled into the job.

When I began as a patrol officer in Edina, MN, a suburb of Minneapolis, I wasn't planning on staying. I simply needed a job. But I soon got hooked. Policing was exciting. It was teamwork and it was making things right—doing justice. Just like in *Gung Ho: work together–work in harmony.* My studies in sociology and deviant behavior intermingled with what I was learning as a brand-new cop.

After two years in Edina, I joined the Minneapolis department. I spent seven years there patrolling a beat, training recruit officers, and investigating crimes. I made arrests, got involved in high-speed chases, gave emergency aid at accidents, was shot at (never seriously injured), and helped people— yes, helped them. For the first time, I realized that policing was all about protecting people and their rights.

In 1968, I applied for my first chief's job in Burnsville, MN, another Minneapolis suburb, population 15,000. I had a master's degree in sociology, time in the ranks, and I was eager to be in charge. This time I would be working with a forward-thinking city manager who would let me try out some radical ideas I was developing about police.

First, they could be much better; second, police should always obey the law while enforcing it; third, police should treat everyone they encounter with dignity and respect; fourth, the ranks of police should be more diversified to reflect the communities they serve; fifth (in these times of civil protest), police should always first attempt to handle demonstrators in a soft, persuasive, and gentle manner; and sixth, police officers deserve to work for leaders who treat them as adults, with respect, and listen to them and their ideas.

I didn't encounter civil unrest and protest in Burnsville, but it didn't prevent me from thinking during this time about what I would do if I were a chief in such a situation.

Two opportunities were presented to me in the late '60s. First, would I be interested in leading the campus police at my alma mater, the University of Minnesota? Or would I be interested in applying for the chief's position in Madison, Wisconsin—a city well acquainted with student protest?

The student-faculty selection committee at the University of Minnesota chose me to be their new chief. I had been selected out of a field of candidates that included a chief and a captain from the Minneapolis Police Department. As it turned out, politics were at play, and I never received the appointment.

This left me with the opportunity to apply at Madison. It would be in Madison that I would put my vision for policing into operation over the next 20 years. Changing police takes a long time. I grew to understand that more fully as the years went by.

The Madison police commission wanted peace brought back to their city and to improve police relations with citizens in the community and students on the campus of the University of Wisconsin. They wanted racial minorities and women hired, and improvements in police department operations. Madison was the city that had, since the late 1940s, consistently ranked one of the best cities in America, and the commission expected a police department that reflected that.

It wasn't easy coming to Madison as an outsider at the end of 1972. Soon after I took over command of the department, my assistant chief, Herman Thomas, who created dissension in the ranks, challenged my authority, and ran a covert intelligence operation, actively undermined me. I soon found I had a local version of J. Edgar Hoover to contend with.

My vision for police is that they can be fair, effective, and humanitarian. They can protect our civil rights, work with a variety of people, and take arrested persons into custody with a minimum amount of force. This may differ quite radically from what you may think police should do.

So, what kind of police officer am I talking about? This is what I told citizens who sat on our police selection boards when they asked me that question. Most people don't have a clue about police other than what they have seen on television and in the movies.

I asked them to imagine this scenario: It's after midnight. You are at home waiting for your teenage daughter to return from a date. It's now well past her curfew time. You are thinking about calling the police to report her missing when suddenly she bursts through the front door. She is crying and looks terrible. You notice her blouse has been torn and she has red marks on her face. Your worst fears now have been realized. She has been raped! Now think about the kind of police officer you would like to come into your home and talk with you and your daughter about what happened. That's also the kind of man or woman I would like on the police department.

Five years ago, when I started writing this book, there wasn't much progress going on in policing. It seemed that police were once again in a rut left by that fateful day on September 11, 2001. That day changed just about everything in policing. It changed our nation's police for the worse as they lost their essential role: to protect their citizens and their rights. Rather, they became caught up in "homeland security," outfitted themselves in robot-like body armor, and procured the latest chemical agents and military equipment.

These technological advancements were not only used to control violent people who resist arrest but also those who were not. Often, they are used to punish those who are merely voicing what they think was wrong about our government and its policies—a right guaranteed by our Constitution. What many of us see is a slow but steady shift of our nation's police toward militarization. In 2011, it was most evident in how many police departments responded to the Occupy Wall Street Movement.

Today, I can look back over a half-century of experience working closely with people.

I see police continuing to struggle with four recurring and major obstacles that have literally "arrested" their development:

- Anti-intellectualism.
- Violence.
- Corruption.
- Discourtesy.

Quite frankly, if these obstacles aren't overcome, we are going to experience serious trouble controlling our police. In this book, I specifically identify what's wrong with police today. I also provide an overview of police history and my time in Madison. I believe police can change and I provide seven necessary steps that they need to take to improve. And then I'll tell you about one of the most critical things police do in a free society and how police can do it better—the handling of public protest.

Chapter 1
Stuck in the Rut Again

SOME THINGS PREVENT ORDINARY CITIZENS from even thinking about their police unless they themselves or a loved one has an encounter with them. For most of us who attempt to abide by society's norms, these occurrences are few and far between. But occasionally we have an event or incident that causes us to ask, "What in the world were the police thinking?"

Back in the '60s, it was police dogs, water cannons, and lots of tear gas. More recently, we have seen a variety of police responses to the Occupy Movement in various American cities. Some police responses have been measured and restrained, while others have not.

Now and then, we find an iconic incident like that which happened in November, 2011: a police leader casually walking along a line of students sitting down and linking their arms on the sidewalk on the campus of the University of California at Davis and then spraying them in the face with pepper spray. What was he thinking? And more importantly, how did he and his officers that day understand their job as police officers? Who was being protected and served and who wasn't?

Other events have caught our eyes and ears—widespread law-breaking by police officers involving ticket-fixing, theft, illegal drugs, and trafficking in stolen guns. In other instances, reporters in New York City have been prevented by police from covering public events and demonstrations, and police have actively resisted open-records laws requiring them to release information to the public. And a city newspaper in Milwaukee revealed that far too many police officers continued to work and enforce laws in their city after they had committed crimes that would have resulted in others, who were not police officers, spending time in jail or, at least, being fired from their jobs. Upon my retirement from police, I had imagined our nation's police departments would continue to improve. I especially expected that my own department in Madison, with whom I had worked for over two decades, would continue the path I set of ongoing improvements and continue to serve as a model police department for others.

In fact, many of the innovative policies and practices I put in place—like decentralizing police services, including union representation on the department management team, hiring well-educated and experienced men and women, diversifying the department, and maintaining a sturdy commitment to developing leadership—did carry on.

But other critical practices and approaches didn't. The department didn't continue to randomly survey its customers (those who had used police services or been subject to an encounter with police, including people police had arrested and jailed). Nor did a commitment to systems improvement as taught by Dr. W. Edwards Deming, the renowned professor from the Massachusetts Institute of Technology, remain a part of daily police work, or having both leaders and employees give each other evaluative feedback, so that leaders as well as rank-and-file officers know how they are doing.

When I was chief of police, I made a commitment to share what I was doing in Madison with other police agencies around the country, even internationally. At the time, two professional organizations—the International Association of Chiefs of Police (IACP) and the Police Executive Research Forum (PERF) in Washington, DC—helped me by encouraging me to teach three-day seminars on Quality Leadership and the Madison Experience. During this time, in the mid-1980s, I taught many emerging police leaders throughout the country about what we in Madison were doing. PERF also went on to publish two of my books in which I presented the characteristics of a good police department for citizens and elected officials, and shared what we were doing in Madison.[6]

At the same time, an associate, Herman Goldstein, developer of the problem-oriented policing method, remained a close colleague of mine during the years he taught at the University of Wisconsin Law School in

6. *How to Rate Your Local Police* (1983) and *Quality Policing: The Madison Experience* (1991)

Madison. In 1990, he wrote *Problem-Oriented Policing*,[7] which offered one of the most significant concepts in both American and international policing. Madison, I'm proud to say, was the first department in the country to implement his ideas. For over 20 years there has been an international conference highlighting work police have done using this method. And in 2003, a national center for problem-oriented policing was established in Madison, and its popular website receives over 10,000 inquiries every month. In addition, the center has distributed over 900,000 guides and publications about the method. The guidebooks they publish are peer-reviewed and cover solutions to hundreds of police problems from handling aggressive panhandlers to preventing armed robberies.

Despite this decades-long effort to train and provide resources for police officers and their agencies, the method has yet to be standardized among American police. Links between practitioners and academics in the police field are few and far between. The police field has yet to identify a standard body of knowledge on which both practitioners and academics can build. This has been the primary motivator for me in writing this book. Unless police have these links and learn from and document their experiences, we won't see them rise above the level they are today. And that will be tragic for our nation.

Years ago, as a young police officer, I remember finding myself being profoundly enmeshed in the life of being a cop. I soon realized that my identity, social life, and even family life revolved around me being a cop. I worked every day with police and socialized with them when I was off-duty. My preferred company was other police. I also realized I was closer to the man I was paired with at work—my partner—than I was to the woman to whom I was married. I shared more of my thoughts, feelings, hopes, and dreams with him than I did with her. Each day at work, I trusted my partner with my life. And then I realized that if he did something wrong, I would no more give him up than I would my own mother.

This is the power of a subculture. At the same time, I also felt that being a police officer was a very special, critical, and necessary function within

7. Herman Goldstein. *Problem-Oriented Policing*. Philadelphia: Temple University Press. 1990.

our society. Yet I had become a fully-fledged member of what sociologists call subculture: a distinct group of people who have patterns of behavior and beliefs that set them apart from society.

Subcultures can emerge because of the age, ethnicity, class, employment, geographical location, gender, or sexual orientation of their members.

Members may wear a style of clothing, display certain symbols, or use mannerisms, language, or patterns of speech to signal their belonging to a subculture. Police work is a subculture.

I came to see that joining the police was more than a job. It's a life-changing event; an event that finds one initiated into a very distinct group in which certain expectations exist. For example, you have the right to use coercive and even deadly force in your work. You use certain distinct words to describe the work you do and different groups of people you encounter. Police officers have intimate knowledge about the behavior of others, and elements of both danger and secrecy exist in their work. All of this easily sets the police apart from normal society. And when you add to it irregular working hours, a lengthy selection and training process, taking of an oath of office, and wearing a badge, a uniform, and a gun, police are distinguished from most any other occupation in our society.

I came to realize the uniqueness of this subculture one night standing outside our patrol shift briefing room in downtown Minneapolis when one of the officers on my shift made a derogatory remark about my partner. It was 1965, and I had been on the Minneapolis department for three years. The speaker was one of those officers who would show up late on a call, after we had gotten things settled down, and then proceed to agitate the citizens with whom we were working. He was a troublemaker. Often, he would get a conflict going again and then make a physical arrest. In such situations, my partner and I could do little but help him out, even though we knew it was a bad arrest—not an illegal one, but a cheap one, because he had caused the problem. He was wrong, but we never criticized him in front of the public or to any of our supervisors.

One time this guy was verbally poking me outside of roll call and trying to agitate me like I was some guy he ran into on the street. He was getting to me. I could sense my fellow officers looking to see what I was going to do. But I calmed down and slowly turned to him. "Look, asshole. See this badge on my chest? It's just like your badge. And if you keep provoking me, I'm not going to act like some poor mope on the street you can push around. I'm going to rip your badge off and shove it up your ass. Understand? And stop butting in on our calls."

It was quiet. Our sergeant came out, looked at the two of us, and called us in to the briefing. Later, many of my colleagues thanked me for doing what they should have done. *Doing what they should have done*—one or more of us should have dealt with this bad apple much sooner.

Somebody should have told him to quit jumping calls and irritating people. But we didn't. We didn't because he was a fellow officer. So, for the first time, I began to see not only the positive camaraderie of policing, but also the dark side of it—what this subculture could do to any one of us, how it could change us and keep us from doing the right thing.

Police work is seductive. Even outsiders fall prey to it. During the years of federal funding in the late 1960s, there appeared a lot of researchers and academics at the police station wanting to study us and what we did. Almost every outside academic or researcher who wanted to study us quickly became co-opted—became a supporter. On ride-alongs, such a person might say, "If I were you, I wouldn't have taken that from that guy—I'd have punched him in the face and arrested him!" This kind of seductiveness is especially dangerous in police work.

Egon Bittner, a prominent sociologist who had studied police for many years, observed that the core of the police role is the non-negotiable use of force.[8] He was right. No one else besides police in our society has the authority to place their hands on us, restrain, or arrest us without our permission. That makes police unique in our society.

There are few people who can legally touch us without our consent and force us to comply with their orders. Police can. They can stop us, ask us questions, put their hands on us, search us, arrest us, and put us in jail. The force they use doesn't have to be physical (though the threat of physical force is always there); police can ask questions of us that no one else has

---

8. Egon Bittner. *The Functions of Police in Modern Society*. New York: Routledge. 1970.

the right to ask. And if we refuse to answer them, we could be arrested, handcuffed, put in the back seat of a patrol car, and taken to jail, where we are strip-searched, photographed, fingerprinted, and placed in a cell until we can bail out. If we can't bail out because we don't have the money, we will stay in jail overnight until we appear before a judge in the morning.

This authority to use both physical and psychological force necessitates that police have adequate training and that the training continues throughout their career. Socializing police trainees into the work of policing is a lengthy process that begins even during the application process. And that socialization can work to ensure either good or bad policing.

Because the selection and training processes for police are so intense and, after graduation, the work schedule so unique (with shifts on nights, weekends, and often holidays), new police officers soon find they have few people to socialize with outside of their colleagues. This too makes the job of a police officer quite unique, along with the emotional and physical intensity of the work. Most officers even see their relationships with old friends and acquaintances severed once they become police. Their friends and family begin to see them as different—even spouses.

For example, on weekend nights, when most people socialize, police are often working. And if police officers are invited to friends' social events, they may be confronted with violations of the law—which, before they were hired and trained as police, they had no responsibility to intervene in. They may be confronted with excessive alcohol consumption, underage drinkers present, or their friends' recreational use of marijuana or other illegal drugs.

Police recruits are told early in the academy that they will most likely not be able to keep their old friends, and that their old friends will even steer clear of them, now that they are cops. Recruits are also reminded that department regulations require them to be on-duty 24 hours a day, to report any criminal activity they see, even when off-duty.

Failure to do so could result in their termination.

This puts police officers in an uncomfortable position: they should leave the party.

And even if they do leave, once having known what went on there, they risk being reported for overlooking criminal activity. It soon becomes apparent to new officers that it is a lot easier and safer to socialize with fellow police than with their old friends and acquaintances. It just avoids potential conflicts. And, besides, their old friends can't understand what being a cop is really like.

In a partnered assignment, such as in a two-officer patrol car, an officer begins to realize that he (or she) not only spends most of his waking life with his partner, but also depends upon that partner for his personal safety and even for his job retention, in the case of junior officers on probation. When one depends so much on another person for their economic and personal safety, it is easy to see why police misconduct is tolerated within the ranks. If a partner's behavior doesn't negatively impact another officer's safety, it is often tolerated and not reported.

While new police officers often think putting on a badge and carrying a firearm won't change them, their friends, or their lifestyles, they are sadly mistaken. New police officers quickly find out that, to a large degree, the only other people who can understand their lot in life are other police officers. Becoming a police officer is a robust, indelible socialization process.

But of course, what is taught in the police academy regarding proper norms for police behavior may not be what police recruits experience once they are assigned to the station house. The first major incidence of police corruption that caught my attention was in the very early months of my police career. It was early in 1960, and the Edina police had just hired me. I still vividly recall that situation to this day.[9]

It was disgraceful. It was reported in the national news that a burglary ring was discovered inside the Denver Police Department. Off- and on-duty officers operated it. When the investigation was finished, 35 officers were arrested. Over a seven-year period, these rogue cops had committed more than 100 thefts from citizens they had sworn to protect and serve. One of their crimes was (at the time) the largest burglary take in the city's history. They broke in and cracked the safe in a local supermarket and pocketed $40,000. When Denver citizens found out their police officers

9. *Time Magazine*, October 13, 1961

were the same people perpetrating this crime wave, they were outraged and remained so for some time.

When the investigation by the police department finally got under way, investigators uncovered a well-organized and staffed burglary ring. The officers involved looked for burglary opportunities while on duty.

When they decided to break into a business, they posted lookout officers and carefully monitored the police radio for any indication that they had been spotted. Once their crimes were discovered and reported, many times the same officers returned to investigate it. If any evidence was inadvertently left behind, they simply destroyed it.

Over the years, these crooked cops experienced few failures in their well-planned crimes. That's hardly surprising: they had become the crime experts. They committed crimes based on what they knew. But one night, it all changed. They got caught. It wasn't a citizen, but a fellow officer.

Unfortunately for them, they ran into an honest cop. After spotting a business being burglarized, he spotted the perpetrators and gave chase.

During the chase, the safe they had stolen fell out of the trunk of the fleeing vehicle. The officer was eluded, and when he circled back, he saw a man about to retrieve the safe. When the officer moved to arrest him, the man identified himself as a fellow Denver police officer. This was the time the subculture kicked in for this officer. What was he to do? He pondered the matter. But in the morning, he reported what he had witnessed to his chief.

Upon listening to the officer, the chief (not believing him) sent him to see a psychiatrist instead of launching an investigation. The chief wasn't suspicious of the facts reported to him but of the officer's mental stability. The psychiatrist, however, reported back to the chief that he believed the officer. He wasn't lying, nor was he mentally ill. It was then, and only then, that the Denver Police Department began an investigation.

Nevertheless, the investigation took almost a year. During that time, the department found that not only was corruption rampant, but it also had spread to other police departments in the area. After the Denver officers were arrested, an elected sheriff and five county deputies joined them in jail.

There was a tremendous public outcry. And after being severely criticized for his laxity, the chief resigned. The greatest loss, however, wasn't the events themselves as much as the loss of trust that the citizens of Denver had in their police.

For many years afterwards, every Denver police officer has had to live with this shameful blemish. When two officers answered a call at a construction site a few weeks after the arrests were made public, it was reported that workers on the site shouted, "Hey, guys, lock up your cars. Cops in the neighborhood."

At the same time, a thousand miles away in Edina, I also heard these kinds of comments from some people I arrested—was I one of those cop burglars? At the time, I felt the shame those Denver officers caused all of us who wore a badge. Denver wasn't as far away as I thought—bad cops impact all cops.

Throughout my career, I learned that without effective oversight, adequate salaries, and high public expectations, police will slide backwards—because left alone, isolated, underpaid, and with low public expectations, these police won't be the kind of people we want to protect us and our way of life.

Thankfully, an honest man in Denver, who happened to be a police officer, had the integrity and courage to ignore the subculture he was part of and blow the whistle on his corrupt colleagues. Yet we must realize that even in the case of a police burglary ring, it is difficult for any other officer to complain and break the code of silence that informally exists within most police departments.

For some months, before all this was uncovered, Denver officers, it was speculated, had talked about the rumors they heard, maybe even joked about them. But who took the next step and considered whether they were true? If the police are to be kept free from corruption, honesty and integrity must be among their fiercest internal values. If integrity had been a prime value among Denver police at the time, then it wouldn't have been so difficult for a good cop to turn in a bad one. For police to be above reproach in their conduct, they themselves must be willing to turn in a colleague who is dishonest. Unless honesty is a prime working value held by police, honest police departments cannot exist.

I don't remember having many ethical challenges when I first began policing at Edina, but one occasion comes to mind. It was one night when a car roared by my marked squad car. It obviously was exceeding the speed limit. I was new on the job, only a few weeks, but I knew what to do. I pursued the vehicle, turned on my red lights and siren, and notified the dispatcher I was in pursuit. The driver would not stop. I called into the dispatcher again that I was in a chase, and I requested backup.

After a mile or two, the car finally stopped. When I cautiously approached the vehicle, I heard laughing and found the three occupants having a good chuckle. I was wondering where my backup was when I recognized the occupants—colleagues from the afternoon shift I had just relieved.

I don't remember having had to think about my response. Sure, I could ignore this and have a good laugh, be one of the boys—no harm, no foul, ha-ha. Or I could report their illegal behavior to the chief. Looking back, maybe I should have. I chose to do something else. I told them I was highly pissed off and that what they had done was dangerous and not so funny. I let them know in no uncertain terms that if they *ever* did something like that to me again, I would arrest them.

I don't know what they were expecting from me. Maybe it was a test. If it was, I didn't pass. Or did I? Afterward, we never talked about the incident again, and we continued to have a good working relationship. What those officers did was both illegal and improper.

I decided to use my discretion. I gave them a warning. If I had gone along with their antics, they would have continued to play their little jokes on me and perhaps other officers. If I had turned them in to the chief, I would have been ostracized as a guy who couldn't take a joke and would have lost their support at work—and maybe even their backup protection if I needed help. It was a difficult decision. I think I made the right one. They didn't screw around with me again.

When I was an officer in Minneapolis, it was a little different. If we encountered off-duty officers who were drunk, we parked their cars and took them home. The stakes were much higher in a big-city department.

Police work was far more dangerous there. I do, however, distinctly remember one incursion into the blue subculture. While working on the tactical squad (dubbed the "Flying Squad"), my partner and I took down an after-hours tippling house—an unlicensed establishment that illegally served alcohol after hours. When I entered and asked for the person in charge, a man came forward, looked at me, and asked who I was and what unit I came from. Then he said something strange: "Does Captain Heilen know you are doing this?"

Now, I knew this captain wasn't in charge of this precinct. He worked downtown. I told the owner that, no, the captain didn't know about this, and that if he did, so what? Then he told me I should call the captain. I ignored his request.

As we were processing the arrests, I noticed Captain Heilen driving up to the establishment we had taken down. Instead of arriving in a department vehicle, he was in his personal car. It was after 3 a.m. and well outside of his normal work hours. He called me over and said, "Do you know what you are doing?" I said yes, I did, and told him what we had found and that I was surprised to see him out so early in the morning. He paused, stared, and then, without a word, drove away.

My colleagues looked at me, wondering what was going to happen. Nothing ever did. No one at headquarters or my supervisor ever discussed the arrests with me. Even today, I have a deep-seated feeling that those of us on the tactical squad that early morning so long ago made the blue subculture a little less threatening.

That's because we were the new breed, the different ones, college cops. That night, those of us on that new tactical squad defined ourselves as to who we were. I'd like to think that night made a difference in Minneapolis. I always wondered how much of a payoff the captain got for what appeared to be a police protection racket. I hope the proprietor thought he was a bad investment and quit paying him.

Minneapolis was different for me. In Minneapolis, I had to work with drunks and sadists on my shift. I also had colleagues who took things that weren't theirs to take. They used their badges to get free meals from restaurants, free drinks, and free admission to movies. Some of them were even so bold as to bring their families into a restaurant when they were off-duty and expect the owner to pick up the tab. And the waitresses never saw a tip on the table.

Interestingly, they were also the guys who were fast with their fists, not the tough guys you'd like to see show up on a tense call. No, they were the guys who were quick to punch a mouthy drunk or a bad guy in handcuffs. I came to see that they were cowards. They needed to be watched because they would start trouble on the street, particularly with people of color—like that colleague of mine I had to confront outside of roll call.

When I started studying the sociology of police at the University of Minnesota, I came to understand the subtle nature of corruption and the police culture. I read studies about "honest cops" who were on the take.

Usually, the unit or precinct in which they worked had been historically crooked, and the officers who had to work there found that, to be accepted, they were expected to receive their part of the take. Within the culture of corruption, taking money means that the person receiving it is just as guilty as the others. Some cops took the money but gave their share to their church or a charity to stay clean and still be accepted by their peers. While this might have been good for their consciences, they were still crooked cops.

What I have just stated may be quite foreign to people who don't carefully read daily news or scan the internet. If you do, however, you will see a steady stream of reports throughout the country regarding police corruption, abuse of force, and other illegal behavior. In each of these instances, plaintiffs receive large cash settlements, and some police officers go to jail. Corruption isn't something that happened in the 1930s—it goes on today in many of our nation's cities and police departments. But remember, when police officers must depend on their fellow officers to help them when they are in danger, taking their share of the take, going along with petty thievery, and overlooking a few protection schemes often becomes an acceptable trade-off for one's personal safety.

In Minneapolis, coffee was always free to police—my colleagues told me the owners of these businesses wanted police to stop by and be seen; it was cheap protection. But when I was on the street and a restaurant owner picked up my tab, my policy was to leave a tip for the server equal to the cost of the meal rather than cause a scene. I did tell them that if they wanted me to return, they needed to let me pay for my meal.

The question I had about these freebies was perhaps quite different from that of my colleagues. It was: what does it do to the police to be put in such a situation? To be considered such a low-caste member of the community that they are thought to be too poor to pay for their own food—or, worse yet, considered moochers?

Occasionally in Minneapolis, I showed up at burglaries, and the owner of the victimized business or home hadn't yet arrived, I noticed some cops taking things. If it was my call, I put a stop to it because I had to write the report—I was in charge here until detectives arrived. But if it wasn't my call, I simply turned away and left. Unfortunately, some business owners, when they did arrive at the scene of a break-in, encouraged police to take things. "Take something," they'd say. "I'll just claim it on my insurance." Partners in crime. When I refused to stop by liquor stores on my beat and pick up my Christmas present (one or more bottles of liquor), my colleagues griped that I was ruining it for them.

One of the more difficult areas of improving police is dealing with corruption when it is embedded in the police subculture. I use the term 'corruption' broadly to include acts such as stealing things, receiving regular payoffs—enforcing or not enforcing the law, accepting gifts and favors not afforded the public, disregarding departmental rules and orders, lying, issuing false reports, giving false testimony, or committing other acts a person knows are dishonest or morally wrong. Corruption exists when police break the law, whether in pursuit of enforcing it or to enhance their own lives by accepting special favors like free food, liquor, or other things of value.

On the other hand, proper professional police work involves scrupulous adherence to the law while enforcing it. It is being honest to a fault. Because of the disparity in power between police and citizens, the lack of transparency in most police organizations, and few public mechanisms to effectively regulate or control police behavior, the problem still exists as to how to reduce and eliminate police corruption effectively.

I have mentioned some ways an individual officer—myself—dealt with corrupt practices he encountered. Ultimately, though, the goal shouldn't be to learn how an officer might effectively deal with a corrupt police culture but rather to figure out how that culture can be eliminated through the introduction of new professional ethical expectations in the police department.

This, of course, goes back to the way these ethical practices are taught to entry-level police and reinforced within the station house. But the primary failure of most efforts to reduce or eliminate corruption and other misconduct in a police department is that they usually fail to acknowledge the power of the police subculture I have described. When dishonesty is a matter of common practice, and when it significantly supplements the income and lifestyle of those who practice it, it is very difficult to eliminate.

However, an article in the July, 2009 issue of the *Harvard Business Review* gives me encouragement that honest organizations can be developed.[10] The authors, James O'Toole and Warren Bennis, addressed the problem of trust in our nation's corporations—specifically, our financial institutions. (The situation that inspired it was, of course, the meltdown of our nation's financial system in 2008, which plunged us into the most significant period of economic downturn since the Great Depression of the 1930s.)

The authors noted that our culture has tended to evaluate executive performance based on one criterion: the extent to which an executive created wealth for their investors. But today, they said, all that is changing. Thanks to the new forces of globalization, executive performance should now be evaluated by the extent to which they create organizations that are economically, ethically, and socially sustainable.

This is a radical change, and a new definition, brought about by a very new way of looking at leadership in our society. According to O'Toole and Bennis, the way out of the mind-set that drove us into economic crisis is the way of organizational transparency—as they call it, a culture of candor:

---

10. James O'Toole and Warren Bennis. "What's Needed Next: A Culture of Candor." *Harvard Business Review,* July 2009.

No organization can be honest with the public if it is not honest with itself...leaders need to make a conscious decision to support transparency and create a culture of candor... Organizations that fail to achieve transparency will have it forced upon them. There's no way to keep a lot of secrets in the age of the Internet.[11]

So how can this apply to the police? Well, like Wall Street, police organizations are bastions of secrecy and opaqueness. Some secrecy, of course, is necessary for police, such as in the ongoing investigation of a crime. But for much of what police do, it isn't. Police would benefit ethically by opening their practices up to public view.

And if we are serious about transparency and a developing a culture of candor within the police, it must begin from the top. Police leaders must start telling the truth and being truthful. They must desist from keeping organizational secrets long after they could be shared with the community.

This especially includes secrets about mistakes. Leaders who can admit mistakes will tend to encourage others in their organization to own up to their own mistakes. The objective here isn't organizational or personal catharsis, but rather that mistakes be acknowledged and identified with the purpose of improving the process or system that caused them: admitting mistakes so that they aren't made again.

It's not that bad people try to get into police departments or financial organizations and then do bad things. In fact, the opposite is true: good people with good intentions are hired to work in organizations that unfortunately have poor systems in operation or organizations in which the existing culture is harmful.

And it is simply not enough to talk to new police officers about values, ethics, and guidelines or have them swear to and sign the *Law Enforcement Code of Ethics*. It is more, much more. Those are significant, but courses or discussions about ethical problems can't eliminate deep-rooted issues and corrupt organizational practices. Instead, more must be done to create

---

11. *Ibid.*

police organizations that encourage good people to continue to be good. And it starts when police seriously begin to police themselves.

While there may not exist an empirical police personality, there are several qualitative studies existing which further describe the socialization process new police officers undergo which contributes to the development of a specific police subculture.[12] This socialization encourages a worldview that can override an individual's upbringing, prior experience in life, and education. In many instances, police attitudes are very like those of white blue-collar workers: experience, not education, is the finest teacher, racial and ethnic minorities are to be avoided, and the highest personal achievement is to be *respected* by those with whom you work.

But police officers additionally see themselves as being up against a world that is hostile, and this affects how they behave toward others in that world. Understandably, along with being respected, bravery and courage are critical personal attributes to them as well. If an officer isn't considered brave and courageous, how can other police depend on him or her?

Combine this aggregate of personal attributes of police with the danger and secrecy of their work, their isolation, the scarcity of their numbers, and the carrying of a firearm during and after working hours, and it is easy to see why police perceive themselves as the thin blue line.

Christopher Cooper, an African American and former Washington, DC police officer, offers some glaring examples of the police subculture in operation. The article from which the following editorial appeared in *The Philadelphia Inquirer* in 2000 appears below. His remarks pertain to the arrest by Philadelphia police of a citizen named Thomas Jones.[13] The

12. International Association of Chiefs of Police, 1957.

13. One of the first to write about the working personality of police was Jerome Skolnick, "A Sketch of a Policeman's Working Personality." A copy of this manuscript can be found at: http://cw.marianuniversity.edu/tpluzinski/SelectedR/Police%20Personality.pdf January 1, 2011, 1138 hrs. See also Jonathan Rubinstein's chapter, "Cops Rules" in *City Police*. New York: Farrar, Strauss, Giroux, 1973. I would also suggest the reader be aware of the classic work by John Van Maanen on "The Asshole" in *Policing: A View from the Street*. Peter Manning and John Van Maanen, eds. New York: Random House. 1978.

arrest was documented on video by several other citizens and posted on the Internet.[14]

Regardless of the severity of Jones' alleged actions, his having been set upon by a mob composed of law enforcement agents indicates cowardice and a lack of professionalism by the officers involved…

Sadly, in our early tenure as cops, we are instructed on the "code" of the police subculture. These are norms that are almost always perverse… The first is that if a citizen runs from one of us, we are to beat him severely… And if that citizen has killed a cop, he shouldn't make it to the station alive…

Some police officers, fortunately, decide to resist such norms…

A different perspective is held by people and academicians of color, as well as some whites. We recognize that American policing suffers from a perverse subculture, and that all too often, individual officers lack the courage to stand up to that code. The result is a too-frequent lack of integrity and respect for human life, a lack of respect that all too often exacerbates the racial tensions that still exist in our society.

John Van Maanen is a sociologist who has written extensively on the police subculture. He incisively describes the view many police officers have of those they call "assholes" and the importance of getting them off the street. Who or what in police jargon is an asshole? This term isn't just for a regular crook, but a person who pushes other people around and who doesn't submit to the police definition of the situation—that is, what's *really* going on.

In my experience, the term has meant someone who is both a trouble-maker and challenges police authority. To Van Maanen, however, the label, as used by police, is a distinct and formal label; he identifies a tri-party typology consisting of 1) suspicious persons, 2) know-nothings, and 3) assholes. That is, a person may be one of three types in an encounter with police: a suspicious person, a person who knows nothing about police work or what's going on, or, worst of all, someone who refuses to submit to

14. You can see the two-minute video at: http://www.break.com/ usercontent/2008/5/Police-Beating-Caught-By-News-Helicopter-505411. December 28, 2010; 1212 hrs.

police authority, a person who disrespects police and/or pushes other people around. How does this happen? Van Maanen writes:

> *By virtue of [police] independence from superiors, their carefully guarded autonomy in the field, their deeply felt notions about real police work and those who would interfere with it, and their increasing isolation from the public they serve... police view their critics as threatening and as persons who generally should be taught or castigated, [in such a situation] one could argue that the explosive potential of citizen-police encounters will grow.*[15]

Attitudes like these on the part of police can lead to or cover up the continual problem police have—corruption. Wrongdoing by police, therefore, is both aided and abetted by a distinct, separate, and impenetrable police subculture—one that does not hold honesty and impeccable professional behavior as working values and, instead, sees critics as threatening and needing to be taught a lesson.[16]

One experiment I encountered during my studies at the University of Minnesota educated me about the power of subculture. It was called the Stanford Prison Experiment.[17] In 1971, social psychologist Philip Zimbardo conducted an experiment having to do with power and authority. Every

15. John Van Maanen. "The Asshole." *Policing: A View from the Street.* Peter K. Manning and John Van Maanen, eds. New York: Random House. 1978.

16. For a deeper exploration into police subculture see: Elizabeth Reuss-Iianni and Francis A.J. Iianni. "Street Cops and Management Cops: The Two Cultures of Policing." *Control in the Police Organization*, Maurice Punch, ed. Cambridge, MA: MIT Press. 1983, Peter K. Manning. *Police Work: The Social Organization of Policing.* Cambridge, MA: MIT Press. 1977, Maurice Punch. *Policing the Inner City.* London: McMillan. 1979, and John Van Maanen. "Working the Street: A Development View of Police Behavior." *The Potential for Reform in Criminal Justice.* Herbert Jacob, ed. Beverley Hills, CA: Sage Press. 1974.

17. A complete discussion of the experiment can be found at http://www.prisonexp.org.

police officer should be aware of it because it applies so much to police work.

As part of the experiment, Zimbardo and his staff put together a prison-like structure in the basement of a Stanford University building. Then they randomly selected college students who were paid to play the role of either a guard or a prisoner.

Within a few days, the scheduled two-week experiment had to be called off because the randomly-selected student-guards had begun to mentally—and even physically—abuse fellow students who had been randomly chosen to serve as the inmates.

Zimbardo concluded that most all of us are susceptible to acting in such a way because our behavior is determined more by the situation in which we find ourselves—its various group dynamics, organizational cultures, and our own need to be accepted—than by our inherent nature or professed values.

This finding makes sense and can easily be applied to Nazi concentration camps, My Lai, Rwanda, Abu Ghraib, and Darfur. It is far too easy to create systems and situations in which good people simply acquiesce and find themselves unable to resist what they know is wrong or unable to do what they know is right because of the perceived power of the group or the need to be accepted.

I had a similar experience early in my Marine career when I was assigned as a brig guard on the *U.S.S. Boxer*. I was 19 at the time. I soon experienced the same pressures that Zimbardo mentioned. I found myself becoming hardened toward the prisoners and a willing participant in maintaining the harsh and inmate-harassing climate of a ship's brig. I was becoming a person I didn't want to be. Luckily, an opportunity arose for me to work as an orderly to the ship's captain. I was glad I got out of there when I did.

What is needed is to develop policing systems that are essentially ethical in nature—systems that will lead to virtuous and transparent conduct, reinforce the good most people try to accomplish in their lives, and implement the culture of candor noted earlier.

While it may be difficult to imagine a secretive, hierarchical organization like a police department being transparent and speaking openly with its community, it isn't an impossibility. But to make it happen, police leaders, especially a department's chief, must cultivate a culture in which it is permissible to speak truth to power, and an organizational culture that supports honest behaviors that are consistent with the *Law Enforcement Code of Ethics*.

While codes of ethics are nice to post on the walls of a police station, it is far more crucial for them to be practiced on the street. For it is only within this kind of transparent and democratic organization that police will be able to reach their highest level of performance. It is only within this kind of organization that police will find the freedom to innovate, effectively solve problems, meet tomorrow's challenges, and enjoy the respect and trust of the communities they serve.

If a police department publicly articulates, supports, and practices such aims, incidents of willful misconduct will become few and far between. But if the department does not—its culture continues to be closed and secretive, and it cannot learn to police itself—its community will one day suffer the negative effects if it hasn't already.

Misconduct, of course, can occur both inside and outside the police department. It isn't just that some bad police officers in the organization may have problems or difficulty carrying out their duties, but that how they conduct their work may be predicated on how they feel about a certain person or group of people.

When citizens feel they have been subjected to improper behavior by the police, it takes a lot of courage and effort to do something about it. Often police departments close ranks against complainants. The presumption such a department holds is that it couldn't have done anything wrong, and so there must be something wrong with the complainant. Just like when the Denver chief sent the officer who complained about the burglary ring within his department to a psychiatrist.

In responding to complaining citizens, police often check whether the complainant has a police record. Meaning, essentially, that the person then can be labeled unreliable. Further questioning is along the line of whether the person is trying to get out of an arrest charge or is one of those cop haters. As a result, the first part of an investigation into a complaint against police is often an examination of the complainant's possible motives.

A citizen quickly picks up on this and then concludes that they are no longer so much a victim of police misconduct as someone who has offended the police. It takes a professional internal affairs investigator to not act in such a way that a complainant feels like they have done something wrong.

It is true that some people bring false charges against police, and that some people try to fabricate cases against police to receive monetary settlements or to get charges against them reduced. Regardless, it is extremely important that police departments always operate from the assumption that a complaint is worthy of a prompt and thorough investigation.

Unfortunately, the traditional police subculture, not the police administration, has its ways of deciding which police behaviors are serious cause for concern. For example, the police officer who shoplifts $100 in merchandise from a clothing store while off-duty is often perceived differently from an officer who, while on-duty, accepts $100 in cash or goods from a merchant for not enforcing the parking regulations in front of his business. The former usually will find little support among fellow officers, while the latter, because the offense occurred while he was on-duty, may in fact be supported by colleagues who have also engaged in similar misconduct.

Another example is that officers who assault their spouses or children in domestic quarrels that occur off-duty won't get as much support from peers as officers who use excessive force during the arrest of a known troublemaker. The former is understandable, but the latter is excusable, if not expected.

Whether fellow officers will come to the defense of colleagues accused of misconduct is often determined by the unwritten but widely known behavioral norms of the police organization. If rank-and-file officers view a merchant's cash payment of $100 to an officer for ignoring parking violators in front of his business as inappropriate and wrong, the practice of accepting such payments most likely will be rare or nonexistent.

The same applies to using extra force when a person resists an arrest, runs from police, or fights with them. Many departments have problems with officers using excessive force in these situations to punish offenders.

When this is a department-wide problem and not just one officer's, it will usually be found that it is an accepted practice among the rank and file, and that officers *expect* their colleagues to use extra force in such situations.[18] Of course, many departments look the other way when bad behavior happens, simply calling it understandable. But with the advent of new technology, complaints are no longer simply the assertions of bad guys who ran from police. Now, thanks to not only department-mounted video cameras on squad cars but also the video-recording capability citizen bystanders have on their cell phones, it is easy to make records of such events.[19]

In cases in which an officer exhibited bad behavior while following the unwritten norms of doing real police work, a department often closes ranks to protect the officers. We may even hear the chief saying something like "We have a tough job to do out there. That guy chose to run away and resist arrest from my officers, and he simply got what was coming. If you don't understand this, I'm sorry, but *you* try and go out on patrol at night and deal with the people we do."

And if it was just one or two officers making an arrest, perhaps their use of extra force won't be an issue. But if there were several officers at the scene, all doing the beating—and especially if the person being beaten belongs to a racial minority group—the incident could go public and create widespread disorder in the community.

This happened in 1991 after a videotape of the beating of Rodney King

---

18. For a good illustration, go to YouTube on the internet and search "police brutality." Within seconds, you'll see a huge number of videos showing officers, after a high-speed chase, running up to the vehicle they've pursued and pummeling the driver. This wasn't what they were taught to do, and no doubt department rules prohibit such behavior—yet it happens because it's simply what many police, as a subculture, do when a chase ends (or even when a person verbally abuses police). In all but the finest police departments there will be a summary beating awaiting those who disregard police authority—that is, "assholes."

19. As a response, many police departments have put video cameras in their patrol cars that record not only outside activity but also behavior that occurs within the police vehicle.

by Los Angeles police was publicly released and, as I mentioned earlier, after the public beating of Thomas Jones by police in Philadelphia. Often these situations lead to public inquiries and lawsuits that result in million-dollar settlements.[20] Afterward, police and city leaders may be required to sign consent decrees promising they'll make changes in their police departments. Over the years, cities throughout the nation have been forced by courts of law to make specific improvements to their police departments. In almost every instance, these court-ordered efforts to try to change police behavior on the street have been ineffective.

The way to improve police behavior is for leaders to always practice the behavior expected of officers. Eliminating existing inappropriate and illegal practices on the street will require that all supervisors and officers be informed that such practices are no longer condoned or protected. Once the rank and file understand that their supervisors won't overlook these kinds of behaviors, there will be fewer cases of misconduct than when these behaviors are protected or overlooked by senior officers.

But getting to that point can be arduous and will take solid commitment and personal modeling on the part of police leaders. What must be crystal-clear is that command and supervisory officers support ethical behavior at all times. They all must know that the department has specific rules and that those who don't follow them will be disciplined.

Never must mean never, and a gratuity must be understood to be anything of value—even a cup of coffee—not afforded the public. When officers see themselves as moral agents, formally educated, uniquely trained, prepared to withstand the temptations that will be presented to them, and they are adequately compensated for their work, misconduct will no longer be the problem it is today but rather an occasional stumble on the part of

20. Nearly $1 billion has been paid over the past decade to resolve claims against the New York City Police Department according to an investigation by the Associated Press. The total spending outstrips that of other U.S. cities, though some smaller cities and departments also shell out tens of millions of dollars a year in payouts. http://www.huffingtonpost.com/2010/10/14/ap-investigation-nearly-1_n_763008.html, December 30, 2010; 1008 hrs.

an individual officer. Officers will make mistakes. When they do, police leaders need to be able to assure them they will be dealt with fairly.

For too long, both police departments and their communities have looked the other way when confronted with so-called petty police misconduct: free coffee and meals, special discounts, and favors.

Misconduct and endemic corruption are close bedfellows. One precedes the other, and the difference between them is a matter of degree. If a little bit is tolerated by department leadership or by the community, it soon will grow into a larger problem.

Those we select to be our police cannot bend the truth just a little, throw one extra punch at a suspect, or only take small things. Preventing these things from occurring in the first place is much, much easier than weeding out such practices in an historically corrupt police department.

Shortly after I left the Minneapolis Police Department and went to Burnsville, I raised some concerns in the city's newspapers about how the police were using force to suppress dissent on the University of Minnesota campus. A few weeks later, a spaghetti dinner benefit was held for Walt Dziedzic, an officer I had served with who was running for the Minneapolis City Council. It was one of those legendary police get-togethers—lots of storytelling and beer drinking. I was reminiscing with some of my old buddies on the tactical squad when the discussion got around to some of the things I had recently written and the changes I was making in Burnsville.

One officer, after listening to our conversation, turned to me and said with a puzzled look on his face, "Couper, I thought youse was one of us—a 'stone copper.'"

At first I didn't understand what he was saying. What on earth was a stone copper? My friend Dave Gorski, with whom I had worked on the tactical squad and who now was with me in Burnsville, explained. "You were known as a tough street cop—a 'stone copper.' And now he doesn't understand how you could have changed, how you turned your back on them." Now I understood. "I used to kick ass and now I don't," I said with a smile. "What's the matter with me?" Later, I was to hear the term *dinosaurs* when police officers were describing other officers who were having trouble with change or refusing to change.

If police are going to evolve and grow—that is, improve—they will have to replace the public's image of them as stone coppers. This isn't an impossible task; other occupational fields have, over the course of the years, continually improved not only their public images but also their capabilities. For instance, ambulance drivers are now well-trained, tested, and licensed emergency medical technicians. In the past, almost anyone could practice medicine, with barbers performing minor surgical procedures, until professionally-minded physicians called for education, training and the licensing of those who wished to practice their art.

Don't get me wrong—things have progressed in the police field since I entered it in the 1960s. In those days, I went to injury accidents, applied first aid, and then rushed the victim to the hospital in my police car with little or no training. Today, this would be ground for legal action.

The year I joined the police, a street officer was quoted in *The New York Times* complaining about the passing of the good old days: the time when police handled most things with a nightstick and administered curbstone justice. He complained:

> *The only time [a police officer] took anything to court was when he couldn't handle it with his nightstick. But today the commissioner says it's not the job of a policeman to adjudicate anything. All we are here for is to make an arrest and take the case to court. The more arrests we make, the better he thinks we are doing our job. In the old days, if some bum came in here and told me that he was robbed of a thousand dollars, I'd toss him out on his ear. Not today. Today if he comes in and tells me someone stole his purple Pekinese, I got to make out a complaint and go looking for it.[21]*

In the 1950s through the '70s, few governmental leaders made the case that control of police could be accomplished internally by developing, training, and reinforcing a set of professional ethics, and that these ethics could be continuously reinforced by supervisors and managers committed

---

21. *New York Times.* December 5, 1960.

to coaching, developing, and leading their officers. Instead, most police leaders created more ways to impose control over their officers, such as centralization and patrol cars with radios. This is consistent with the way we have tended to do things in America—bosses exist to control their workers.

Much of this thinking comes from Frederick Winslow Taylor at the dawn of the Industrial Age in the early 20th century. Taylor was a mechanical engineer who sought to improve the efficiency of work, primarily in the industrial setting, through what he called "scientific management." Even though his ideas seem crude today, he was one of the first to examine work as a phenomenon worthy of systematic observation and study, and his studies influenced our nation's thinking about work.

Taylor's philosophy of scientific management is driven by four major principles: 1) Work can be scientifically studied and methods of work developed, 2) it is wiser to select and train employees rather than leave them to train themselves, 3) workers should be given detailed instruction on how to perform their assigned work, and 4) work should be divided between managers and workers—managers plan the work and workers do it.[22]

Even in today's light, Taylor's concepts seem reasonable in that workers should be trained and their work should be planned and directed. However, in its application, Taylor's work translated primarily into *control* and did not anticipate the emergence today of an educated workforce. Educated and trained workers today can play a critical role in improving the quality of their work. Taylor's ideas about work still dominate the thinking of many leaders in industry, business, the military, and, yes, the police. We can still see Taylor's ideas at work in police departments when we hear that it is management's job to supervise and direct officers because they are incapable of understanding the nature of their work.

Taylor wrote:

---

22. Frederick Winslow Taylor. *The Principles of Scientific Management*. New York: Harper & Brothers. 1911.

I can say without the slightest hesitation that the science of handling pig-iron is so great that the man who is…physically able to handle pig-iron and is sufficiently phlegmatic and stupid to choose this for his occupation—is rarely able to comprehend the science of handling pig-iron.[23]

Now, although these comments sound extreme, there initially was some reason for Taylor to develop the ideas he did. At the turn of the 20th century, many workers were illiterate—unable to read or write or even speak English. Consequently, they needed close supervision and direction. Leaders were smart, workers were not. But we can no longer say this about today's highly skilled and educated workforce, and we most certainly cannot say it about today's police.

Even in Taylor's day, workers and their unions viewed scientific management with suspicion. While Taylor truly believed that the worker was worthy of his hire and that a worker's pay should be linked to his productivity, he never thought they had anything to offer about improving things or the systems in which they work.

We can see Taylor's influence in response to police corruption during the time of Prohibition. Police reformers began to centralize operations, removed officers from foot beats and put them into radio-controlled patrol vehicles, and instituted military-style rank and command systems. We see vestiges of Taylor's influence when some police departments have their rank-and-file officers wear blue shirts and their supervisors wear white, or when police departments require officers to punch a time clock before work or adopt other workplace practices that more resemble those of a factory. If police supervisors wear white shirts, it is implied that they are not expected to get them dirty doing the work of policing. And if police officers punch time clocks when they show up for work, it will be very difficult to get them to think of themselves as professionals.

Controlling police officers by such external measures—namely, unnec-

---

23. *Ibid.* p. 59.

essary rules and regulations, and class distinctions—continues to be the way many police chiefs respond to two of the major behavioral problems that have always challenged police: corruption and inefficiency.

No matter how effective police may appear to their citizens, if they are on the take, they aren't good. No matter how busy police may appear, if they are not concerned about continuously improving the services they deliver, they are not as effective as they could be. This is something citizens should be aware of.

Historically, rather than improve the quality of officers in the ranks, reformers have often tried to implement more rules and regulations, more supervisory control, and the demeaning of officers on the street for their inability to control crime. But all that external control eventually backfires on police administrators and supervisors. How rank-and-file officers are treated by their leaders impacts those whom police encounter on the street. It is simply a fact of human nature.

So how do the police move from being the kind of cop who used his nightstick as a primary tool and meted out curbstone justice? How do we move into today's world, which demands well-educated and trained police officers who are, in fact, professionals committed to the rule of law and preserving and maintaining the values articulated in our nation's Constitution and especially the Bill of Rights?

In most professional organizations, training and education are central to who they are. This is accomplished by working closely with academic institutions and training academies, and maintaining high standards for recognition and accreditation in a field. A profession's key values are also usually highly publicized and known by those whom they serve, e.g. a physician's commitment to do no harm.[24] This can be accomplished through something as simple as a short statement about the way the work should be practiced, how people ought to be treated, and how new ideas and challenges should be approached and responded to.

When I first joined the police, the talk in the field was about bringing

24. The physician's Hippocratic Oath,, while it does not assure correct ethical behavior or competency on the part of the practitioner, does set forward a basic moral construct for the practice of medicine.

professionalism into law enforcement. At that time, a professional was an educated person who practiced from an empirically-based body of knowledge, and was licensed by a state board to practice. A professional could also be disciplined by that board for acts of malpractice or for violating the public's trust. Other occupations like medicine and law—occupations that *served* people—historically fell into this category. Police didn't seem to fit in.

Professionals perform necessary social functions in our society; they help people.

Police, on the other hand, were seen more as controlling people and not necessarily helping them. Worse yet, they hurt them—using threats, fines, physical force, and arrest to carry out their work.

In the wake of Lyndon Johnson's presidential commission, federal money in the 1970s and '80s enabled the development of thousands of police academic programs in our nation's colleges and universities that assisted in the education of tens of thousands of police officers. While we have seen a rise in the educational level of our American police officers during the past 40 years, there is a troubling side to it as well.

With the availability of college tuition assistance, many police officers demanded special courses. They were not interested in a liberal arts education, but rather in hands-on police science courses. Only a few were interested in literature, languages, or social sciences. And even fewer leading law enforcement officers stood up and stressed the significant role a general liberal arts education could have in preparing men and women to function as police officers in a complex and diverse society such as ours. (Perhaps this was because many police leaders themselves didn't have a college education or an appreciation of higher education and therefore couldn't speak to its importance.) To me, it was another aspect of the blue subculture's tendency to keep itself isolated and not have to confront the impact of education that, at the university level, was liberal in scope and nature.

While many universities and colleges established four-year degree programs in criminal justice, such as the University of Minnesota did, it wasn't the case nationally as the two-year college system agreed to develop special curricula for police officers and granted college credits for police experience and training academy courses. Many of these courses had the intellectual rigor of a commercial trade school and were designed and taught by active-duty police officers rather than college professors.

That isn't to say some of these classes were not essential for police to attend, just that they would have been more appropriately taught in the police academy rather than a college classroom.

One of the fallouts of this emphasis on police science was the demand from police to drop the requirement of a foreign language, otherwise a key component in most liberal arts curricula. Police argued that they didn't want a language requirement and that there was no reason to mandate one. Looking back, though, what could be more critical in our nation's cities now than having multilingual police officers on patrol?

Thankfully, some urban departments, like New York, with 138 languages spoken in the borough of Queens alone, are willing to pay a premium for bilingual officers.

So while it is true that many police officers attended local colleges and universities over the past 40 years, relatively few received a broad education. To make a long story short, the tail wagged the dog as many of our academic institutions capitulated to the lure of federal dollars and complaints from police officers and offered the classes police demanded. What was often missing, however, was an education.

I'm not saying that police have not improved over the years but rather that their improvement has been slow, too slow, in a fast-changing, 21st-century environment. As an example, I would like to offer the following comparison: football and policing.

From time to time in the past I have used a sports illustration to make my point about the need for continuous improvement. I use professional football as an example because a good part of my early life prior to becoming a police officer was spent playing football, and the game has mushroomed in popularity in the United States. I played football throughout high school and college, and in the Marines. I also played a season of semi-professional football in California.

If we compare the top football team in 1960, the Philadelphia Eagles, who beat my home-state Green Bay Packers 17–13 that year in the National

Football League (NFL) championship game, with the top team in 2011, the Green Bay Packers, we can see some major performance differences in both size, speed, and technique between these two teams a half-century apart.

If we could somehow resurrect the 1960 Philadelphia Eagles and put them on the same field with today's Packer team, who do you think would win and by how large a score? If you were to make a wager, which team would you put your money on? I don't think many of us would choose to bet against the Packers. In just about every statistical area, the 2011 Packers substantially outperform the 1960 Eagles. I would maintain that all of today's NFL teams are bigger, stronger, and faster, not just the Packers.

They pass and kick farther and more accurately. They have more training, better play strategies, and more financial resources than their predecessors in 1960. Therefore, one can safely say that the game of football has significantly improved during the past half-century, and the 2011 Packers would therefore be expected to trounce the 1960 Eagles.

Now let's go back again to 1960. It was the year I entered policing. Would it be fair to make comparisons between police departments of then and now? Are the police departments on which I first began serving in the '60s of higher quality, fairer and more effective today than they were then?

To be fair, police departments don't have to compete against one another each week, nor do their reported statistics easily measure their effectiveness. If we were to measure reported crime rates between the two eras, it would probably not be fair. But if we could compare today's and yesterday's police departments, we would see much *less* difference between police departments than we would between the Eagles and the Packers.

Whether it is fair to compare police departments from decade to decade might be arguable. But the amount of improvement that has or has not occurred within police departments during this period may be worth thinking about. Should police departments be judged on how well they maintain the *status quo* or by how much they have improved?

Comparing police to football players is, of course, somewhat like comparing apples and oranges. The skills required to be a successful professional football player, I would argue, are much fewer and more narrowly focused than the many skills required of a competent police officer. During my football career as an offensive tackle and defensive end, I didn't have to pass or kick the ball; my job was to keep the opposing player in front of me from tackling our ball carrier or, on defense, to tackle the person with the ball. I was expected to play both offense and defense, to be on the kickoff or return teams, and to line up to either defend or try to score an extra point. Today, most college and professional football teams have special teams to perform those functions that are clearly defined units that usually don't consist of the same players.

When I came into the police, on the other hand, I couldn't just be good at a couple of functions. I had to "play" both offense and defense. I had to be able to drive a police vehicle, talk on a radio, investigate crimes, write reports, give chase to suspects, defend myself, and make arrests without seriously injuring others. I also had to be able to provide first aid to injured persons, convey them to a hospital, know state laws, city ordinances, and rules of arrest, search and seizure, be a referee during neighborhood squabbles and marital disputes, and be able to settle a host of messes that people get themselves into.

In comparison, the job competencies required of me as a football player seemed rather narrow compared with those that citizens expected and required of me when I became a police officer.

Three other job aspects stand out regarding excelling at the game of football or policing: tenure, leadership, and training.

As to tenure, there are few, if any, professional coaches who will take a head coaching job without a contract. They know that building a good team takes time and that any coaching job has its ups and downs.

As to leadership, I'm sure that all managing directors, owners, and/or presidents of professional sports teams and their shareholders believe that the leadership skill of the coach and his staff are one of the most significant factors in the team's success.

Shareholders and fans know that it's not just what the coach says but how the coach leads that determines performance.

As to training, I often wonder how many hours of practice (both on- and off-season) it takes to be a successful professional athlete. We can probably agree that most likely, thousands and thousands of hours of both intensive play and practice are involved. Many Olympic athletes have written about their single-mindedness in preparing for the games—swimmers who spent six hours a day in the pool, runners who trained mile after mile, and cyclists who rode hundreds of intense training miles every week. Some successful players began playing football about the time they entered elementary school and have played the sport for most of their life.

Brett Favre retired from football , then rejoined another team and was again one of the top NFL quarterbacks as he approached 40 years of age. He went on to "un-retire" two more times until he quit for good at age 42.

If we compare the training of football players with that of police officers (or compare police with physicians, lawyers, or other professionals), we will find there is a tremendous difference in both their training and preparation. It is such a difference that it would be difficult to argue that, given all their public responsibilities, police are well trained.

How many hours of training are required for a person to practice the art of policing? In some places, the answer is "none." The average length of initial police training in the United States is less than five months. When compared to other professionals today, the current length of police training is highly insufficient.

Given the numerous responsibilities assigned to police, the high expectations the public has of them, and the many situations they can face requiring life-or-death decisions, how should police be trained? What level of formal education should they reach? How long should their initial academy training last? And what provisions should be made for periodic in-service training throughout their career?

In each of the areas I mentioned above—tenure, leadership, and training—everything that seemed right and reasonable to expect from a high-performance sports team or a corporation ought to also be expected of a critical public agency like the police. If you thoroughly studied what police are expected to do in our society and then devised education and training to meet those expectations, I'm confident that the standards you would set would significantly exceed the current standards for our nation's police.

Perhaps an argument could be made that high expectations regarding police are not reasonable—that policing is, by its nature, an elementary task not suited to people with educations and career aspirations.

I can tell you that from my review of police misconduct around the country, to continue to think this way is both unfortunate and costly. Cities around the country have had to respond to police misconduct cases that often cost them tens of millions of dollars. In Minneapolis, a department in which I served for several years, the city has paid out over $13 million during the past seven years to victims of police misconduct. Larger cities like New York, Los Angles, Philadelphia, and Washington, DC, often pay out millions of dollars each year to settle mistakes made by police.[25]

I don't recommend that we lower our expectations of police but rather that we raise them. We should expect first-class behavior from police officers because they ultimately represent who we are as a people and as a society. At a minimum, we should expect police to accurately identify and apprehend criminals with a minimal amount of physical force. They should be able to write full and truthful reports of their activities and give honest testimony in court. We also should expect them to possess skills that help in the prevention of crime, to be able to aid individuals who are in danger of harm, and to assist people who cannot care for themselves. We should further expect police to know the laws they are to enforce, protect our civil rights, and to be able to do many other tasks such as directing and controlling traffic, resolving interpersonal conflicts, identifying community problems, and preserving order. But overall, we should expect our police officers to be educated, honest, competent, and courteous—respectful in every way to everyone they encounter. They should do so because police are often the most visible representatives of our system of government—of America itself.

These skill sets and functions are so complex and difficult to perform today that only those who are academically prepared, intensely trained, and properly directed should be given such responsibilities.

In turn, citizens should demand that only the kind of people I outlined

25. http://www.startribune.com/local/minneapolis/126494938.html. January 3, 2012; 0645 hrs.

above are hired as police officers and then given both the necessary training and leadership to meet community expectations. We should also make sure that police officers have the kind of internal leadership that treats them with respect, listens to them, helps them grow professionally, and permits them to participate in workplace decisions. These are the qualities that will get police moving forward and out of the ruts they continue to be stuck in—subculture, corruption, and low expectations.

Chapter 2
The Circle Goes Round and Round

You CANNOT WRITE ABOUT THE development of police in America without knowing about Robert Peel and the London Metropolitan Police. The development of uniformed public police took place much more slowly in England than in the rest of Europe. Public police were already established in Paris by the time the English began. Before this time, a system of privately funded rewards was created to apprehend thieves and burglars. This private model continued well into the 19th century. There were privately-funded police organizations in no fewer than 45 governmental units or parishes within a 10-mile radius of London. As one can imagine, there was little coordination, information-sharing, or discipline among or in these jurisdictions.

However, in 1829, the Metropolitan Police Act was passed by Parliament, which enabled the Home Secretary to establish a unified public police force in London. This significantly reduced the function of private police and brought the modern governmental function of policing a democracy into existence. Robert Peel was the Home Secretary.

As time went on, the London Metropolitan Police essentially became the model for police forces in most democracies around the world, including ours. Our system of policing and the United Kingdom's differ significantly from many other countries' in that our police exist to protect a citizen's rights just as much as those of the state. This is what makes policing a democracy unique among the world's police—the function isn't just about order but also about rights.

It is what makes it a challenging enterprise.

Peel's nine principles laid out the framework for police conduct in any society in which it is necessary for the police to work closely with citizens and have their respect. Remarkably, these principles are as valid today as they were when they were first developed over 150 years ago.[26]

The first principle is a powerful statement regarding the role of police: they are to *prevent* crime and disorder as well as apprehend offenders. They don't serve primarily to control and arrest criminals. Instead, they have a responsibility to prevent crime from ever happening in the first place, which means police must be willing and able to work upstream in society regarding the causes of crime, and create and maintain an effective system of preventing it.

The second and third principles state that police cannot function effectively in society unless they have the approval of the public. Good relationships, cooperation, trust, and confidence between the community and the police are paramount to having effective police. Ultimately, the greatest way to foster adherence to the rule of law isn't through threats but by creating a social climate wherein people *voluntarily* observe the law because they can see that it benefits themselves as well as the society of which they consider themselves to be members.

The fourth and sixth principles are the result of a wise observation about human behavior and the use of force. The public's cooperation with the police diminishes as increased force is used by the police. How police make arrests and take offenders into custody is often an area of contention and conflict between police and the community. The fourth principle states that if police want cooperation from the community, they need to use coercive force carefully and judiciously. The sixth notes that when physical force must be used, it should only be when persuasion, advice, and warning are found to be insufficient—that is, as a last resort.

The fifth principle is one of the primary ethical principles of democratic policing.

Images of Lady Justice can be seen in many of our nation's courtrooms,

---

26. Lentz, Susan A. and Robert H. Chaires, The invention of Peel's principles: A study of policing 'textbook' history. *Journal of Criminal Justice* 35: 69–79. 2007. doi:10.1016/j.jcrimjus.2006.11.016. *Note: While Robert Peel has received the lion's share of citations down through the years, the Principles were a collaborative effort of Peel, Richard Mayne, and Charles Rowan.*

with the scales of justice in her hands but her eyes blindfolded so she cannot see whether those who come before her seeking justice are young or old, rich or poor. She also cannot see the color of their skin. So, too, police must be like Lady Justice, blind to an individual's race, gender, or socioeconomic class. They must be impartial when operating as agents of government and not be influenced by illegal or improper public pressure or prejudicial attitudes.

The seventh principle reminds us that *everyone* is responsible for the peace, welfare, and harmony of our society, not just the police. As representatives of that society, police must be recruited from the community to serve the community. Police are those who are paid to give full-time attention to the public's responsibility of maintaining a safe, peaceful, and orderly society. The police are the public and the public are the police.

The eighth principle identifies the necessary checks and balances that need to exist between the police and those of the judiciary. This necessary separation helps balance the power that each possesses: one to arrest, the other to judge. In America, we intentionally created a separation of the three powers of government: executive, legislative, and judicial.

Each balances the others' unique powers. The executive power of the police is balanced by that of the legislature and the judiciary. The legislature creates the law, the police enforce it, and the judiciary reviews it.

The ninth principle reiterates what the first principle says about the primary role of police. Police should be judged by the absence of crime and disorder in their community, not by their activity or how many arrests they make. Although it is necessary and essential for police to apprehend criminals, an ideal community isn't one in which police focus on apprehension. An ideal community exists when police and citizens work together to prevent crime from ever occurring in the first place.

These are the kind of principles that are needed to guide police in a democracy—they seem reasonable and clear. Why, then, do police often fall short of them?

In a totalitarian system of government, the harsh treatment by police of perceived offenders is the way business is done. In a democracy, however, social control must be accomplished by government while individual rights are protected, and police are expected to be fair and just. Therefore, people who live in democracies have a different set of expectations than those living under other forms of government.

In a democracy, police have a very complex role compared to what is expected of the police in other systems. The power of the state must be balanced with the rights of an individual; other systems have no balance requirement—the police only use the power given them by the state.

As previously noted, police in a democracy don't exist solely to maintain order on behalf of the state but also to assure that the fundamental rights guaranteed to every citizen are protected in the process.

This is never more evident as when a totalitarian state responds to public protest. In this instance, the goal of the police is to prevent or repress, not facilitate, protest. We see that in today in Syria, China, and other less-than-democratic governments. In these instances, the very act of disagreeing with the government is illegal and subject to police action.

A democratic state and its police ensure its citizens the right of speech, public assembly, and the airing of grievances. This is essential in a democracy because citizens are ultimately in charge through their elected representatives and must have the right to speak out and organize to make their desires known. While the state itself has the monopoly on the use of force, that monopoly must be used sparingly in a democracy and only in accordance with the rule of law—there are no sovereign rights except those held by the people. In fact, as President Lincoln noted in his Gettysburg Address, ours is a government of the people, by the people, and for the people. How police in a democracy respond to public protest is a key indicator of their competency.

In the course of our nation's history, police seem to have been unaware of Peel's guiding principles. The legacy of American police during the past 150 years has not been one of civility, honesty, and maintaining the respect of those whom they serve. Bad policing by some police departments and their officers has significantly tainted how citizens throughout our country view police today.

In December 2011 Nicholas Peart, a young college student in New York, reported to *The New York Times* that he had been stopped and frisked by police officers at least five times. He is one of more than 600,000 citizens of color stopped by police in New York last year; 84 percent of those stops involved blacks or Latinos. He wrote about his experience:

> *The police use the excuse that they're fighting crime to continue the practice, but no one has ever actually proved that it reduces crime or makes the city safer. Those of us who live in the neighborhoods where stop-and-frisks are a basic fact of daily life don't feel safer as a result.*

> *We need change. When I was young I thought cops were cool. They had a respectable and honorable job to keep people safe and fight crime. Now, I think their tactics are unfair and they abuse their authority. The police should consider the consequences of a generation of young people who want nothing to do with them—distrust, alienation and more crime.*[27]

To illustrate this problem further, a recent study at Columbia Law School and, reported in *The New York Times*, found that tens of thousands of times over a six-year period the police stopped and questioned people on New York City streets without the legal justification for doing so. And residents in an area of Brooklyn's 73rd Precinct, an area in which the residents are predominately poor and black, were the most likely in the city to be stopped and frisked by police officers.[28]

If, over the years, our nation's police leaders had internalized Peel's nine principles, trained on those principles, and made operational decisions based on them, I believe we would have a system of policing in America today that would be noted for its wisdom, skill in peacekeeping, courtesy, and respect from the communities it serves.

When we look at the system of American policing today, we find a wide range of organizational functions, structures, and sizes operated by

27. Peart, Nicholas K. "Why is the N.Y.P.D After Me?" *The New York Times*, December 17, 2011.

28. Study Finds Street Stops by N.Y. Police Unjustified. *The New York Times*, October 26, 2010.

multiple layers of government, and a wide variation in organizational competencies and capabilities.

Supplementing American policing today is the growing area of private security. In many cities, private guards sit comfortably in climate-controlled buildings behind secure doors aided by electronic monitoring systems while city police patrol the streets outside in all kinds of weather, without advanced technologies, and they are responsible primarily for those who will never be able to work in climate-controlled offices.

Policing in America is local and difficult to either control or coordinate. While consolidated or regional police forces can be found in Great Britain and other European countries, they are virtually nonexistent in our nation. Instead, we are a nation of small, fragmented, localized police organizations. Almost every city, village, and township has its own police department. There are 2,000 police departments in this country that have only *one* police officer in their employment. This balkanization of small and uncoordinated police departments results in a police function that has difficulty with coordination, conducting training, sharing information, reducing redundancy, and being as effective as it could be.

This is true whether we are talking about jurisdictions that share borders or that operate at different levels of government.

To get a grasp on this fragmentation of law enforcement jurisdictions in the United States, consider this: there are more than 18,000 police departments staffed by more than 600,000 officers. The overwhelming majority (87 percent) of these departments are local and small—that is, they employ 25 or fewer police.

In contrast, only one percent of the nation's police departments employ 1,000 or more officers. The very largest of these departments is in New York City. The police department there employs around 35,000 officers. Compared with most police departments in the country, the departments in our nation's largest cities are virtual armies in size and scope, and have little in common with the overwhelming majority of American police departments. But thanks to television and the movies, these departments have tended to exert a distorted impact on the rest of the country (including police themselves), who get their impressions about policing from them.

One way to ensure more effective coordination and efficiency of the police function would be to require police to consolidate into regional area departments of not less than, say, 100-500 officers. I'm not the first person to suggest this; many independent studies of our nation's police have recommended it. This was a major recommendation in the report of the President's Crime Commission in 1967. Since that time, there have been few regional consolidations of police services.

I must also highlight that the local nature of our nation's police can also be an asset. There are small police departments that are close and responsive to the people they serve. Unfortunately, those police departments most often serve the wealthier neighborhoods of suburban America.

I don't expect that what I say will significantly alter the day-to-day functioning of our large, army-sized police departments in our major cities. It would be nice if it were so. But my focus here is primarily on those smaller departments in American cities—departments of 500 or fewer officers who have concern for, understanding of, and connection with their communities. It is for the police officers in those ranks and their leaders that my remarks are primarily intended: those men and women who, day in and day out, deliver direct services to most of us who live in America. The style of American policing as we know it today has been intensely influenced by police in our large cities.

At the beginning of the 20th century, our nation experienced large-scale immigration of workers into those cities, the expansion of urban areas, and the rise, correspondingly, of political bosses. Employment as a police officer in those cities frequently came about because of patronage—police jobs were handed out by a city's political bosses. These jobs were not sought out by educated men or those who wished to rise in American society. As might be expected, there were major scandals involving the police during this time, and often an entire police department would be dismissed and new officers appointed after a city election. The purpose of this wasn't to reform the department but rather to hand out political favors and install officers in a police department sympathetic to a new mayor's agenda—good or bad. Policing wasn't about protecting the rights of individual citizens. It was more about what violations should be overlooked and what laws should be enforced according to the wishes and benefit of local ward bosses.

In the mid-1850s, New York and Boston acquired our nation's first organized police departments. In each instance, public police officers replaced private night watchmen just as in London. These men were either volunteers or partially paid by business owners. They didn't carry firearms; indeed, for many years, the only weapon American police had at their disposal was a nightstick. Arming police with guns came much later in our history—usually after an unarmed officer was slain while making an arrest.

The New York Police Department was closely modeled after the consolidated Metropolitan Police Force in London. Like London, New York consolidated separate police jurisdictions like Brooklyn, Staten Island, and others into one department. This consolidation was exactly what the British had done in bringing together the numerous police agencies that surrounded London. What seemed to be missing, however, was a set of overriding ethical principles, or a Robert Peel, that who could overcome petty partisanship, the abuses of local political bosses, and, particularly, the troubles the Prohibition Era brought on in the 1930s.

While we would hope that police leaders of this era would have been aware of Peel's principles of policing, it is necessary to remember they were not educated men. They didn't have a good grasp of European history, the Enlightenment, or the legal thinking that would have identified the dangers inherent in fielding a police organization which operated more by political whim than by the rule of law.

Since that time, few large metropolitan areas in our nation have been able to consolidate the scores of police departments that surround almost every one of them. The 1967 President's Commission's report on the police tried to address this situation by recommending consolidation of police in major metropolitan areas. The report cited not only cost savings but also operational efficiencies in effectiveness as benefits of consolidation. As an example, the commission described the police departments in and around the metropolitan area of Detroit. At the time, this area contained 85 separate police jurisdictions, 40 of which employed fewer than 20 police officers. Detroit wasn't unusual. The same situation exists today in almost every large metropolitan area in the United States. We have a penchant for small, localized government. While police consolidation seems to make sense, we avoid doing it.

Looking back, American policing has had—and missed—many opportunities to advance. One came in the 1930s during Prohibition, after a presidential commission found most police had been corrupted by criminal syndicates that had moved in to provide now-illegal alcoholic beverages to a thirsty population. In addition, it found that police were often using torture to extract confessions from suspects. Reforms were demanded, but few of them survived.

Another opportunity came along in the late 1960s while the nation was being torn apart by urban racial violence and an unpopular war in Southeast Asia. Another presidential commission was convened which recommended a series of changes police should undertake. Few of their 23 recommendations were ever implemented, but these recommendations continue to remain the major issues in policing. A spin-off of the 1967 report came to light again in the 1980s when it was realized that police needed to be more community-oriented and to work towards solving problems. Even today, it remains to be seen whether those recommendations will be tried, let alone sustained.

I feel we are still in the rippling effect of the major forces that drove the presidential commission in 1967. The question is whether or not our nation's police will be able to effectively work in a diverse, multicultural society, keep the peace during times of civil protest, vigorously protect citizens' civil rights, and have close relationships with immigrant communities including recruiting their sons and daughters to serve proudly as police.

Over the years, and since the '60s, some police practices have become more effective. As a case in point, police forces in most of our major cities are now more integrated regarding race and gender. They have also begun to use technology more effectively, especially communications, as in the case of enhanced 911 emergency systems and personal radios. Police also use modern-day methods of identification and scientific methods of investigation.

One of the most notable changes came about through a federal allocation in the 1960s—grants for rank-and-file police officers who wanted to obtain a college education. I was one of those who took advantage of this program. It changed my life. As I mentioned earlier, serving as a student by day and a cop by night, I came to see police work in a new light. I began to see and understand that big changes were needed not only in American police departments but throughout our entire criminal justice system.

If our nation's police don't work on improving themselves before there is another major problem like Prohibition or a surge of massive protests in our streets, they will continue to repeat the cycle, the circle going around again, just as they have done in the past. Yet another opportunity will have been missed.

Now, let's get to that first missed opportunity—the Wickersham Commission in the 1930s. To investigate the problems with enforcing prohibition laws, President Herbert Hoover appointed a commission—the National Commission of Law Observance and Enforcement—headed by former U.S. Attorney General George Wickersham.[29]

It was the problem of police corruption that came to a head during those years, 1920–1933. A constitutional amendment was our country's response to the problem of alcohol abuse. Though the law was well-intentioned, it ultimately had unanticipated consequences. Prohibition resulted in blatant disregard for the law in many sectors of our society and widespread corruption on the part of the police who were expected to enforce it.

The commission's report was written by August Vollmer,[30] a police chief himself, and not only highlighted the nation's disregard for the law but also, for the first time, documented the illegal use of torture by our

---

29. National Commission on Law Observance and Enforcement (Wickersham Commission). 1931.

30. August Vollmer served as chief of the Berkeley (CA) police department in the early 1900s and taught at the University of California School of Criminology. He went to Wichita (KS) in the early 1930s and established the four-year college degree as an entrance requirement. He was one of the first major police reformers in this country and consulted with many cities in regard to improving their police departments.

nation's police in extracting confessions from suspects. This practice, called 'the third degree'—the infliction of physical or mental pain to extract confessions—was identified by the commission as being widespread throughout the country.

In the desperate effort to compel obedience to law, experience has shown that those charged with the high function of enforcing the law sometimes stoop to attain their ends by means as illegal as the acts they seek to punish or suppress.[31]

The best-known argument isn't unfamiliar to police leaders: "Chief, if you knew for sure the person you have arrested was the person who had kidnapped and buried a little girl underground, and time is a factor because she will soon suffocate, wouldn't you use any means necessary to find that little girl and save her?"

But both international law and common moral decency prohibit the use of torture in any circumstance—even in the circumstance of an endangered child. The following is the definition of torture that comes from the United Nations' convention on the subject:

> *Torture means any act by which severe pain or suffering, whether physical or mental, is intentionally inflicted on a person for such purposes as obtaining from him or a third person information or a confession.*[32]

There are some horrendous incidents that have ended up in civil actions against police that might raise the question whether torture totally left the police station in the 1930s. Surveying the media during the last few years will show that torture continues to be a problem today in police ranks.

While the Wickersham Commission documented widespread evasion of the Prohibition laws and the counterproductive effect this was having on society, it surprisingly didn't recommend that the law be repealed. Instead,

31. National Commission on Law Observance and Enforcement, 1931.

32. Convention Against Torture and Other Cruel, Inhuman or Degrading Treatment or Punishment. United Nations. Part 1, Article 1. 1987

it recommended a more aggressive and extensive law enforcement effort to force the public's compliance. There are certainly some parallels here with how our nation continues to respond to illegal drugs. With regard to marijuana, we could say today that there is similar widespread evasion of the law, and that this too has resulted in widespread corruption of those charged with enforcing these laws. We could also document that enforcement is both ineffective and counterproductive.

The work of the Wickersham Commission, however, remains one of the most significant steps in our nation's history toward improving our nation's police. It was the first systematic investigation and documentation of police misconduct in the United States. It brought to light the illegal use of torture by police to extract confessions and information from suspects. And the work of the commission became a catalyst for later reform efforts, which called for police to be more accountable to their communities.

Four decades later, another opportunity arose. This time it wasn't about police corruption but about a growing rate of crime in America fueled by civil rights and war protesters. In the 1960s and '70s, many major events occurred that caused our nation to snap out of its doldrums. It became a major opportunity for police reform. The events were related to the growing movement to end institutionalized racism and racial segregation in our nation, and a growing discontent with the course of the war in Vietnam. These two movements taxed and challenged the centralized police model that was a response to the charges leveled against the nation's police by the Wickersham Commission.

During this period police found themselves having poor relations with minority communities. Their hiring and promotional practices were criticized. Their crowd-control tactics left much to be desired. It was also revealed that many police departments had gathered a large amount of illegal intelligence regarding protest leaders who had not committed any criminal acts.

Those of us who lived through that period can remember that to many, protest was first viewed as un-American, even equivalent to being a communist. Leaders of national protest movements, such as Dr. Martin Luther King Jr. and Malcolm X, were labeled as being influenced and funded by outside agitators or foreign governments; therefore, American police (who were predominately white and working class) had little sympathy for protesters and their leaders, and this lack of tolerance caused numerous hostile and brutal encounters.

President John F. Kennedy and his brother Attorney General Robert Kennedy, witnessed the civil rights movement in the South, the unacceptable and violent response by police in those cities, and the slow progress of racial integration within our nation. The U.S. Supreme Court had ruled in 1954 that separate schools for black and white children were themselves unequal and unconstitutional. Robert Kennedy struggled continually with the nation's top police officer, FBI Director J. Edgar Hoover, over these issues and the role of the Federal Bureau of Investigation (FBI) in helping the nation uphold its civil rights laws.

After John F. Kennedy was assassinated, President Lyndon Johnson's new administration wished to go further in seeing that civil rights, especially equality and justice, were guaranteed to every American, regardless of the color of their skin, national origin, or economic condition. It was Johnson's dream that our nation could come together and build what he called a Great Society.

This era was also the first time in our nation's history that fear of crime became the No. 1 concern of Americans. Responding to that concern, Johnson established the commission I mentioned earlier, which ultimately presented him with a report. A major part of the commission's work was to examine the state of our nation's criminal justice system, including police, and make recommendations for changes to reduce the threat of crime and social disorder.

The commission's recommendations for the police were developed after a thorough and broad inquiry into existing practices. The commission sought input from academics in the field of crime and criminology, as well as from police administrators. They boldly recommended that police—at this point, years removed from close contact with the people they served—reconnect with their communities, meet regularly, listen to residents, and work out problems together. There was a specific recommendation for special community relations units to engage the community with its police. It was especially targeted at police departments in cities with large minority populations.

The message to our nation's police from the commission was to get back to their communities and hire minority officers. A year later in 1968, the National Advisory Commission on Civil Disorders, called the Kerner Commission after its chairperson, was formed. In their report, they remarked that our nation's police have come to view their communities through the windshields of their patrol cars and hear about their activities over a radio. This is a good description of police in America in the 1960s.[33]

Along with the commission's focus on improving relations with communities came some specific recommendations to hire and promote minority officers, to fully and fairly process citizen complaints, and to develop operational policies that would guide police in the use of what is called police discretion—including the understanding of when to arrest and when not to arrest, as well as the appropriate use of force, both deadly and non-deadly.

An analysis of street riots during that time found that the event that frequently triggered the violence was a questionable arrest made by police or the shooting of a youthful offender. Eventually this resulted in police departments issuing written policies to help direct the actions of their officers in these potentially incendiary circumstances. Prior to this time, most police agencies didn't have written directives regarding when and when not to use force, make an arrest, write a citation, or chase a fleeing vehicle.

The commission also made tough recommendations to raise the educational requirement for police officers to that of a four-year college degree. It recommended three levels of entry into police service: community

33. The commission came to be called the Kerner Commission after its chairman, Otto Kerner, the former governor of Illinois. President Lyndon Johnson appointed the commission amid major civil disorder, much of it racially driven. There were major racial riots in the Watts section of Los Angeles (1965), Chicago's Division Street (1966), and in Detroit and Newark (1967). Johnson asked the commission three questions: "What happened? Why did it happen? What can be done to prevent it from happening again and again?"

service officer, police officer, and police agent. Community service officers were to be police trainees and wouldn't carry a weapon or have the power to make an arrest but would work closely with the community. And police officers would function much as they function today.

The role and function of police agents, however, would be very different. Agents would be given the most complicated, sensitive, and demanding assignments. As an example, agents would serve as juvenile officers, investigatory specialists, and community relations officers. Agents could also work in uniform in high-crime areas of the city. They would possess four-year college degrees, be highly compensated, and encouraged to develop innovative police techniques and procedures. It was also expected that they would require a minimum amount of supervision.

The commission hoped this three-tiered structure would increase the attractiveness of police work by enabling a college graduate without prior police experience, after a short internship, to move into the position of police agent. The commission's recommendation also encouraged existing police officers to pursue college educations and work to become police agents. It further recommended that supervisory and command officers be required to possess a bachelor's degree. Moreover, the commission recommended federal and state tuition assistance programs for current police officers and those seeking to serve as police.

These recommendations shook up the police of my day. There were not only compelling recommendations for college educations throughout the ranks but also for enhanced hiring practices and intensive training programs. There also was a recommendation for legislation that would permit police officers to carry their seniority and pension plans between cities, as do many other professional employees. For me and many other officers, the opportunity for college tuition, increased pay, and the prospect that our promotions would be based on ability over seniority were all music to our ears. It was the realization of a dream—that a professional, competent, legally-grounded police officer would be the norm in our society and not the exception.

Regarding the issue of police discretion and the use of force, the commission specifically recommended that deadly force be used by police only in life-threatening situations. This was a time when most state laws permitted police to use deadly force against any fleeing felon, even those who were fleeing from a property crime and were unarmed.

Additionally, it recommended the use of a new method of organization called "team policing," designed to be more collaborative and community-based. The team-policing concept assigned officers to a team with a geographical responsibility rather than one based on time of day. That is, rather than assigning police to an area for a time of day (a shift), their overall responsibility should be to a specific area of the city—a neighborhood.

There were also recommendations to establish state or regional crime labs and statewide police standards commissions which would provide financial aid to governmental units that wished to implement the recommendations of the commission. The latter, unfortunately, didn't occur, but what did happen was significant. The nation's police started to go back to college and carry degrees from those institutions back to their police departments, and citizens now had a source to refer to regarding what police should be doing—particularly, that they should be working more closely with and listening to their communities.

When the President's Commission released its report in 1967, it recommended that funds be provided to establish police standards boards in each state. These boards would then direct funds they received to police departments to implement the commission's recommendations. This was to provide the financial assistance necessary to create the new professional police model they had recommended.[34]

The strategy, however, didn't pass political muster. Few national police leaders were in favor of the commission's recommendations. The response of Congress was to form a Law Enforcement Assistance Administration (LEAA). It turned out to be an unwieldy and administratively doomed organization.

Between 1969 and 1980, nearly $8 billion was appropriated by Congress to improve police. What happened during those years is now history—an

34. *President's Commission on Law Enforcement and the Administration of Justice.* Task Force Report: The Police. Washington: U.S. Government Printing Office. 1967

unfortunate history. The law enforcement funding effort was changed from implementing the commission's recommendations to one of distributing block grants to the states. It does not take much to figure out what happened here. I heard grumbling about the federal government stepping in to tell local and state police what they should be doing. By going the route of block grants, states would be able to exercise discretion as to how the money would be spent—there were no specific requirements that the money be spent on implementing recommendations of the commission.

What happened was LEAA became a closet revenue-sharing program that did little to help the nation's police except for providing them more gadgets and hardware such as personal radios, computers, patrol boats, and weaponry.

To be fair, one part of the program was of significant help to our nation's police and to me personally: the funding of formal education for police. Yet overall, most citizens witnessed little improvement in the quality of their local police services because of a national expenditure of $8 billion dollars.

Following the work of President Johnson's commission, the American Bar Association (ABA) considered the various functions expected of police, something Johnson's commission had not done. The ABA's report, *Standards Relating to the Urban Police Function*, was made public in 1971.[35]

The ABA project was the collaborative work of both scholars and practitioners. This was the first deep inquiry into the nature and expectations of urban policing—what the public should expect city police to be able to do. It went on to identify the primary functions of policing in cities. Professor Frank Remington of the University of Wisconsin Law School chaired the project.

Two eras have now gone by for our nation's police: Wickersham and the 1967 President's Commission. Wickersham addressed the police corruption brought about by Prohibition. The 1967 commission addressed the growing problem of police-community relations in our nation's cities.

We now are in the third era of policing—an era that, so far, is still evolving. It is the era I call "community policing." Community policing

35. Standards Relating to the Urban Police Function. American Bar
    Association. 1971

emphasizes closer relationships between the police, their communities and a response to community-identified problems.[36] It may become another missed opportunity by our nation's police.

It remains to be seen whether police will take advantage of this opportunity or go to something entirely different. Currently, police have spent over three decades ostensibly doing community-oriented policing; however, there are limited data available to measure the success of their efforts. A new development could overshadow the work that has been done to implement a style of policing that has been in progress since the early 1980s. That development is the overwhelming dependence upon technology to conduct police work.

Many people, myself included, believe that this development was triggered by that day in September 2001, when terrorists attacked our nation. After the attacks, and even into the present day, our nation has been in a constant state of fear that, sadly, has been exploited by some of our nation's political leaders. While the attacks were certainly of a very low-tech nature—commandeering commercial airliners and flying them into buildings—our nation's response was to unleash the power of our technology: electronic surveillance, video cameras, security checkpoints, preventative detention, and massive military retaliation in the Middle East.

A large amount of this technology surge filtered down to the nation's police in the form of new weaponry and methods of intelligence-gathering and surveillance. Yet in community policing, police officers' dependence isn't on technology but on people. The theory is that respectful working relations between police and citizens lead to safer communities because

36. Herman Goldstein. *Problem-Oriented Policing*. Philadelphia: Temple University Press. 1990. I need to emphasize the critical connection between Goldstein's problem-oriented policing and community (or neighborhood) policing. The community looks to police to solve problems; Goldstein's method most effectively and in the long-run focuses on those community problems. Community, or neighborhood policing, decentralizes police to work in small geographical areas of the city—movement from doing work based on time of day to geographical area. I strongly supported the neighborhood policing concept in my article, "The Delivery of Neighborhood Police Services: A Challenge for Today's Professional," in the March 1972 issue of *The Police Chief* magazine.

safety and order are everyone's goals. When police and citizens work together on community-identified problems, they get resolved. The problem with dependence upon technology, on the other hand, is that it tends to draw police away from their community and essentially distances them from those whom they are to serve.

One of the top examples to enhance community-oriented policing is the problem-oriented method established by Herman Goldstein in the late 1970s.[37] It was then that many police, researchers, and policymakers became interested in improving the effectiveness of police. Research during this period pointed out the limitations of some very sacred assumptions police held—assumptions about random patrol, rapid response to calls, and follow-up investigations. These sacred cows of policing had been the basis for police practices for many years.

Instead, there was a new recognition that:

- Police deal with a range of community problems, many of which are not strictly criminal in nature. Arrest and prosecution alone—the traditional functions of the criminal justice system—do not always effectively resolve problems.

- Giving police officers, who have great insight into community problems, the discretion to design solutions is extremely valuable for solving the problems.

- Police can use a variety of methods to redress recurrent problems.

- The community values police involvement in noncriminal problems and recognizes the contribution police can make to solve these problems.[38]

---

37. Herman Goldstein. *Problem-Oriented Policing.* New York: McGraw-Hill, 1990.

38. http://www.popcenter.org/about/?p=history. December 27, 2010; 2205 hrs. Also, the work of James Skolnick and David Bayley in 1986: *The New Blue Line: Police Innovation in Six American Cities.* New York: The Free Press

Early experiments in problem-oriented policing occurred while I was chief in Madison, as well as in Baltimore County, Maryland, and the United Kingdom. My favorite story about the problem-oriented method was about an officer who found himself responding to a noise disturbance call at the same address night after night. Responding to noise complaints is part and parcel of urban policing. Noise complaints had become so routine that every night-shift officer knew they would get one or more calls about noise to that address before the night was over.

In each instance, the complainants came from an elderly woman who lived above a tavern. Just about every night, she would call the police to complain about the loud noise from the tavern's jukebox. And night after night, officers would respond to the call, talk to her, and then routinely go downstairs and tell the bartender to turn down the music. The bartender would often wonder why he was turning down the jukebox because it didn't seem to be very loud. Nevertheless, the jukebox would be turned down, and the police officer would write a report. In fact, both the police officer and bartender knew that no matter how much the volume on the jukebox was lowered, another call would soon be forthcoming.

Finally, in exasperation, one of the officers decided to tally all the noise calls related to that address. When he added them all up, he was astounded— during the past three months, there had been scores of multiple calls to this address. When he reviewed the reports as to what officers had done in response to the calls, he found that most of them did as he did: they told the bartender to turn down the jukebox and went back on patrol.

So the officer decided to go farther, to begin to work upstream to determine what was really causing this problem that was excessively taxing police resources. He talked to the woman and even listened from her apartment before and after he asked the bartender to turn the jukebox down. Then he talked to the owner of the tavern. The owner defended himself and his employees by saying that no matter how low they turned the jukebox down, the lady upstairs would continue to complain and call police.

Now the officer had some data. He began investigating and checking the noise level of the jukebox in the tavern and in the woman's apartment.

It really didn't seem to be very loud in the tavern, but in the apartment, it truly was a problem.

At this point, some police officers might have just advised the lady to buy some earplugs or to find another residence. But that, of course, would only forestall the problem until the next resident moved in and the unrelenting cycle of noise complaints continued.

Instead, this officer used the problem-solving method to address the situation. He began by looking at the nature of the problem, talking again with the bartenders and the patrons, as well as the woman upstairs. Then, after going over what he had learned from tallying the complaints and talking to the people involved, he began to look for causes.

At first, he thought the cause was the jukebox. But it turned out he was wrong. No matter how low it was turned down, it still resulted in a noise level that was too high on the second floor. Further investigation, which involved working with the tavern owner, revealed the problem to be the location of the jukebox: heating ducts next to the wall by the jukebox functioned as a noise amplifier on their way to the second floor.

The officer made some suggestions to the owner about moving the jukebox and placing a rubber pad under it. The owner agreed. The next night, there was no noise complaint from that address, and none in the following months. The officer's problem-oriented investigation reduced hundreds of police calls to that address. And the solution was simple.

This is a small illustration of how one officer worked upstream and did some very basic problem-solving that reduced frustration for a citizen, a business owner, and his employees, and freed officers for other calls.[39]

As problem-oriented policing has evolved over the last two decades, it has emphasized evaluation of problems and the importance of solid analysis, development of pragmatic responses to the problem, and the need to strategically engage other resources such as members of the community and

---

39. Over the years, one's memory often blends. I at first thought this situation involved one of my officers in Madison. However, Herman Goldstein reminded me of a similar story from Philadelphia he noted in his book, *Problem-Oriented Policing.*

other city departments as well as local businesses and service organizations, as partners.

While many other new policing orientations have emerged over the years (such as values-based policing, intelligence-based policing, and COMP-STAT),[40] none has the potential of improving policing more than the problem-oriented approach. So why is it not standard operating procedure for our nation's police?

There are many reasons new ideas in policing don't thrive, not the least of which is the American political penchant for throwing out everything your predecessor did, effective or not. But I suggest that the failure of this method to become standard practice among our nation's police is due to the fact that it directly challenges the police organization itself by empowering rank-and-file police officers—not just command officers—to develop effective and successful responses to problems in collaboration with community members. It also challenges one of those Four Obstacles to improving policing—anti-intellectualism.

I say this because I don't believe the lower ranks of officers are the basis of the problem. Whenever I have watched rank-and-file police officers being introduced to the concept of problem-oriented policing (either by reading articles on the subject or visiting their website,[41] attending the national conference on problem-oriented policing, or being specifically trained in it, they become excited and invigorated about their work. A national problem-oriented policing conference has been held annually since 1990.

During the conference, attendees who listen to success stories told by other rank-and-file officers who practice the method come to believe in its effectiveness. When police officers come to see their work as solving problems, and criminal behavior as not the problem but simply part of it, they start to work more effectively to find causes and prevent the problems from happening in the first place. But it appears that when these officers return to their departments, they often don't find open minds or

---

40.   COMPSTAT: Computer Statistics; a method developed at the NYPD to hold officers and commanders responsible for crime increases and quality of life issues in their precincts.

41.   http://popcenter.org

understanding leaders willing to make the necessary organizational changes so that they can practice the method.

Nevertheless, something is happening in the police field regarding this method, as the national Problem-Oriented Policing Center demonstrates. Despite the failure of our nation's police to shift from responding to incidents to becoming more problem-oriented, officers around the country have continued to show tremendous interest in this method.

Since the publication in 2001 of the first problem-oriented policing guide, nearly *one million* copies of the guides and other publications offered by the center have been sent out to individual officers and police agencies. These materials are now widely used in police training and college courses. Two years later, the center launched its website which provides curriculum guides, teaching aids, problem analysis tools, innovative learning experiences, and an immense range of information. Today, the site receives an average of 1.5 million visits each month, offers more than 3,000 full-text PDF files for download, and has more than 2,000 files downloaded daily.[42]

With all this interest and activity, one would think this method would begin to take hold and modify the traditional police response to incidents. But doing problem-oriented policing means that police officers, supervisors, and commanders must change their ways. And change in policing isn't something that begins easily or is able to sustain itself without considerable long-term commitment and persistence.

Problem-oriented policing can thus help police to build that critical body of knowledge that will improve their effectiveness in most of the things they do, something vitally necessary for the future.

According to Goldstein, there are four major impediments to problem-oriented policing.

- The absence of a long-term commitment on the part of police leaders.

- The lack of analytical skills within a police agency.

---

42. http://popcenter.org and my conversations with Michael Scott, director of the Problem-Oriented Policing Center.

- The lack of a clear academic connection.
- The current police subculture.[43]

So why has the problem-oriented method not become the standard method of policing? Goldstein goes on:

> *Improvements in policing… will not come about by simply increasing the numbers of police and by augmenting and modernizing the equipment they use. We need to invest proportionately and more heavily in thinking—in an organized, systematic, and sustained way—about what it is that the police are called on to do—and how they should do it.*[44]

What he is saying is that these things have, so far, proved insurmountable: the commitment of police leadership, the failure to train the necessary skills for problem-solving (primarily analysis and evaluation), the lack of a formal relationship with academia, and the oppressive nature of the police culture. Fortunately, the problems he cites can be resolved through sustained leadership, training, and public education—subjects that will be addressed in the chapters that follow along with the Seven Steps necessary to improve our nation's police.

A vast body of research has demonstrated that the problem-oriented policing method works, that it is effective in managing and controlling a wide range of crime and disorder. This isn't a new method anymore—it has been around for three decades.

Departments that have never attempted to implement it should;

---

43. *Ibid.* On Further Developing Problem-Oriented Policing: The Most Critical Need, The Major Impediments, and a Proposal. *Crime Prevention Studies*, vol. 15. 2003.

44. Herman Goldstein: On Further Developing Problem-Oriented Policing: The Most Critical Need, the Major Impediments, and a Proposal in *Mainstreaming Problem-Oriented Policing*, Crime Prevention Studies, Volume 15, edited by Johannes Knutsson, Criminal Justice Press, Monsey, New York, U.S.A. 2002.

departments that have tried to implement it should now do it again—and, this time, do it correctly—with leadership.

These are a few of the prominent historical legacies that have prevented our nation's police from improving. In some instances, it has been the political system in which they have had to work. In others, it has been the police themselves and their leaders. There is really nothing—other than a lack of will, discipline, and persistence—that prevents our nation's police from moving forward.

For too long, there has existed a more effective way of implanting community-oriented policing. It is now a major part of our history. Police have now, through practice and academic research, developed a significant and established body of knowledge about community-oriented policing. It won't supplant the critical emergency or tactical functions of police such as responding to crimes in progress, accidents, and other civic needs.

Instead, it will broaden the number of effective strategies and responses police can use to effectively solve problems.

Problem-oriented policing changes the way police do their daily work— their work becomes more creative, effective, collaborative with community members, and, ultimately, personally and professionally rewarding. The problem is that this body of knowledge is essentially unknown to most of the police field. Now is the time to change that, to make that knowledge more accessible, to put it into practice and, thereby, get our nation's police off the circular merry-go-round and moving forward.

Chapter 3
Growing a Leader

EVEN AS A YOUNGSTER, I was a defender of the underdog. I remember being emotionally impacted when, as a boy traveling in the South with my parents, I was confronted by two drinking fountains: one signed "white" and the other "colored." I had to ask my father what they were. Why were there two drinking fountains? After my father told me, I wondered what kind of country was I living in: a land of free men and women?

By the time I got out of the Marines in 1960 and enrolled at the University of Minnesota it seemed as though everything was changing around me. I felt I was in a time of promise. Yet it was also a time of chaos. There was a struggle for civil rights, a youth revolution, and a war that soon became unbearable. All those contemporary forces affected me. I became more and more interested in policing and less interested in returning to the Marines. I had to, nevertheless, confront the historical legacy of the job I was doing, the rules I was enforcing.

Looking back over those turbulent decades of American history in which I carried a badge and a gun, I'm still amazed at everything that happened. They were times of uncertainty, yet tremendous opportunity. I felt I was in the center of these movements. I would feel at times more aligned with those who participated in them than the police with whom I worked.

Edina, MN, was a very good place to start. In 1960, it was a very progressive police department. It had an excellent reputation in the Minneapolis-St. Paul metropolitan area. It was a wealthy suburb and paid a good monthly salary for that time: $450. The department had a professional air to it, an educated chief—Wayne Bennett—and was academically tied to the programs and certification offered by the Northwestern Traffic Institute in Illinois. Nonetheless, I wasn't sent to any formal training before I went out on patrol. My recruit training consisted of riding with a sergeant for a week. The next day back at work, I was out on my own, keys to a squad car, street map, and ticket book in hand.

What I did carry away with me from my Edina experience was a good set of ethics—they instilled in me the deep belief that police were to obey the law while they enforced it and to treat everyone with courtesy. This was to help me immensely two years later when I joined the police department in Minneapolis.

There had been a successful citywide referendum in nearby Minneapolis to increase the size of the police department by 100 officers. I was a member of the second class hired. In our ranks was Ray Presley, the second African-American police officer hired by the Minneapolis Police Department. All those who took the police examination who were veterans of World War II or the Korean War, and had made a passing score of 70 or more, went to the top of the list. They had what was called absolute veterans' preference. My class came right behind them. Many of us were veterans too, but we were too young for either World War II or the Korean War. We were not eligible for veterans' preference.

Looking back, my class was a wave that turned into a tsunami. We were quite different from the rest of the police hired that year. Our class had the highest scores on the civil service examination, we were younger, and many of us had some college experience (although few of us had degrees). Of the 400 members of the department, fewer than five officers held a college degree. Only two came from a racial minority group, and women could serve only in the youth bureau or as jailers in the women's section—never as patrol officers. That was the environment in which I worked and began to think more profoundly about policing.

In Minneapolis, I did have a formal, four-week recruit school. The director was Deputy Inspector Ed Farrell, a college graduate. While a few of us attended classes at the nearby campus of the University of Minnesota, we never thought of staying on the police department after receiving our college degree. A college degree was considered a ticket out of the police department.

I continued to take classes at the university, but soon ran out of money. Paying tuition and supporting a growing family on a patrolman's salary at that time was getting to be too much of a financial burden. At first, I must admit I was more interested in being a tough street cop than one with a degree. If I did get my degree, I thought, I was going to join a federal law enforcement agency—certainly not remain on the street.

My original plan to return to the Marines soon faded away in the excitement of city police work. While I didn't see myself remaining as a patrol officer for my career, police work had gotten into my blood.

Then President Lyndon Johnson's proposal for a Great Society changed all that. With the passage of the Omnibus Crime Control and Safe Streets Acts in 1968, grant monies became available for me and other front-line cops to attend college. Now I could afford to finish my education and support my family.

After reading the report from President Johnson's commission,[45] taking classes at the university in sociology, crime and deviant behavior, and personally supporting our nation's civil-rights movement, I came to view the potential of my job in a new and very different way. It is safe to say that all these events coming together triggered an epiphany for me. It transformed my view of what police could be in our society, especially the critical role they could play in protecting the rights of citizens and ensuring justice.

Like everyone else, I saw the troubling behavior of Southern police each night on national television—how they fought to uphold local and state racial segregation laws and how they worked to demean and disfranchise black citizens, even though the highest court of our nation had clearly stated that separate wasn't equal and that everyone had a right to vote and be treated equally. I soon came to see that other police officers (especially those from my recruit class) were beginning to think the same way I did. We were different—a new breed. We didn't think like most of the other senior officers with whom we worked.

As one of this new breed of college cops, I worked nights on the tactical

45. President's Commission on Law Enforcement and the Administration of Justice. Task Force Report: The Police. Washington: U.S. Government Printing Office. 1967.

squad and went to school during the day. These were busy days of adrenaline-pumping night patrol, being challenged by new ideas in the classroom, learning new ways of thinking, and finding new friends. Many of those new friends were members of the Students for a Democratic Society (SDS) and active in campus antiwar groups. They were my classmates, and we had engaging conversations at lunchtime. From me, I think they gained a different perspective on the police. From them, I came to understand the anger and frustration they were feeling about police and their role in repressing protest, and the gap they perceived between what our nation said and what it was doing. Today, I sense a similar attitude from those who are participating in our nation's Occupy Movement.

All these experiences started to broaden my perspective and views about dissent, freedom, and the role of police. What we Americans said we were (and what we valued) seemed to be terribly out of sync with how we, the police, were conducting business.

While finishing my degree, I left the tactical squad to try out some ideas I had about foot patrol—especially a foot patrol on Plymouth Avenue on the north side of Minneapolis. Plymouth Avenue was an area of the city that was predominately black and earlier had been the location of the frequent civil rights disturbances that culminated in a night of arson that took place after Dr. Martin Luther King Jr. was slain in Memphis.

I could try out my ideas because of an unusual leader at the north side precinct, Captain Ken Moore. He was a stand-up guy and agreed to my request to walk a beat on Plymouth Avenue, which was in his precinct. To anyone's recollection, it was the first foot beat in an all-black area of the city. This neighborhood resented police and, only a year or so earlier, had torched many white-owned businesses in the district.

This was a good place to try and put my new ideas about neighborhood policing into practice.

The central location on my beat was a newly established neighborhood center called The Way. When I started walking the beat on Plymouth Avenue, I went around and introduced myself. That was my first encounter with community policing. I remember that I didn't want to wear my uniform hat because I wanted people on my beat to know who I was—that

I wasn't a faceless member of an occupation force. I wanted them to know I wasn't going to act like other cops they had encountered. I wanted to be there to help and work with this community. So I went about establishing relationships (like any good community organizer) and tried to listen, meet community needs, and work to solve the problems in the neighborhood.

One day a sergeant drove by and saw me walking my beat. I wasn't wearing my hat.

Now, this sergeant wasn't well-liked by the community in which I worked. His attitude and conduct in the community left much to be desired. He stopped and ordered me to go back to the station, get my hat, and put it on. I respectfully told him I thought it was better that I not wear my hat while walking this beat. He asked why. I replied that I didn't want to wear my hat because I was afraid people in the neighborhood might not recognize me and accidentally shoot me. "They might think I was you." He glared at me and quietly drove away. He knew what I was talking about. He also knew that the captain needed me on this beat, and that I was the only one in the precinct who would volunteer to walk in this part of the city.

My experience on that foot beat, working intimately with people in the neighborhood, caused me to think about police-community relations in a real sense. I knew that without officers who forged good relationships with the people they served and who could gain their trust, the police could do little to solve neighborhood problems, control crime, or keep peace in those neighborhoods.

Walking my beat alone one day, I thought of a book I had recently read for one of my classes. It was James Baldwin's *Nobody Knows My Name*.[46] Baldwin gave a stunning account of being black in America.

There is a statement he makes about Harlem swinging hipsters and the police; I remember it even to this day. According to Baldwin, the white police officers he knew had to walk in twos and threes in his neighborhood. They had to do so for safety reasons. They couldn't walk alone because, Baldwin said, the only thing police knew to swing in Harlem was a nightstick. I didn't want that to be me.

---

46. James Baldwin. *Nobody Knows My Name*. New York: Dial Press. 1961.

It was also during this time that I was formulating some ideas about the proper police response to protest. I was beginning to see that proximity mattered; being close was safe—just like on the beat. Get close, talk, and stay in contact. The further the police positioned themselves from people in the crowd, the greater the chance the crowd would depersonalize them: see them as objects and not people. Therefore, getting closer to the people, whether in managing crowds or patrolling neighborhoods on foot, seemed to be a good basic strategy that needed to be experimented with.

When I was promoted to detective, I moved from my foot beat on Plymouth Avenue to the detective bureau. Knowing that I now was, in their terms, a college boy, my fellow detectives, all of them my father's age, would ask me when I was planning to leave.

Evidently there had been several situations in the past when men joined the police department, attended the university, got a degree, and then immediately left for a better job that paid more. Internally, no one expected a college boy to remain working in the police department. I informed my co-workers that I was never leaving. That I loved police work. There was stunned silence. They looked at each other, and I knew what they were thinking—now they had to compete with guys like me for promotions. They wanted me to take my degree and leave. All guys like me will do is cause trouble for them, try and change things. They were right.

After seven years with the Minneapolis department and with my baccalaureate degree in hand, I was awarded a graduate fellowship from the National Institute for Mental Health (NIMH). This grant would support me through a master's degree and on to a Ph.D. in sociology.

My professors wrote convincing letters of recommendation to the police department in support of me taking a leave of absence for academic studies. Unexpectedly, the department granted me a leave for a year, permitting me to devote full time to my studies, doing research, and writing my thesis.

Being a NIMH fellow at the university and working with other students in the program made another lasting impression on me. Even more so than before, I began to see police with a new understanding of their potential role in making America a fairer and more equal society. Cops with degrees could make a difference.

During my years as an undergraduate and graduate student, I had the opportunity to work with and learn from not only some outstanding academics like David Ward and John Clark, but also world-renowned criminologists like Donald Cressey, Tom Murton, and Ula Bondeson from Sweden. I became the graduate student representative to the faculty committee. I had friends who were faculty members—friends I introduced to my colleagues still working the streets of Minneapolis. I still had not left the police department. But then, that was before I met Patrick McInnis.

I soon had a chance to put my ideas into practice. I had written some commentaries in the *Minneapolis Tribune* about my thoughts concerning the pressing need for improved police-community relations with the black community. They caught the eye of the new city manager of Burnsville, Patrick McInnis. McInnis asked to meet with me. After lunch, and before he offered me the job, we discussed leadership, operational policy, training, and police use of force. I remember him writing my job offer on a napkin. It was about 40 percent more than I was making as a detective. I accepted.

McInnis was in his mid-30s, only a few years older than I was, smart, and a forward thinker. And Burnsville was a growing city. From that group of 100 new police officers hired in Minneapolis, I was the first to serve as a chief. Many others, in later years, however, would go on to head up police departments in other cities.[47]

Other things were happening in the Minneapolis-St. Paul metropolitan area as police officers started to get their college degrees. Change was in the air. The first wave of college cops, so evident in the civil service scores of the Minneapolis hiring process in 1962, was now being positioned to make a difference.

Burnsville gave me my first opportunity in 1969 to walk my talk: test ideas that were formed by seven years as a street cop in the high-crime and multiracial areas of Minneapolis and five years as an undergraduate

---

47. Fellow Marine and tactical squad officer David Gorski joined me in Burnsville and then went on to serve as chief of police in Golden Valley, MN; at Harvard University in Cambridge, MA; and finally in Appleton, WI. Jim Mossey, also a fellow tactical squad officer, served as chief of police in Crystal, MN, a suburb of Minneapolis, for many years.

and graduate student. These experiences gave me the opportunity to study police work not only as a practitioner but also as a sociologist. I could test both my experience and my education. I repeatedly asked myself: is this true to my experience, and, if not, why not? If it isn't, do I have data to support this new learning which may be a major change in the way I have always done things?

Even in Burnsville, I was feeling the emotional effects of the civil rights and antiwar protests that I directly experienced in Minneapolis and when I was on campus. I knew I was in a time of major social upheaval, and this was, perhaps, the only chance I would get.

The kind of police we needed were police with formal educations—they would be the most likely to be open to what I was trying to do; they would be the most flexible. A higher educational requirement seemed to be the first and finest step toward getting my department to where I wanted it. In Burnsville, police were to be highly educated before they started to practice. With the support of McInnis and the city council, I established a four-year college degree requirement. Today, Burnsville still maintains the four-year degree entrance requirement we established in early 1969. They are one of the few departments in the nation to do so.

Right away, any person could tell the police in Burnsville were different. We did away with traditional military-style uniforms. Instead, we wore navy-blue blazers, French-blue trousers, and name tags declaring "Public Safety Officer. Our patrol vehicles were white with gold reflective tape along the sides. Our unique approach received national attention in *News-week* magazine that noted:

> *From Clancy Cop, circa 1890, to gray jumpsuits in Menlo Park and blue blazers in Burnsville: Policemen are becoming respectable, just like doctors, schoolteachers and the corner druggist.*

It was a sign of things to come. For me, it was a preferred future. In that same article, I was quoted:

If we change our dress and titles, maybe we'll get some changes in behavior from both the officers and the community.

It turned out to be true. Burnsville officers immediately noticed a change in attitude from the people they contacted while wearing their blue blazers. The city was proud of their officers.

In Burnsville, I drew many students and college graduates to our department. The students worked as community service officers (CSOs) while they were in school; they didn't carry a firearm or have the arrest power. Still, they could handle minor traffic accidents and other incidents. When CSOs received their four-year degrees, they were appointed as sworn officers. We attracted applicants from racial minority groups and from broad and diverse backgrounds—everyone I hired who carried a gun and had arrest power had a four-year college degree.

I was looking for applicants who had broad liberal arts educations. I wasn't especially looking for graduates in police science. One of my recruiting posters called college graduates to "Join the other Peace Corps." I was looking for the same kind of educated, sensitive person who might also be attracted to join that organization.

We are looking for college graduates who want to make a significant contribution to our society by helping build a model of police professionalism… if you are one of our "new breed," the kind of man [sic] that can handle responsibility and authority, make important decisions, and (most important), the kind that likes people, we will accept your application as a public safety officer in our management training program.

These were heady days for those of us who considered ourselves to be a new breed of police. We were convinced that police in our generation, and in the generations to come, would be very different from the past; they would be educated, they would protect the rights of all people, and they would work smarter. I would use that recruiting theme again in Madison.

I thought about recruiting women into the department, but I couldn't convince McInnis that it was a good idea. At this same time, the final report of the 1967 President's Commission made it clear that they also didn't think women police were a good idea. The use of women as patrol officers was never mentioned in their report. As it was, uniformed women patrol officers would break the gender barrier a few years later.

One thing McInnis and I did agree upon with conviction was that our department must be racially inclusive. He and I made that happen, even in mostly all-white Burnsville. The racial and gender integration of our nation's police may seem rather passé today, but I can tell you that this was a long and often agonizing goal to accomplish.

Sexism and racism were alive and well during those days, and the unsung heroes of this story are the women, minorities, and gays who stepped into policing and those in the department who stood up for them. Without this integration of our nation's police, the prospect of improving them would be far more difficult, if not impossible.

Burnsville turned out to be my first experimental police department. In 1971, I put into practice the idea of neighborhood-oriented police services. I called it the "neighborhood safety officer program" and divided the city into sections that were policed not by time of day but by turf. One officer would be responsible for handling all incidents and providing more efficient person-to-person contact with the residents, business owners, and school principals in his district without regard to time of day—turf over time.[48]

A year later, I was a speaker at a seminar during a meeting of United States Conference of Mayors (USCM) in Kansas City. The topic? Changing police.

Looking back at the publication that came out of that meeting, I realized that I had already begun to identify the tension between fighting crime and serving people:

> *Cops are strange people. We are the dilemma of a free society. We are a dilemma because we should not be needed... But here we are...*

48. Neighborhood Safety Program Inaugurated in Burnsville. *Dakota County Tribune,* July 8, 1971.

The issues are glaring and frightening—we struggle between the roles of crime fighter and social worker and we struggle with unionization, professionalization, civilianization, standards, career development, mobility, community relations, and delivery of people-oriented services, conflict management, and change.[49]

While at Burnsville, I also tried to open the minds of my fellow police chiefs. I was now a member of the Minnesota Chiefs of Police Association. In that capacity, I was asked to chair the program committee for their annual meeting in the Twin Cities. This was during the late 1960s, when problems between various protest and civil rights groups were heating up and coming to the forefront.

As in most major cities, police in our area were clashing with protesters almost daily. It was expected that antiwar activists at the University of Minnesota would soon call for a strike and shut down the university. When this happened at other universities, the state governor would activate the National Guard and send them in to restore order. Soon this occurred on the campus of my own university.

I convinced my committee of chiefs that we should offer several low-key listening opportunities for our colleagues so that they could hear what various community leaders were saying about the issues of the day.

The theme I suggested was "Let's talk to them now, rather than on the street." I contacted various community activists I had come to know over the years. They included leaders of the American Indian Movement, gay rights organizations, and campus antiwar groups. When I asked them to participate, every one of them agreed.

When the president of the chiefs' association found out about the training program my committee was offering, he wasn't happy. A few others were also upset. Why would you do something like this? This is crazy and will only lead to trouble. I calmly explained both my thinking and the fact that my committee had approved this program. I further told them that this was an opportunity. It would help chiefs do their jobs more effectively

49. *Ibid.*

by understanding what is going on today. They remained unconvinced, "We hope you're right, Couper," they warned. "If not, you may have one of the shortest memberships on record in our organization."

This caused me some concern, and I started second-guessing myself. Would my colleagues boycott these discussion sessions? Would they not show up? Would they argue with the discussion leaders? Would some of them walk out? I hoped not.

As the start of the day's program drew near, I went around and checked the discussion rooms. As I glanced into the first room, I relaxed. Many of the chiefs had already arrived and had taken their seats. Some had even begun conversations with the presenters. Later, as I moved from room to room, I saw that they were packed, the chiefs were attentive, and very good questions were being asked. The atmosphere was cordial and respectful. When the time came to rotate to another discussion room, the chiefs moved to other rooms and listened to another community activist.

It was probably the first time many of them had talked face-to-face with an antiwar activist, an American Indian leader, or a person who championed rights for gay, lesbian, bisexual, and transgendered people.

The chiefs came through for me, and it gave me hope for the future. I said to myself, yes, this was something police leaders need to do—to talk with people who don't share their views or opinions—even those who even oppose them and what they do. I was encouraged that my vision for police may one day happen.

The most noteworthy part of this day was that the discussion took place in a respectful atmosphere, something that couldn't happen at the scene of a protest. It is too easy for police leaders to become isolated, to see the world as consisting of two groups: them and us. On that training day many years ago, I learned that structured community dialogue could happen. It was one way to break down barriers between people. That lesson would also serve me well later.

While I enjoyed the opportunity I had to lead the Burnsville department, I longed for a bigger challenge—a larger, more urban police department to test my ideas about crowd control, conflict management, breaking down racial and gender barriers, and neighborhood policing. My first opportunity came when the chief of the University of Minnesota police department retired. I thought this was a job that was tailor-made for me. Many of my friends, faculty members, and fellow students at the university thought so too and urged me to apply. It made sense. If I was interested in trying out my ideas on handling protest, the university was certainly the place to be.

What could be better? The university was my *alma mater*. I knew not only the campus but the cities and culture that surrounded it as well. And now in our nation's history, since the first days of the free speech movement in Berkeley, CA, colleges and universities were hotbeds of protest and conflict. What could be more challenging at this point in my career? At the time, I had just completed my master's degree in sociology.

I was also working for the university on a part-time basis, counseling students interested in a police career and helping establish the newly-created Criminal Justice Studies Department with my former graduate professor and friend, David A. Ward. The establishment of a criminal justice studies department on campus wasn't without its opponents. At one time, we had a sit-in protest in our office by the SDS, who were actively opposing the department's presence on campus. I saw some familiar faces among the protesters.

It was during my oral interview for the university police chief's position that I first met Frank Remington, who had also chaired the ABA project on standards relating to the urban police function. Remington was a member of the student-faculty committee appointed to select a new chief and make its recommendation to the president of the university, Malcolm Moos. Remington was serving as a visiting professor at the time, but his academic home was the law school of the University of Wisconsin in Madison.

After interviews and various background investigations were conducted, my name was forwarded to the president as the committee's choice. In the meantime, I met with the university director of personnel concerning salary, benefits, and a starting date.

Everything seemed to be going well. I was told President Moos would call me for a meeting and announce my appointment. I went back to Burnsville and waited.

As often happens, information concerning a pending appointment was released to the campus newspaper and then to Twin Cities media.

Within a day or two, my photo was in the campus and city newspapers indicating I was to be the new campus police chief. Soon after, I received a hard lesson in politics.

An old adversary from my days in Minneapolis had left his position as detective on the police department, run for the office of mayor in Minneapolis, and gotten elected.

Detective Chuck Stenvig had headed the city's police union for years. He and I had frequently clashed over issues like the necessity for police higher education and relations with the black community. One of the things Stenvig vehemently disagreed with was my forming a local chapter of the national law enforcement fraternity, Lambda Alpha Epsilon, which intensely supported higher education and professionalization of police. To him, it was another union. To me, it was a national academic fraternity. Soon the fraternity had members from all over the metropolitan area, not just from Minneapolis police. We not only championed higher education for police, but also sincere relations with the citizens—particularly those in the minority community.

As president of the fraternity, I had written an op-ed article that appeared in the *Minneapolis Tribune*. It addressed the need for police change in many areas. I also had an article in the publication of the International Association of Chiefs of Police concerning new ways to police our college campuses. Basically, Stenvig was opposed to any reform of police. As union head, his position was that the police were doing just fine—leave us alone.

Now, as mayor of the city, Stenvig used his new political muscle to go after me with a vengeance. When he found out about my candidacy at the university, he immediately contacted the media and told them that if I was appointed police chief at the university they would get no help from the Minneapolis police in the event of trouble on campus, meaning that in the event the university needed help, he as mayor would prohibit them from coming on campus. Other universities around the country were experiencing strikes, and most everyone assumed there would soon be one at the University of Minnesota.

While the possibility of a strike was real, Stenvig's threat wasn't. I knew it was a bluff because all metropolitan area police departments, including the university department, had signed mutual aid contracts to help one another in the event of an emergency such as a student strike.

Stenvig really couldn't pull off what he threated to do. But his bluff grabbed the headlines that week. It also grabbed the attention of Malcolm Moos, who now was reconsidering the recommendation of his student-faculty committee.

When the students heard Stenvig's threat, they were elated. What better endorsement of me than this? By all means, they said, keep the Minneapolis police off campus. At the time, there was increasing tension and some clashes between the Minneapolis police and university students over the war and racism in areas surrounding the campus.

I didn't think Stenvig's threat would sway Moos. Through all this, the university personnel director advised me to sit tight. I would receive the call from Moos. I never did.[50]

During this waiting time, I came under pressure from McInnis. He said I should make up my mind as to what I was going to do—now. I had talked with him before I applied and had thought I had his support, but now I felt the situation had dramatically shifted.

I was sensing my position at Burnsville might be in jeopardy if I continued in the university process. I worked solely at McInnis' pleasure. So, with a large family (now consisting of six children), I withdrew my name from consideration. I got back to work in Burnsville until I received a call two years later from Madison. It was in early 1972.

The call was from Frank Remington. As I mentioned earlier, I had met him when I interviewed with the campus committee he chaired to select the university police chief. Remington had returned to the University of

---

50. Charles Stenvig went on to be elected to a second mayoral term in 1971. He began with little political experience beyond police union politics or party affiliation. He lost a third bid for office in 1973, came back to win again in 1975, then lost again in 1979. For a decade, Stenvig used public concern about crime and social unrest as a major part of his candidacy. He retired to Arizona and died in January 2010. http://www.startribune.com/local/85040487.html.

Wisconsin and told me that the city of Madison was about to begin the process of hiring a new chief of police. Would I be interested in applying? I said yes.

When I told McInnis I was going to apply for the chief's job in Madison he was not happy. In fact, he told me I had better get that job. This put some stress into my life, and I now resolved that I had better put all my efforts into Madison.

When I considered Madison, I found a report on the department that the city had commissioned a few years earlier. It was a general analysis of structure and rules of the department. Things looked okay, but the report didn't look deep into the organization. Nor did it mention any of its problems. Little did I know there was deep trouble brewing inside the department. Trouble that had been brewing for some time. I didn't know at the time that I was going to be the one to have to deal with it.

Chapter 4
The Madison Story

BEFORE I LEFT BURNSVILLE, McINNIS finally gave me his blessing. I remember him telling me that I was going to "have my hands full" there. He was right.

It wasn't long afterward that I had a chance to observe what I might be getting into. In the late spring of 1972, I flew to Madison from Minneapolis for my first interview with the Board of Police and Fire Commissioners (PFC). According to Wisconsin state law, commission members are appointed for five-year terms by mayors in cities over 5,000 in population. They serve as the hiring authority for the police and fire departments in those cities. Also according to state law, chiefs in these cities have tenure and cannot be removed except for cause. A tenured police chief was an unusual finding in an American city. At the time, I didn't think much of it. Whoever thinks he won't be successful? Not me. Later, tenure, for me, would make all the difference in the world.

It was an early Friday evening when I arrived. I was staying at a hotel just off State Street, the main avenue between the university and the Capitol. My interview was to be the following morning. It was a warm night and before I settled in for the evening, I walked along State Street to see the sights and have a beer. The sidewalks were packed with students and other young people; it reminded me of my trip to the Berkeley campus a few years earlier when I was sent there by my chief in Minneapolis to observe and take notes on crowd-control tactics we could use. I noticed a very familiar sight—two students sitting on the sidewalk with their backs against a building conversing. It was a wide sidewalk, and there was plenty of room for others to pass by. Two large Madison police officers walking down the sidewalk stopped and looked at the two college-age people.

"Get off the sidewalk!" one of them barked. The two jumped up and quickly retreated without a word.

Interesting, I thought. What if they had refused? What if instead, they had said, "But, Officer, we are simply sitting here talking, not bothering anyone, and not blocking the sidewalk. We don't think what we are doing is illegal." What would the officers have done? I think I knew. If the students had challenged their authority, someone would have gone to jail or worse.

From my first observation of Madison police in action, I started to think about what I might be getting into. When I reviewed department reports and documents the PFC sent me, the department appeared traditional but well organized. While it may have had problems controlling its use of force in handling student protests, the department apparently had a clean record with regard to corruption. The recent evaluation of the department a year or two earlier by the Public Administration Service, a nonprofit organization in Chicago, gave the department good marks. But what I witnessed that first night in Madison left me somewhat uneasy.

When the biographies of the top candidates were printed in the newspaper, I certainly appeared different from the others who had applied. I was the youngest and had less police and supervisory experience. But what I did have was more education, a national and world view of policing, and some new ideas about managing conflict and working closely with the community. They were the cards I was going to play during my interviews. In any other city, these kinds of credentials could be the kiss of death. But in Madison, they became assets.

What I saw on the street my first night in Madison was more consistent with the department's practices with the community than not. I later found out that, over the years, the department had lost the trust and confidence of a good portion of the community because of the rough tactics they used in handling public demonstrations and protests and the way they related to young people. There was also low-level racism in the city, and it was most obvious in the face of the police department. At the time I applied, the police department had only one black officer in its ranks, and persons of color were virtually absent among those employed by the city or county governments.

Geographically, there appeared to be some racial segregation.

Quite often in the past the department had overreacted when trying to control protests. The first major incident was the response of the department to the Oct. 18, 1967 demonstration against Dow Chemical Company. On that day, Dow was recruiting on the campus of the University of Wisconsin. This was at the height of the Vietnam War. Dow was the primary manufacturer of napalm, a jellied gasoline our forces used in Vietnam. Although it wasn't designed to be an antipersonnel weapon, it often was used that way. And when it was, it inflicted horrendous burns on whoever was in the general vicinity—enemy soldiers or civilians.

After I was appointed chief, I found and reviewed the video coverage of what had happened that day. It was brutal for me to witness. It magnified the department's lack of preparation, planning, training, options regarding the use of force, and leadership. It seemed so obvious to me that we, the police, had to change our tactics in response to situations like this. Unfortunately, I later found out that not everyone in the police department agreed with my thoughts on how the department handled Dow. While the incident had happened five years before, for many officers on the department it was more like yesterday.

Now there wasn't only a war in Southeast Asia, but also a growing, sometimes violent public reaction against racial segregation and racism in our society. I wasn't shy in articulating to the police commission how I believed the police needed to improve in both areas. I said that if I were appointed chief, I would work to make a good police department better and bring racial minorities and women into the department. I saw my role in Madison as not only a change agent committed to justice but also that of a peacekeeper—I would work to bring peace to the city.

While some in the community and in the department considered me to be soft on policing—that is, being more liberal than conservative in my worldviews—there was also a hard side to me: tactical squad officer, martial arts and firearms expert, commendations for bravery and meritorious service. I had also authored a training manual on crowd control and trained others in its methods. This permitted me to, as Teddy Roosevelt had suggested, speak softly while carrying a big stick.

Through my conversations with Tom Stephens, president of the PFC, I felt I had his support. He agreed with what I was maintaining needed to be done with the department. Later, I came to understand Stephens was very much in tune with what citizens in Madison wanted. He knew Madison residents were tired of the continuing conflict and animosity between students and police. Earlier public hearings the commission had held made that clear to him. But the current mayor, William Dyke, as well as most of the command staff of the police department, was still in battle mode. On the day of my swearing-in, the evening newspaper reported: "Absent from the swearing-in ceremony was Mayor William Dyke, who according to reliable sources was furious over the choice of Couper. Dyke, who wanted the commission to name his assistant, Robert Heck, tried unsuccessfully to downgrade Couper, apparently because he feels the young chief is too liberal."[51] Madison, after almost five years of continuous conflict, wanted peace but didn't know how to disengage. I presented a way out.

The police commission was composed of a diverse group of citizens. Stephens was the director of transportation for Oscar Mayer Foods, a local, nationally-known meatpacking business that had a long-term economic and historical relationship with the community. Other members of the five-person commission were Stuart Becker and Andy Somers, both attorneys, Lois Liddicoat, an insurance salesperson, and Ellsworth Swenson, a man with an organized-labor background. This was the traditional composition of the commission: lawyer, business owner, woman, and labor

---

51. On the day of my swearing-in, the evening newspaper reported:
    "Absent from the swearing-in ceremony was Mayor William Dyke, who according to reliable sources was furious over the choice of Couper. Dyke, who wanted the commission to name his assistant, Robert Heck, tried unsuccessfully to downgrade Couper, apparently because he feels the young chief is too liberal.

    "What particularly angers the mayor is that four out of the five commissioners are his own appointees… Dyke, in his vehement opposition to Couper, appeared to be in a very small minority in the city." (*The Capital Times* newspaper, December 20, 1972.) Dyke was beaten by Alderman Paul Soglin four months later in the spring election. He currently serves as a county judge in Iowa County, just west of Madison.

representative. For the most part, this balance, with the later addition of a minority representative, continued throughout my years in Madison.

The three final candidates for the chief's job were Herman Thomas, the acting chief of the department (William Emery had retired after 15 years as chief because of medical problems. Many people in Madison were of the opinion that the antiwar years, the infamous bombing of Sterling Hall, and continuing street battles with the students had severely impacted his health); Assistant Chief Edward Daley; and William Heck, a former out-of-state police officer who was now an aide to Mayor Dyke.

Stephens later confided to me that on the first round of voting, I had only one vote—his. Later, during a second round of voting, I found out I'd received Stuart Becker's vote. The three remaining votes were distributed among Thomas Daley, and Heck. None of the candidates had the three votes necessary to be appointed. Stephens and Becker then played a waiting game. I was the only candidate with two votes; the others only had one each. Stephens and Becker needed one more commissioner to come on board with them for the third, winning vote.

During the waiting game, the wild card in the selection process came to be held by the police union, the Madison Professional Police Officers Association (MPPOA). When I learned about this, I remembered my losing battle with Stenvig back in Minneapolis. Were my disagreements with him again going to thwart my goal to lead a larger police department? Was a police union again going to be able to keep me out?

A very bright and charismatic detective by the name of Roth "Buzz" Watson headed the police union. He made it publicly clear that the MPPOA was dead set against Herman Thomas becoming chief. Thomas was known for his hard-handed, uncompromising management style, both inside and outside the department. The union wanted no more of that. But the union also was unsure of mayoral aide Bob Heck, despite their close relationship with Dyke. Heck's police experience seemed to be limited to that of being a police dog handler for a state highway patrol on the East Coast.

I wasn't privy to the discussions between Watson and commission members, but gradually the police union began to consider me as a possibility. Perhaps with me, they would have a chance at a new start: someone from outside the department and not aligned with anyone.

I learned later that Lois Liddicoat approached Stephens with the MPPOA proposal.

She would be willing to support me under two conditions: first, that Watson would get a private meeting with me before I met anyone else in the department, and second, that I would be hired on a six-month probationary basis. When these two requests were first forwarded to me, I thought they were unusual but reasonable. They didn't, at the time, appear to be harmful—or so I thought.

I'm speculating here, but I think the union thought having first contact with me would be in their best interest and that I would be more open to working with them than the other two candidates would be—especially if Watson could claim to have control of the swing vote during my probationary period. If all this was true, Watson had the potential power to get me to do what he wanted or see me go.

I agreed to the conditions the commission presented, and they publicly announced my appointment on Dec. 20, 1972. The vote was 3–2. As often happens in these matters, there wasn't a coming-together vote, a second, unanimous vote for purposes of solidarity. At the time this occurred, I had a lot of self-confidence and, quite frankly, the fact that I had two votes against me on the commission didn't faze me. I would get to work and win the opposition over just like I had done in Burnsville. They were cops and so was I—cops stick together. I thought this would be the situation in Madison. I was dead wrong.

I never thought any of my officers would actively oppose me to the lengths they did. Moreover, I never imagined a situation in which a group of police officers would turn against their chief. I knew there were regulations against that. And wasn't that like mutiny? But this was Madison. And in Madison, some people were about to play hardball with me. I was to learn another hard lesson or two in politics.

Within a few weeks after taking over the department, I went about the task of interviewing all the department leaders. It was an eye-opening experience. While the top leaders of the department were bright and above-average in intelligence, most all had a very narrow view of the police function and very few of them could articulate what needed to be done to reduce the acrimony between the police department and the student and racial minority communities. Most of them clearly defended the past and simply couldn't see doing anything different than they had. But I knew the department had to change if we were going to be able to keep peace in the city. I also came to see that peacekeeping was as needed inside the department as much as it was in the community.

This was the time in America that has since been described as the "War at Home." The apogee of this war in Madison was the bombing of Sterling Hall, the home of the Army Math Research Center, on the nearby campus of the University of Wisconsin. The bombing happened two years before I arrived. The bombing resulted in the accidental death of Robert Fassnacht, a researcher who was unfortunately working late that night. The bombers, directed by a local activist by the name of Karleton Armstrong, thought the building was empty. The bombing and Fassnacht's death were a shock to the city and to its image.

Since the late 1960s, the Madison department had been responding to student protests on campus and in the city. I sensed distinct feelings of both resentment and revenge among a significant number of officers who were assigned to police these events. At the same time, among the more junior officers, there was a growing discomfort concerning the way they were ordered to respond. Thankfully, one of my three top assistants, Ed Daley, was one who did question the department's protest strategies. Daley was a breath of fresh air. Without his support and the support of a core of other forward-thinking officers like Sergeants Jim Scrivner and Tom Hischke, Detective Jack Heibel, and Policewoman Morlynn Frankey, I might not have survived long enough to make the necessary changes that I did. During my watch, all of them rose to the rank of captain or higher.

I did a lot of work inside and outside the department during those first months. Apparently, Mayor Dyke had a problem with me. He didn't appear at my swearing-in ceremony and then avoided meeting with me. Stuart Becker, commission member and friend of the mayor, unsuccessfully tried to arrange a *rapprochement* between us. At the last minute, the mayor would always cancel.

Another problem was Herman Thomas, who was acting chief until my appointment. Now he became my second-in-command—a civil service position; he didn't serve at my pleasure. During the selection process I was promised that Thomas would retire as soon as I came aboard. He didn't.

And it was obvious he wasn't going to. He wasn't supportive and wouldn't tell me when he was going to retire.

Regardless of Thomas, I continued talking to both department and community members about the future of the department. I confidently believed both Dyke and Thomas would come around. The mayor faced re-election in only a few months, and I figured Thomas would eventually support me. Isn't that what subordinates are supposed to do?

Soon things began to heat up. Early one afternoon, Liddicoat asked to meet with me. She awkwardly requested that the two of us have a meeting alone with no staff members present. When she came into my office, she quickly came to the point. She asked me to promote Detective Roth Watson to the rank of captain, a position I was in the process of filling. It also was a position that needed approval from her and other commission members. I quickly understood where she was going with this. I listened to her request and told her why I thought it wasn't a good idea.

She left my office disappointed. I would soon learn how disappointed she was.

When I brought my first promotional requests to the commission a few days later for their approval, they were rejected—I couldn't get the three votes I needed. Stephens and Becker voted for my recommendations, but Liddicoat didn't. She had jumped ship and joined Somers and Swenson. I no longer had the support of the commission.

When Liddicoat cast her vote against my promotions, I knew there was going to be a new game in town. The promotions' rejection was front-page news in the *Wisconsin State Journal*, the city's morning paper, and local radio stations, pro and con, reported on the conflict throughout the day.

Still, I could advance after I found I had the authority to make acting promotions in the interim, so I could carry on the work of the department.

But only the commission could make a promotion permanent. I then withdrew my recommendations and offered to work with commission members to clear up any misunderstandings or concerns they might have regarding my choices and the process I used.

My appointees now had to serve in an acting capacity until I could work this through. Still, this was an unusual event—no one could ever remember the last time a police commission had rejected a chief's promotions. It was the casting of the first stone, one of many to be hurled during the next two years.

Dyke, who had yet to warm up to me, ran for re-election in April. I had thought he might lose because I knew what had happened in the county elections five months earlier. At that time, Dane County voters (including voters from Madison) had swept most of the conservatives off the county board and elected liberals to leading positions in the county: county executive, district attorney, and sheriff. The first winds of change had already blown through Madison. Everyone was waiting for the spring election in the city for the second wind of change to blow.

During Dyke's campaign speeches, he often made fun of me by making light of my use of the term "conflict management" to describe the way we were now going to approach protest in the city. He made every effort to challenge me, undermine me, and underplay my authority within the department. Looking for continued support from officers in the department, he had continued to refuse to meet with me, and everyone in town knew it. It was a tense four months.

Soon Ald. Paul Soglin, a university student representing the campus district, announced he was running for mayor—and appeared to be holding his own against Dyke. Now, being aware of the shifting preference of Madison voters and my popularity with the media, Dyke became less hostile.

As election day drew closer, it looked like Dyke was going to be beaten, and I could feel the tension within the police department. Most of the officers were formidable Dyke supporters, and hardly anyone within the department voiced support for Soglin. They knew him from his earlier days on campus. He was a rebel, a student activist. He had the additional credentials in the student district he represented of being arrested and jailed by Madison police during a campus demonstration. His long hair had been shaved while he was in custody—one more way to demean those who were causing trouble for the police. It had to be done, the former sheriff said, for "health" reasons.

Soglin was overwhelmingly elected mayor. Understandably, he didn't hold positive feelings about police. But because I was younger, had some interesting ideas about policing the city, and wasn't from the department, he was more than willing to work with me. We first met the day after his election. I had wisely stayed out of the mayor's race. Of course, I wanted to see Dyke ousted. I had my preference and felt empowered on the morning of election day when I cast my vote for Soglin.

I had remained apolitical since I arrived, and I worked to maintain that position throughout my years in Madison. Instead, I worked on the issues—community relations, peacekeeping, and conflict management.

And I worked with the local media to gain support for my ideas in the community. Most of the members of the media agreed with me that the police department needed to change. And it was evident, overall, in most of their reporting.

Looking back, I used the same tactics I used in dealing with hostility: move closer; closer is safer. While it may appear paradoxical, getting close to a crowd *is* safer. When close to others, officers are not depersonalized. It is when they stand back or hide behind shields and face masks that their job becomes dangerous. So when I came under fire in Madison, I stepped up my public contacts and appearances—closer is safer. I sought out interviews, called press conferences, and offered to give talks to community groups about my vision and plans for the department. As I moved out into the community, I felt much more comfortable. I felt the community supported the direction I was taking the department.

A young, liberal police chief was one thing in Madison, but when Paul Soglin was elected mayor, there was a firestorm from conservatives in town. These folks, including many officers on the police department, were outraged by his election. Now there wasn't only open disagreement with me but also with our new mayor. After Soglin's election, Chicken Little would have had a great time in Madison crying out, "The sky is falling, the sky is falling!" The winds of change had now blown through Madison as it had through the county five months earlier.

The war inside the police department now began in earnest. Those who opposed me knew they could muster three votes from the commission to oppose my policies or even get rid of me in a few months. Very soon, a petition was circulated by some officers who asked those in the department who didn't agree with me or my policies to sign on and indicate their displeasure. One hundred and fifty-three officers did—slightly less than a majority. The petition was forwarded to the PFC in August 1973.

The internal and external opposition forces were now joining together. Every change in the police department was now described as my criticism of the department. While the opposition couldn't get rid of Soglin until the end of his two-year term, they could get rid of me—the six-month probationary clause that I'd thought unimportant now became their target.

I survived the probationary period, but the war continued for the next three years. There were investigations, hearings, depositions, trials, orders, and restraining orders as forces within the department, aided by conservatives in the community, came together to oust me.

The atmosphere within the department was often cold and brittle. I'll never forget two early and significant department staff meetings. At the first meeting with my new staff, Thomas, my second-in-command, turned to me and said in a loud voice, "Chief, your mustache does not conform to our grooming code."

I couldn't believe what I had just heard. Was he joking? No, he wasn't. He never joked. Silence filled the room. All eyes turned on me. What was I going to do? "Well," I remember slowly and carefully replying, "thanks for bringing this to my attention. I guess we will just have to change the grooming code, won't we?" And it was done.

I had the grooming code relaxed to permit officers and employees of the police department to look more like the rest of the community in hairstyle, length, and the wearing of moustaches. My thinking was that if the department was going to become part of the community, it should start *looking* like the community. My mustache stayed.

A second challenge soon followed. This time the stakes were much higher than hair length and moustaches. It was during a joint meeting of my staff with command members of the sheriff's and university police departments. We had come together to plan a response to a large upcoming march and protest. My department was the lead agency, and as I started the discussion, Thomas interrupted and again asked me another pointed question: "Chief, we want you to know that we have fought long and hard to enforce our policy that the students must walk on sidewalks and not in the street during these protests. I hope you are not going to change that policy." Again, all eyes on me.

Silence in the room. Now, for the second time in as many weeks, Thomas had openly and publicly challenged me.

But I began to see that these challenges could be turned into teaching moments. I again carefully replied, "Gentlemen, I know you have had a struggle over the past years with students, with protests, and many of you have suffered injuries. I know it has not been easy. But I want you to know that I tend to look at these things differently. I don't think our job is to keep the students out of the street. Instead, I think our job is to see that they have a safe environment in which they can exercise their rights to free speech, assembly, and petition. I don't want to fight over the street. It's not that significant. But what is significant is that we help them exercise their rights without anyone being hurt or property being damaged. We will no longer fight to keep protesters on the sidewalk."

I sensed a feeling of relief from many in the room, especially from University of Wisconsin Police Chief Ralph Hanson and our new sheriff, Bill Ferris. Hanson, with many others from the university administration, had struggled with the harsh and often combative street policies of the Madison Police Department. And Ferris—a young liberal, basically inexperienced, and newly elected—also seemed relieved. Many of the officers sitting around the table that morning knew that the policy of keeping marching protesters out of the street wasn't only dangerous but foolish. I even sensed some support from my own staff—but not from Thomas. I now knew he was dangerous and that I needed to keep him off the street and away from protesters.

So that became our street policy and practice for over 20 years: people matter more than property, and civil rights have precedence over local traffic laws. From that day forward and into the years I was chief of police, Madison never suffered property damage or had any of its police officers injured during a protest, on or off campus.

It didn't take me long to know what needed to be done; by listening to community and department members, I knew what I had to do. What I didn't know then was how long it would take. Over the years, I have questioned whether the size of a police department is a barrier to its improvement. I think it is. In police departments with more than 500 officers it is difficult, if not impossible, to initiate lasting change. Their size, span of control, and internal culture simply prohibit any lasting improvements from being made.

The Madison department had fewer than 500 employees. It had an intelligent and well-trained workforce and no history of internal corruption. Or so I thought until I stumbled upon a very dirty little operation in Madison—the undercover work of Herman Thomas' Affinity Squad and its secret files. And when I set out to tackle this problem, it helped me tackle another big one: the man who created the squad, kept its files, and was now trying to oust me—Assistant Chief Herman Thomas.

The problem identified to me by many members of the community was the secret reports the squad was generating. I doubt if the prior chief, Bill Emery, knew the range of its activities. Thomas had organized a focused intelligence-gathering effort staffed by police officers who dressed as hippies, students, or street people to infiltrate and gather information in the student community regarding campus protests.

Their ability to infiltrate came from their long hair. Cops didn't wear long hair—remember the department policy on hair length?—but long hair could gain them acceptance from those in the student community. But I soon found out there was a much darker side to the Affinity Squad than this almost comical description.

Officers assigned to the unit would join campus groups and submit reports based on who was there and what was said. These undercover officers attended as many community and student activities as they saw fit and reported their activities directly to Thomas. To keep the identity of those officers secret, even from other members of the department, many of them went undercover without formal training, immediately after being hired. Their names were even kept out of city and department personnel records. Some of them were students willing to inform on other students.

When I first heard about the squad and how it worked, it reminded me of what I saw earlier in Berkeley. I witnessed how police had used undercover officers to make arrests on campus. I saw how much animosity it created with the students. I vowed then that I wouldn't use this kind of tactic if I ever was a chief.

I terminated the program, and these undercover officers came in from the cold, attended the police academy, and became regular police officers. I, of course, was wary about them, especially the negative impact this early experience might have had on their attitude about policing. I worried that the department had created a group of officers who thought their role in society was to spy on people rather than to serve and work with them. When these officers finally came back from undercover duty and became uniformed officers in the ranks of the police department, many seemed to have considered Thomas to be their leader and not me. Very few of them were supporters of what I was trying to do and the changes I was bringing to the department.

The actual work of this undercover effort—the reports they produced—contained more gossip than fact. Years later, I had to publicly disclose the contents of those files under the Wisconsin open records law after several community activists had filed a request. In order not to damage the reputations of those on whom the squad reported, I went to great lengths to see that names were edited out of these files prior to release. And on the long-anticipated day the media was waiting for, those edited files turned out to produce more of a whimper than a bang except for one thing. Someone on the editing team had overlooked one of the informants' names in the report: a woman who lived in the student community and provided information on people she knew to the police. Her name was not blacked out in a report that was released. This resulted in the city having to pay a large cash settlement in 1980. I'll always wonder if the failure to edit her name was accidental or not.

One report in the files documented an encounter between uniformed and undercover police officers. After a street demonstration in which undercover officers had infiltrated the crowd unknown to uniformed officers, the undercover officers were standing on a sidewalk near the campus when police assigned to the protest approached them.

Even though the protest was over, they were set upon and beaten by uniformed officers. There was a code word the undercover officers were to use. They told me they had shouted the word, but none of the uniformed officers said they heard it.

The interesting thing is that none of the undercover officers had done anything illegal—they were just hanging out in the area, and they all received a sound beating. Two of those young undercover officers who got a beating that day later became outstanding command officers. They, of all people, personally knew things needed to change.

But there was a much darker and evil side to the Affinity Squad. It wasn't very long after my appointment that I heard from community members that they strongly believed the department had dossiers that contained negative and personal information on members of the community, including elected officials. This, of course, was a serious charge and not unlike charges that have been made about the FBI during the tenure of Director J. Edgar Hoover. It was alleged that Hoover used his secret files to keep members of Congress in line and supporting him.

When I would ask Thomas about this, he told me that the documents in his files were not about individuals but about illegal assemblies. He maintained there were no dossiers, no personal files on individuals. Still, the rumors abounded that personal information had been illegally gathered and used to force support from local politicians regarding police department matters—essentially to blackmail them into supporting the police department. This was a very serious allegation. But at the time, no one seemed to have any specific evidence. I would soon find out Thomas was lying. He was in a bind. If he told me the truth, he and his intelligence officers would have been subject to not only internal discipline but also the possibility of criminal charges.

Early one Saturday morning, I had read in the newspaper there was going to be a campus march into and through the city. It was a celebration of an international event called China Day. I went to the planning meeting, and some students asked who I was. I told them I was the new chief of police. I don't think any of them believed me because they ignored me and went on talking about the demonstration. Their leaders even announced that they were going to try to take the street in opposition to city rules and that some of them might be arrested. When the march began, I gravitated to the front. I wanted to see what was going to happen.

The demonstration went well until we approached the corner of Park Street and University Avenue. At that location, Madison officers from the day shift had assembled and formed a barrier to prevent the students from moving forward into the street. The tension was high as I walked up to the officers, identified myself, and asked them to let us pass. I asked them to help us get to the South Student Union a half-mile down the street. The officers stepped aside, and the rest of the march was uneventful. The demonstration ended when we arrived at our destination.

My first protest demonstration in Madison had ended without incident. After the demonstration, reporters contacted me and asked what had happened. Why hadn't I stopped the students as the department had always tried to do in the past? Why weren't they kept out of the street?

It was again a teachable moment of the type I would frequently take advantage of during my career. I told the reporters I believed it was the job of police in a democracy such as ours to protect demonstrators and, if necessary, to facilitate their right to protest as guaranteed in our Constitution. Rather than to block or suppress these events, the role of the police is to assist and protect. What I said made headlines in the *Wisconsin State Journal*. Not everyone in the city was pleased with what they read.

I later found out that I wasn't the only police officer at that student meeting. An undercover officer, unknown to me, was present. I was about to be the subject of an intelligence report submitted to Thomas. What concerned me most was what the officer reported about the nature and atmosphere of the meeting. At best, he didn't know what was going on. In the worst case, he submitted a false report.

At work on Monday, Thomas informed me he had received a report that said I was in physical danger during that meeting. It was from that undercover officer. Thomas went on to say that there were people there who were planning on physically harming me and that I shouldn't be out there in the community like that. This was strange, but even stranger because I was personally present, and it was in direct contradiction to what I experienced at the meeting. The students present at the meeting were cordial, friendly, and respectful, and I was never at any time in any danger.

I reminded Thomas that I had been a street cop for many years and knew danger and what that felt like. I told Thomas he needed to evaluate the intelligence he was receiving because it wasn't correct. In fact, I said, what was written in that report was false. I also reminded him that while I was the new kid in town, I wasn't stupid—and that group had not been dangerous to me or anyone else. What I didn't tell him was that he was the one I felt was most dangerous—not those students.

What was Thomas trying to do? Control me? Keep me in my office and off the street? Yes, I concluded, that's what he was trying to do. Just like he had done to Mayor Dyke. If I stayed in my office, I could be watched, isolated, and controlled.

I later learned that the police department, under Thomas, had, in fact, used these same kinds of tactics on Dyke. During those intense years of street protest, a police officer would be periodically sent out to check the undercarriage of the mayor's car for a bomb. This would, of course, cause the mayor to be more worried and dependent upon the police department and Thomas for his safety. Wouldn't this cause the mayor to begin to fear the community? Maybe to stay out of the community? To see the police as the only ones he could trust?

If a police leader or mayor is kept in fear and encouraged to stay in his or her office, then the police department can, perhaps, be free to do whatever it wants without supervision. But Thomas's scare tactics were not going to work with me.

All this intrigue came to a head a few months later, just before the spring election. I had heard still another rumor about the dossiers. Even though I had served as chief only a few months, if it was to come out that the department was gathering dossiers on citizens, it could be a mark against my leadership. That night, I ordered one of my assistants to enter Thomas's office with a master key and check whether those files kept in his office contained dossiers on individuals or not. He reported to me later that night that there were dossiers, about people by name, containing information about non-criminal matters—matters that essentially could be used for blackmail, just as had been alleged.

I specifically remember him telling me the contents of one file. It involved a prominent member of the city council. It contained damaging information about the alderman's daughter. According to the file, she was working as a prostitute in a city in California. This kind of information, should the police threaten to release it, could become an instrument of political bullying. Its release, during those days, could significantly damage or end the career of a local politician. Worse yet, it could be used to influence voting in a way favorable to the police department.

By the time I moved to take possession of the files, they were gone from Thomas's office. I then received a report that Thomas had been seen during election night loading boxes of files into his personal vehicle. Later I learned he had taken these files to his home and hidden them in his basement.

The next morning, I went to his home with investigatory officers and questioned him about the files. He said he had them in the basement of his home. His defense was that he was afraid that the newly-elected mayor would take control of them and release the names of undercover officers, thereby endangering them. When I asked about dossiers, he again denied that he or any officers under his control had compiled information on people; he insisted it was only events. He then turned the files over to me. When I returned to the station and examined the files, the dossiers were gone—including the one about the alderman's daughter.

The act of taking, hiding, or destroying official police files, even if they were improperly gathered, is a criminal act. This was an indication of a serious ethical breach within the department, an instance of corruption.

Therefore, I took the information I had to the district attorney for his review and for a decision on whether to criminally prosecute Thomas. After reviewing the matter, the District Attorney, Humphrey "Jerry" Lynch, declined to prosecute. I still wonder today if that was the right decision for the Madison community. Thankfully, Thomas immediately resigned, and the files were locked away in a bank safety deposit box for a time in the future when a decision would be made by a court concerning their disposition. Two problems had now been solved—Thomas and the files.

It was now time to forge ahead. I didn't find any other major ethical breach within the police department as potentially deep and destructive as Thomas' operation. Thomas had stayed around for the first four months of my administration, instigating trouble for me within the ranks, sowing seeds of discord that were to grow during the coming months and have an impact on me long after his retirement.

When leaders focus on the little things like dress codes and street use, it's easy for them to be distracted from what they really should be doing. Even when leaders get tied up on the big things like illegal intelligence gathering, it is easy for them to get sidetracked. But the job of a leader is always to move forward. There is truth in the saying "When you are up to your rear end in alligators, it's difficult to remember that your initial goal was to drain the swamp!" Alligators surrounded me, but I still had to drain the swamp.

A few months after the spring election, I had a key opportunity to share my ideas with the community about draining the swamp. I was asked by Madison's Downtown Rotary Club to talk about the policing needs of our city. The Rotary Club brought together men and women each week from business, education, and government. It was a stellar opportunity for me to share my vision with them and the rest of the city through the various media outlets sure to show up on that day.

I titled my talk "The First Seven Months and the Next Seven Years." In it, I attempted to set forth my vision for the police department—where Madison's police needed to go. That day, I felt a real sense of urgency as opposition continued to build against me within the police department and in some segments of the community. I knew I needed to lay out an exciting future with lots of enthusiasm on my part, then convince Madison residents that I could deliver on it. Two of my closest advisors in the community, Professors Remington and Goldstein, gave me wise advice: "David, this is a time when the community needs to know what will be lost if you are forced out and leave. You need to tell them now."

I laid out three directions that I planned on taking the department in the coming years. I told the Rotarians that I needed their help and support in doing so:

- Decentralize police services and develop neighborhood and team policing. The police department has been centralized since the mid-1800s. We need to get out of a centralized location and work closer to the people we serve.

- Build a people orientation—a sensitivity to and understanding of human behavior. I would be recruiting high-quality, educated police officers and training everyone, especially those in leadership positions, about this broader role for police. Traditional policing responded to problems but was not interested in finding their causes. We would work with community members to prevent, diminish, and even eliminate crime and other community disorder.

- Develop our capacity for conflict management and crisis intervention in addition to our traditional law enforcement duties. Reduce the acrimonious relationship that now exists between the police and students. After years of fighting about the war, new strategies and tactics needed to be taken to handle public protests by means other than tear gas and a nightstick.

This was where we needed to start heading now. But I went further and outlined a visionary goal for us seven years into the future. I needed to do this to let the community know what they would most likely miss if I wasn't around to lead the police department. I was, in fact, fighting for my life and my career:

[Eight years from now] we should have successfully made the quantum leap necessary to field a behavior and human services expert which shall be known as a professional police officer... Police officers of the future will be human behavior experts as well as community workers... These future police officers will also have an advocacy role within our communities. They will identify government and social problems and solve them with the resources of the government and the community.

At the end of my talk, I think everyone present, those watching television that evening, and reading about my comments in the *Wisconsin State Journal* and *The Capital Times*, the city's morning and afternoon newspapers, began to realize that the Madison Police Department wasn't going to be their grandfather's police department. Their new chief was calling not just for organizational improvements but also for a massive transformation: creating a new breed of police officers, in a new department, to serve the community in new ways.

Mayor Soglin stood by me during the trials of those early months. I'm still thankful to him. Despite having a hippie-liberal mayor in charge of the city, the city still ran well, and the police department finally came together and did its job. The city didn't fall apart. Soglin had a clear-cut service ethic, having been a city alderman, and he had a deep sense of equality and fairness. I worked closely with him and his team of city managers.

Just about everyone in the city and the police department came to know the two very large posters prominently hanging on the wall of my office. They were pictures of Dr. Martin Luther King Jr. and Mahatma Gandhi. The caption under King read: "No man is free until all men are free!" and the one under Gandhi read: "In a gentle way you can shake the world." They continued to be two crucial office companions during my life in Madison—constantly reminding me about freedom and the practice of nonviolence. They stayed there for my entire 20-year tenure.

But when I showed up at a vigil for peace in Vietnam one evening in the city and a news photographer snapped a picture of me holding a candle after the peace march was breaking up, another firestorm broke out. The picture of me appeared on the front page of the morning paper. Again, some people related to it and expected this of their police chief, while others didn't. Later, it became one of the charges leveled against me—leading a peace march.

At first, I couldn't understand the controversy among my officers. I was a cop; they were cops. Why weren't they supporting me? I was their chief. The proposals I was making and the vision I was casting would enhance their jobs, lead to more respect for them from the community, and even put more money in their pockets through an educational incentive plan. When I had been the chief in Burnsville, I hadn't gotten that kind of resistance and we'd made larger and quicker strides. Burnsville officers and I had agreed we would work together to make Burnsville a world-class department, and all of us would benefit. Why wasn't this happening in Madison? When I was in Burnsville, I never felt I was an outsider—I was a cop just like the rest of them even though I came from the Minneapolis department. But in Madison, things were different. I was beginning to feel like an outsider, and it didn't feel very good.

When I showed up with my family at the summer police union picnic soon after I came to Madison, we were shunned. Hardly anyone would speak to us. When the Madison Fire Department heard about it, the head of the firefighter's union, Ed Durkin—who would later become chief of the department—invited me and my family to their picnic. I soon began to realize that my tenure wasn't going to be assured by senior members of the police department nor the police union. If I were to survive in this job, it would be because the community supported me and wanted me to stay.

Considering the situation created by a proverbial war at home, enlisting the full support of the police department itself may have been impossible. I had to decide. Should I get my support for change and improvement from police officers or community members? The answer was now obvious to me—the Madison community. After all, nearly one-half of the police department had signed a petition against me.

Soon the media began describing the conflict within the police department in sports terms—an "A" team and a "B" team. My supporters were, thankfully, described as the "A" team. The war at home had now established a beachhead within the department. I didn't consider myself an outsider, but I was one. To be an insider, one of the boys, I would have had to accept and bless all that had gone on during the antiwar years. This I couldn't do. And my choosing not to do that meant that a long, protracted internal battle was about to be waged. I had a fight before me, a fight for my life as a police leader. I knew I was going to have to push back hard to survive.

I had to find out who in this police department would join me. I knew who wouldn't. The police union leadership at the time and many officers still in the ranks who held deep-seated and antagonistic feelings about students would most likely not join me. Slowly, I built a small, but solid, coalition of support. I found officers who wanted change. They were mostly younger and few. I needed the finest and the brightest in leadership positions where they could affect and support change, and that meant shortening seniority requirements for promotion and rapidly bringing them into the command structure. These officers, now deemed the "A" team, understood and shared my vision. They knew the department had to change, and they stepped forward to make it happen.

I went about building a team of willing players and bringing women and minorities into the department in large numbers. I don't think those on the "B" team understood the power of the term they chose for themselves. In a big football town like Madison, it's the "A" team who plays the game. They are in the game because the "A" team consists of the elite players. Those whose skills need more development are on the "B" team. The "B" team sits on the bench. The "A" team plays the game.

Demographics were also on my side. I came to Madison just about 30 years after World War II. Those who joined the department during or after World War II were now close to retirement. Within a few years, almost everyone in the top command ranks retired, and that permitted me to fill their places with officers who wanted to work with me and shared my philosophy. When Mayor Soglin went about filling vacancies on the police commission, I went from having two votes in my favor to three, then four and, finally, all five votes in favor of what I was trying to do.

When I met Morlynn Frankey, she was one of six policewomen in the department. All six worked in the juvenile bureau. For a policewoman to be hired in Madison, she had to have a four-year college degree. While these women received detective pay and possessed arrest powers, they were prohibited from carrying a firearm or standing for promotion. One of the first changes I made was to permit them to function fully as police officers—to be able to carry a firearm, to be eligible for promotion as the men were, and to be able to work in other department units if they so choose.

When these changes were approved by the commission, Frankey stepped forward and competed for promotion to lieutenant. Over the years, I promoted her to higher and higher levels of responsibility. She worked closely with me in moving the department. She was a powerful advocate for women on the department, championed my vision, and retired as an assistant chief.

One of first things I had to do along with instituting major changes within the department was to try to manage the uprising against me. The things I needed to immediately do took a considerable amount of my time when I first arrived. I needed to establish written policies and practices regarding how we would go about policing and share them with our community, especially policies regarding the use of deadly force and the pursuit of fleeing motor vehicles. I also had to hire high-quality applicants, both men and women, along with people of color. I needed to bring not only women into the department but remove the restrictions on the women who were already there. So there was a lot of internal conflict during those early days, part of it the youth rebellion within our society and part due to the age difference between older and newly-hired officers. My willingness to relax the department's grooming code created some allies for me and my policies. On the other hand, it irritated many of the older officers. Even so, on any one given day, if a vote had been taken, I would have had difficulty getting 50 percent of the internal vote. In the overall community, on the other hand, I was confident I would have fared much better.

As in most organizations, senior employees in the department controlled its union. Many of those officers sought to get rid of me by all possible means. During my first two years, I had to fight numerous charges they brought against me and my administration.

The conflict escalated from the filing of the petition with the police commission to formal charges being filed against me by seven officers who were looking for more than a review of my leadership. They were hoping to get me fired. It took two years to finally be acquitted of the major charges. Afterward, a newspaper story carried this quote from an officer who had signed the original petition against me:

> So what if you don't like him. The department has leaped forward the past 20 months more than it did in all the 10 years I've been here.[52]

Two days later, an editorial in the *Wisconsin State Journal*, under the headline "Chief Couper Vindicated," correctly observed,

> They resented Couper's style, his philosophy. They were men who thought the polish on an officer's shoes or the length of his sideburns more important than his relationship with the community, the total community… Resentment against Couper was generated by a handful of veterans who saw Couper's progressive law enforcement philosophy as a direct challenge to their viewpoints… Too many smears have been leveled, too many unsubstantiated charges have been circulated, too much vindictiveness has been voiced, to be completely happy over the dismissal of the major charges against the chief. [53]

Those 20 months were a frontal assault against not only my philosophies but also against me and my family. It is one thing to have to go through an ordeal like this and still another thing to see your children suffer. I had six and four of them were attending school during those years. They suffered, too.

Yes, these were hard times, yet predictable, given the job I knew I had to do.

Somehow, in my youth, I thought I could convince the department that what I was doing wasn't only necessary but essential for their future. While I could do that in Burnsville, it didn't initially happen in Madison.

52. *Wisconsin State Journal* newspaper, September 7, 1974.

53. *Ibid.* Editorial, September 9, 1974.

Those years took a personal toll on me as I often spent a full working day in the office followed by a full evening of hearings, investigations, and courtroom battles. John Bowers and Jack Carlson, from the Lawton and Cates law firm, were the two outstanding lawyers who doggedly and expertly defended me. Eventually, I got back to police department business. I wish I could say that the internal conflict ended after this litigation was finished, but it didn't. Even so, as my tenure went on and many these adversaries either left the department or retired. I could replace them with educated and more flexible officers. Slowly, it all began to change. We were progressing.

Still, during those years of acrimony, I was relishing the day the hearings would be over and the charges against me resolved. I held a deep grudge against the officers who had acted against me and was convinced that many of them had given false testimony. I was going to fire them or put them in jail. That old police saying kept ringing in my ears—don't get mad, just get even.

My top staff were behind me on this, and we often talked about the sweetness of revenge. The night I was exonerated, I knew my next step was to go after them.

However, my legal team had other thoughts for me to consider. That evening, they asked to speak with me alone. They reminded me that they were long-time residents of Madison and that what they had to say came from them as members of the community, not just as my lawyers. They advised me not to act against those who had filed charges against me. They went on to say that from their perspective, the city was sick and tired of all the conflict and acrimony within the department. Moving against a few police officers would prolong the internal conflict for months, if not years. It was time, they said, for me to get on with moving the department forward.

When I heard their advice, I was numb. I thought this was now fight time. I had never considered not retaliating. I wanted to go on the offensive. Now it was my turn. But I sincerely respected these two men, and I took their advice. Looking back, it was wise counsel, superlative advice. I thought about it that night and simply knew what I had heard was right.

When I didn't act against those officers, many on my staff intensely disagreed with me. They too had been affected; they too wanted to get even. I had to take the high road and not let my feelings affect the job I now had to do. I had to shift from being a victim to being a leader.

I must admit that when I first came to the department and began to encounter trouble within the ranks, my leadership style became more and more top-down, relying on force to get the job done. I felt threatened, and I fought back in the way I knew at the time—coercion. I now know coercive force might be the *easiest* way for leaders to operate when they encounter resistance, but it isn't the most effective way in the long run.

At a national police chiefs meeting in the late '80s, I distinctly remember a former commissioner of one of the largest police departments in America say he wanted to have leaders that were like junkyard dogs. He wanted bosses who got things done because their officers feared them. I knew he was wrong because the kind of police department I envisioned wasn't going to be led by junkyard dogs that were feared and quick to bite.

They may keep intruders out of the junkyard, but they didn't do much of anything else. You wouldn't want to bring them to a school or a senior center. I didn't want junkyard dogs—I wanted leaders: effective, educated men and women who taught and directed others by being competent and caring.

Thankfully, my inclinations toward using pressure to lead didn't carry over into my interactions with the community. I never felt I was in a struggle with them; instead, I considered them to be my primary supporters and allies in what I was trying to accomplish. So I worked hard to encourage and activate the community to get involved in the police department. Early on, I established several community advisory committees consisting of civic, religious, educational leaders who agreed to give me advice on critical police-community issues. These committees were vital to maintain the support I needed to have among them. I never had to convince them that the department needed improvement.

Beginning in 1978, I had raised the stakes by asking the department to make a firm commitment to what I called a "Decade of Developing Organizational Excellence." I was trying to distinguish differences between the military organizations in which many of my officers had served and those of a modern police department. It was here that I began to see many links between business, industry, and government, few with the military style that was dominant in most police departments. The police were different than the military; they had more things in common with both public and private organizations that deliver customer services. These businesses were asking questions of their customers, finding out what they needed to know to improve.

While policing isn't a competitive business (at least so far), police departments do have customers, community residents who use their services, pay taxes, and act as shareholders—not unlike those in the corporate world. I told the community we needed to de-emphasize the paramilitary traditions of the police—to be more like other organizations in society and to develop enhanced relations with other agencies and the people we serve.[54]

More specifically, I addressed the need to decentralize police services and to be more neighborhood-oriented in our work. I told them we also needed to raise the department's educational standards and to begin to look at crime as a social problem—one that is intensified by causal factors such as poverty, unemployment, racism, and lack of education or job skills. I wanted police officers to use their minds as much as their muscle.

I think it is fair to say that my vision first became the community's and then the department's. I did it by constantly selling my ideas both internally and to the community, and selecting and promoting those who shared my vision. I learned that organizations committed to sustainable improvement must have a clear vision, mission, and definition of which they are, where they are going, and what they will look like when they get there. In Madison, our vision was simple and clear: *Closer to the people. Quality from the inside out.*

This simple vision statement was intended to capture the thrust of the change effort: to improve the *inside* of the organization first—the men and women who work in the police department. I decided to do it this

54. Speech to the Madison Downtown Rotary Club. 1978.

way because I had concluded that most efforts by police organizations to change had failed, even though the ideas involved were good. They failed because leaders didn't prepare and train the men and women who worked for them, and they used force or intimidation to implement the change. Coercive leadership wasn't effective nor sustainable. It didn't work.

Instead, the methods of a more collaborative style of leadership do work and can be sustained if top leaders in the organization are able and willing to first practice the new model and then teach others in the organization what they have learned. Too often, change in a police department has been portrayed to elected officials and the public as something as easy as issuing an order.

We know today that isn't the way it is done. Police departments today are complex organizations, and things don't just happen because the chief orders it. Any effort at changing the police must consider the power of the organization to drag its feet, to resist. That is why any effort to change police must begin *inside* a department and, ultimately, be able to answer this question from the rank and file: "What's in it for us?" If a change-oriented chief and his or her staff cannot effectively answer that question, what is proposed most likely will fail. I advocated that the department take a path that meets the needs of the officers as well as the community—change and self-interest need not be mutually exclusive.

The model I used essentially centered on a clear, highly visible and shared mission. Leaders were expected to walk their talk; to be believably committed to where we were going. The success of the model would ultimately be based on how well they empowered their employees—that was a key.

Police chiefs can improve the quality of our nation's police if they are willing to be persistent in developing work systems that empower their employees, listen to the community, and have the time to accomplish it.

For a city and its leaders to desire the kind of excellence I'm outlining in this book without giving the chief tenure is foolish, short-sighted, and sure to fail. I certainly would have failed if I didn't have both time and tenure.

Michael Scott, director of the Center for Problem-Oriented Policing

(CPOP) and a law school professor, once served with me as a Madison police officer. He went on to work in various police line and executive positions in several cities. He made a noteworthy observation about transformation:

> *How can it be that such a large effort to transform the demographics, education, training and management of American police personnel... cannot be demonstrably linked in improvements in police practices in the field?... No matter who is employed to do the policing job, and how they are educated and trained, so long as the police job remains so challenging, so much in conflict, and so wedded to fundamentally flawed strategies, police performance will remain wanting. Put another way, changing the players won't make much difference if the game remains the same.*[55]

The job of a leader is, and always had been, to change the game; particularly if the results are not acceptable. That's what happens at halftime. If you are behind, you change how you are playing the game. In Madison, I changed the game and others can do it, too. Scott's question is still valid today: can police really change? Or was my experience in Madison just an anomaly?

55. Michael Scott. "Progress in American Policing?: Reviewing the National Reviews." *Law and Social Inquiry*, vol. 34, issue 1, Winter, 2008.

Chapter 5
How Many Chiefs Does It Take
to Change a Department?

TOO MANY PEOPLE BELIEVE THAT our police cannot change, they cannot improve. It's just the way it is. I believe police can improve if certain factors are present. I thought those factors were in place when I retired in 1993. I thought police were on a new path toward improving the way they did business. But they weren't. They were once again going back to old practices, circling around and not moving forward. I was invited to join our nation's leading police chiefs at a summit meeting on police improvement in Washington, DC in March 2005.[56] The conference was sponsored by the Police Executive Research Forum, an organization in which I was an active member for many years, that had a history of helping police improve.

What I heard and saw there that day caused me to reflect on my career in policing and all that I had hoped for. Had I retired too early from the game? I looked around the conference table and wondered why my former colleagues had not moved on from the point I had left them when I retired. Overall, things were not improving; it was the same-old, same-old. On the other hand, that day in Washington was a turning point that motivated me to put my thoughts together and write this book.

The purpose of this gathering was to discuss what Jim Collins had written concerning successful business organizations in his widely-acclaimed book,

---

56. Chuck Wexler, Mary Ann Wycoff, and Craig Fischer. *Good to Great Policing: Application of Business Management Principles in the Public Sector.* U.S. Department of Justice, Office of Community Oriented Policing Services: Washington, D.C. 2007.

Good to Great: Why Some Companies Make the Leap and Others Don't.[57] When I received my copy and read it, I was excited about what Collins had uncovered. I thought there were some things police could learn and apply from what he had found about high-performance companies. Why do some police departments make the leap while others don't? Why can't all police departments be great—exceptions to the mediocrity that seems to dominate the field?

But when I got to the meeting, it didn't take me long to realize that few of the chiefs in attendance had read the book. Fewer still were interested in engaging in the content of the book or discussing it. Even fewer suggested that Collins' work could possibly be applied to their departments.

Now, I knew many of the chiefs sitting around the table that day in Washington, and I must say that my expectation was that by this time in their careers they would be willing and eager to discuss a provocative book such as this. I was wrong.

What Collins did was look for the principal factors that made good companies exceptional ones. He examined organizations that for 15 years tracked or performed *worse* than the stock market, and then went through an internal transition and subsequently outperformed all their competitors. That is where he started to see some remarkable differences. Some companies were good, but there were a few that were great.

Collins found 11 companies that were "outperformers" and so he went on to study them in depth and compare them to their competitors. He wanted to know what these companies did that enabled them to transform and outperform their competitors. One of his key findings, naturally, had to do with leaders.

He called Level 5 Leaders those who created companies that outperformed their rivals. These leaders were found to be humble, willful, diligent, and hard workers. They knew how to put the right people in place in the organization (and how to remove those who were not). These leaders could almost effortlessly find the accurate information needed to make the

57. Jim Collins. *Good to Great: Why Some Companies Make the Leap and Others Don't.* New York: Harper-Collins. 2001.

necessary decisions. Board members of these companies shied away from selecting celebrity leaders because they knew they failed, in the long run, to create sustained results.

All this, by the way, is contrary to the popular image in America of the business leader (and police chief) who goes into an organization with guns blazing, negotiates a big salary, fires a bunch of people, puts together impressive quarterly performance reports, and then leaves. These leaders are not effective. And whatever they did accomplish wasn't sustainable. They were short-term leaders, and the organizations they led suffered.

The problem of applying what Collins found to a police department is an old one. It is one I had often encountered during my career. It made little difference in practice whether a case study was from the Harvard Business School or the International Chiefs of Police, but police leaders have difficulty accepting findings from other areas of work. Even good practices from other police departments. Over the years, I can't tell you how many times I have heard these responses from police leaders: "Yes, but it doesn't apply to *my* department" or "We tried that, but it didn't work."

The lack of a foundation of rigorous academic training makes it difficult for police leaders to digest any kind of research or case study. This is the continuing and oppressive effect of anti-intellectualism in the police field and why it remains a major obstacle.

This meeting disappointed me. I had expected more, and not much seemed to have changed. A closed mind regarding new ideas and concepts continues to be one of the most dangerous impediments in the police subculture.

On that day in Washington, I sat back and listened to the conversation. It soon drifted away from Collins' book and became a sharing of anecdotes— war stories from the chiefs about *their* department and the fine work *they* were doing. They didn't listen very well to either the presenters or to each other.

When academics are willing to meet and talk with police leaders about their work, they often come away finding the police interesting but uninterested, gregarious but lacking serious engagement. This was the atmosphere I found in that conference room, and it was unsettling. I came away thinking that police were still in trouble and few people in America were aware of it. Something needed to be said and done about their arrested development.

I feared that other matters, like the economy, jobs, health care, immigration, and wars in Iraq and Afghanistan would be more pressing than any need to improve our nation's police. I thought nothing would highlight the problems that continue to plague them.

But then came the Occupy Movement in 2011, and our police were once again on the street responding to public protest in many of our cities. While many citizens didn't know how police should respond to public protest, they knew that what they saw in some of our cities wasn't right. They thought police could do better.

Most citizens may not be able to conceive why highly-trained and competent police are needed, choosing to believe that good is good enough. For many others, at least before the Occupy Movement, police didn't bother them, so what's the problem? But what we are finding today is there are many citizens whom the police do bother, and they bother them daily as Nicholas Peart reminded us earlier. Most of these Americans are poor and/or people of color. As middle-class citizens in this country become less economically advantaged, they may find themselves in similar situations.

Worse yet, some people may feel that building a high-quality police department is simply not worth the effort or cost. Even citizen-activists can be timid about pressing for reform in a police department that isn't supportive of it. In such cases, they fear the pushback that can come from police who define them as troublemakers and know-nothings.

At the same time, American police leaders don't spend much time or effort raising the public's knowledge or expectations of their police either. It is about time to realize that our nation needs police leaders who can initiate and maintain a public conversation as to what citizens should expect from their police. Leaders who ask their communities to partner with them will be able to meet those expectations.

As it stands, police tend to tell citizens what their problems are instead of *asking* them. For example, police may feel there is a problem with burglary in the community only to find out when they get to a community meeting, the real issue is the department's aggressive stop-and-frisk tactics. The burglaries are few and far between, but the department's aggressive tactics are something citizens have had to deal with daily.

In the meantime, our nation's police drift further away from their commitment to solving community problems, working closely with citizens, and zealously protecting their rights. It is my belief that left alone, things won't develop. As our nation becomes more populous, undergoes economic downturns and energy shortages, struggles with immigration and an increasing diversity of race and culture in our nation's cities, a higher level of policing will be sorely needed. Good simply won't be good enough.

The challenge to police today if policing is ever going to be considered a profession is rather clear: they will need to develop a system of sustained leadership along with a body of knowledge that is able to fluidly incorporate research findings and to be willing to experiment with this new knowledge and effectively turn it into field practices. This is what professionals do. Thus, every police officer trained anywhere in the country would learn tried and tested methods—best practices—and, in turn, would be expected to practice them during his or her career.

My point is that police leaders have a critical role to play in this society as guardians of our rights. This must never be forgotten by them or by us. Until American police forge and claim that unique role in our society, they will continue to be viewed in the dim light of the past—as somehow being an ongoing part of the problematic historical legacy that I outlined earlier. For without a commitment to, and practice of, the values I have emphasized in this book, police will continue to be bogged down by a combination of poor performance and low expectations from the public. And that is a tragic situation.

Since that time in Washington, I've thought about the things I had learned during my career. Why hadn't these police chiefs learned the same things? I had written books and authored a score of professional articles about change and leadership. I had taught courses around the country in which I shared what I had learned in Madison about leading police and delivering community-based police services. Why wasn't organizational fairness and effectiveness commonly sought among our nation's police leaders? Why were police so slow to improve?

I have no doubt that the attitude which disdains formal education and research and a reliance on coercive leadership are their primary hindrances. I have concluded from my experience and continued observation that this has restrained and arrested their development. It isn't that there has been no improvement; I began police work without a college education, formal training, body armor or a personal radio. My point is that, given the organizational improvements of other institutions in our society, the police have fallen disgracefully behind.

Before any institution can improve, it must identify the obstacles in its way. Some of them I've already identified, such as the power of the police subculture, the negative legacy of their history, and over-reliance on physical force in the field and in the police station. But there are other major impediments American police must also deal with if they want to catch up and stay in front.

Overcoming these obstacles won't be easy. They are sturdily imprinted into our police. Doing so will require a commitment to intellectual excellence, civility, and the rule of law under even the most trying circumstances. It will require police to exhibit a high degree of awareness and self-control as they internally examine and police themselves. It will require that they actively seek to accurately match their communities' complexions and values with the officers they hire and promote.

From time to time, cities and their police have tried to overcome the effects of one or more of these historical, in-bred impediments. Most of the time, they have not applied well-thought-out strategies in doing so, or their efforts have been merely cosmetic. Few attempts have been sustained.

Changing police isn't just about changing a few things, but everything: hiring, training, leadership, solving problems, community orientation, and evaluation. It is about changing the very nature of the police function itself and the changes that will have to be put in place in order to raise the intellectual capacity of police, curtail their use of excessive force, drive out the vestiges of corruption and racism, and implement a new culture of courtesy, customer focus, and restraint in using physical force. They will also have to learn how to properly handle protesting people, not only singularly but in large crowds, and develop on-going formal relationships with academic institutions.

After my graduate education, the University of Minnesota awarded me a grant to study police departments in Europe. It was a vital and essential part of my career development as I began to see police on a larger scale and in different but democratically-influenced surroundings. I chose to study police departments in the cities of Stockholm, Copenhagen, Amsterdam, Hamburg, and London. The university's grant helped me identify and clarify the Four Obstacles that stand in the way of police improvement in America.

Obstacle 1: Anti-Intellectualism

It's 1971. I'm sitting in the office of the commissioner of police in Copenhagen. My eye catches the large oil paintings hanging high on the wall of the office. The paintings are very old, some from a century ago or longer. The commissioner, noticing my interest, says, "I see you are looking at the former commissioners of police in our city. The one over there, on your left, is Police Commissioner Romer. He was also a scientist—in fact, the first to calculate the speed of light." He concludes, "We come from a long line of educated police commissioners."

That moment, with my own recent college education not far from my thoughts, crystallized for me the notion that if we are to have a democratic and effective police institution in our nation, it *must* have higher education as its foundation.

Later, I was to learn more about the police commissioner who also was a scientist.

Ole Christensen Romer (1644–1710), took the first quantitative measurement of the speed of light and was the second commissioner of police in Copenhagen, a position he held until his death. Upon assuming the office of commissioner, Romer fired the entire police force. He did so because he was convinced that morale on the force was so alarmingly low that every police officer needed to be replaced.

Romer didn't abandon his inventive qualities when he joined the police—he used his skills to invent and put into operation the first street-lights and worked to improve the lives of the city's disadvantaged residents: beggars, prostitutes, and the unemployed. He established rules for building new houses, improved the city's water supply and sewage systems, developed new equipment for the city's fire department, and was the moving force behind paving streets and establishing town squares.[58] The police commissioner with whom I was speaking that morning in Copenhagen had not only big shoes to fill but an enormous intellectual legacy to uphold. I thought, if our nation's police leaders were all educated and as creative as Romer, where would we be today?

The negative spirit of anti-intellectualism presents itself in several ways in American policing. It begins with low educational standards for police applicants. Then it continues in police training as the classroom curricula are more oriented towards high school than college. Within police operations, new ideas and creative approaches are neither sought nor encouraged. When it comes to police operations, traditionally-based past experience is valued more highly than research or experience gained by others outside the field—even if it works.

The only way this obstacle is going to be overcome is by requiring our nation's police to have an academically rigorous four-year college education before they are sent into the field. In addition, police departments must have an on-going academic relationship with a college or university to bring together academics and practitioners. The two can then work together to develop, test, and share the most effective methods of policing. This would eventually result in police officers spending time in classrooms and doing research and academics teaching in the training academy and walking a beat.

Obstacle 2: Violence

When I came to Amsterdam in 1971, I noticed their police force's remarkable restraint in handling protests and demonstrations. They had a

58. http://www.amnh.org/education/resources/rfl/web/essaybooks/cosmic/p_roemer.html; January 1, 2011; 1112 hrs.

huge population of hippies, migrants, and street people that had settled in their city. I was commenting on their tolerance to a couple of senior officers when one of them said, "You must realize that many of us were prisoners ourselves. We were arrested and put in prison when the Germans invaded our country. That experience made a difference in how we treat people."

A few weeks later, in Germany, I was amazed how that country's police tried creative ways to prevent having to use force during protests and demonstrations. At the time, the only method used in my country was physical force. The police in Hamburg, however, had developed other methods and strategies. For example, they would field a powerful sound truck when a protest was scheduled. Police in the truck played popular music and bantered with the crowd. They felt it tended to set a positive tone and reduce tension in the crowd. The police officer in the sound truck served as a disk jockey, communicating and sometimes cracking jokes—all of which had a very positive effect and tended to reduce tension and anti-police sentiment within the crowd.

When I related to them what we in America did to control crowds and demonstrations, they looked at me as if I came from another planet. I resolved at that time that I would try to experiment with different methods of crowd control—to use force only as a last resort. That was in the 1970s, and the methods we use today in our country to manage crowds and protests have changed little since then. In fact, they have gotten worse, as police now overly depend on technology to handle crowds and protests.

It is conceivable that we may even see a new device on our streets to control people who protest. The army has developed large microwave transmitters that literally heat people up. I'm not joking. Such a unit can be used as a non-lethal weapon to move people away from an area or deny them access to it.[59] This technology could create a situation in which police no longer must form a line or even be present. The power between police and protesters has dramatically shifted during the past 40 years. There is

---

59. "60 Minutes," CBS television news magazine on June 19, 2009 on a new, non-lethal Army crowd-control weapon. You can see the video at: http://www.youtube.com/watch?v=kkGHgsgc6es.

no need for police to talk to protesters anymore. They don't even have to be close.

Removing the obstacle of violence does not just pertain to handling collective gatherings—it must also apply to police officers' daily interactions and the way they make arrests. Rather than quickly resorting to physical force to accomplish their work, police need to be consistently trained to always use the *least* amount of force necessary to overcome resistance. The abuse of force by police does not only hurt those who are on the receiving end, because when the public determines that police have used unnecessary force, police lose their respect, which ultimately results in less cooperation, thereby diminishing the effectiveness of the police function.

If police should ever be expert on any subjects, it should be persuasion and the use of force. For example, many police use-of-force manuals rank pepper spray below that of using a pressure point to gain compliance. The thinking here is that the pepper spray leaves no permanent damage or continued pain to a person while a pressure point (like a wrist lock) could. This has permitted police to use pepper spray in situations of passive resistance. But the question is: should they? And should they do it in highly public protest situations like many of us recently witnessed on the campus of the University of California at Davis?[60]

Again, whenever police must use force, it must be carefully used and always within the bounds of public approval. Until the use of force is considered a public trust granted to them by the people they serve, it will continue to be a major point of contention between citizens and their police.

Obstacle 3: Corruption

Whenever police act above the law, it is damaging to their effectiveness because it erodes the trust of the people. There are acts of corruption that involve stealing things and money for personal use. There are acts of

---

60. See an article and video of this at: http://www.guardian.co.uk/world/2011/nov/21/uc-davis-police-chief-leave?newsfeed=true). January 5, 2012; 1010 hrs.

corruption in which evidence is tampered with and testimony is untrue. Corruption in our nation's police departments and among its officers is another obstacle to police improvement. We all know that fallible humans like you and me staff public and private organizations. Police will make mistakes.

But what can be done is to significantly reduce the occurrence of both honest mistakes and willful acts. Law-breaking by the police should be an uncommon event. Citizens should always rightfully expect their police to first be honest. Police departments must be committed to effectively and intensively train their officers in the skills necessary to serve as public servants in a democracy. Selecting good people and training them, however, are only the first steps. The organizations in which police work must also be supportive of and practice the values they espouse. This means a police department that is truly committed to openness with the public and transparency in its operations. It means police officials who treat their employees with dignity and respect, and a thorough, fair, and trustworthy system for investigating and resolving complaints of misconduct.

Incidents of corruption and acts of dishonesty were not unknown in the European cities and police departments I visited, yet they appeared to be few and far between.

There was an expectation by citizens in those cities that their government and its officials, including the police, conduct themselves within the rule of law. There was an atmosphere and expectation among the police in each city that I studied that their business was to be conducted in a legal and ethical manner. Suffice it to say that a dishonest police department cannot continue to exist without dishonesty being a deep-seated part of the political culture of that city. If there is widespread corruption in a state, county, or local government, it will be unusual to find an honest police department in that situation and *vice versa*.

Maintaining a culture of honesty is dependent upon police being adequately compensated as law enforcement professionals. A city doesn't save money by underpaying their police. Perhaps the finest advice for police officers regarding ethics is the two commandments I was given as a young recruit: "Remember, everything that was illegal and wrong before you pinned a badge on your chest is still illegal and wrong. Never break the law to enforce it."[61]

Obstacle 4: Discourtesy

Simply put, while it will not leave citizens physically battered, police discourtesy still harms them and the community. This psychologically harmful act means not acting civilly and respectfully toward others.

It was in London, the final city I visited during my study, that the practice of civility was most evident. One day in busy downtown London, I watched a pair of young police constables standing on a corner answering numerous (and sometimes agonizingly repetitive) questions from passersby concerning directions and local landmarks. Every time, I noticed they were respectful and courteous.

Everyone who approached them had their attention, was listened to, and went away feeling that their question had been answered—and in a polite manner. In turn, I noticed that the citizens asking the questions showed a tremendous amount of respect for the officers. Police and citizens were practicing the art of civility.

Now, I know the British police have their problems, just as every police department does, but discourtesy does not seem to be one of them. It is true that civility or politeness is highly valued in British society, and so it is with their police. But isn't civility also one of our values? In our encounters with governmental workers, don't we expect courtesy and politeness from them? A police department that practices civility in its encounters with others will soon find that they, in turn, will be treated civilly. But civility must also be practiced *within* the ranks of the department—how police treat each other and how leaders treat rank-and-file officers is especially crucial. When leaders treat employees with respect they soon find it is reciprocal. It is then

---

61. I believe I received these words of wisdom from Deputy Inspector Edward Farrell, Minneapolis Police Department. Ed was the training director of the first formal police training academy I attended.

much more natural for employees to treat those outside the organization the same way.

I made a commitment to myself that day in London that any police department I would lead would focus on politeness and courtesy as a dominant organizational value. I also knew that if civility was to be an operational value within a police department, it also meant that its *leaders* needed to have polite and courteous interactions with their officers.

Civility is an essential ingredient in both the practice of internal leadership and the conduct of external community relations. Without public cooperation police have little chance of accomplishing their mission, and a discourteous police department much less. This means that a culture of respect and politeness must be created, nurtured, and maintained. While citizens may be expected to react negatively to verbal abuse, the same cannot be expected of a professional police officer. The standard is this: police must be courteous *to a fault*. By that I mean police should never over-react, return insults, or in any way be discourteous—*regardless* of the provocation, situation, or individual.

So far, you may have some doubt as to whether, given the historical background of our nation's police, they are able to adjust to modern times. At one time, I viewed the police as the mythical Sisyphus—reliably going forth each day to push a heavy rock up a hill only to have it slide back down when the day was finished, never being able to push the rock over the hill—only to begin again the next day doing the same thing.

I no longer hold that view. I'm convinced that police can take their place among our most respected public officials. They can push that rock over the hill and move forward. As I will relate in the following materials, we did it in Madison and that improvement continues today, years after my retirement. With the right leadership and a progressive government, it can happen in any city. With the right conditions and the right support, it will only take one chief to change a police department.

Chapter 6
The Seven Improvement Steps

Step One: Envision

Police leaders must cast a bold and breathtaking vision to ensure a distinguished future for policing.

A GOOD VISION STATEMENT SHOULD be short and bold (even breathtaking), and those hearing it for the first time should be able to clearly remember it the next day. One quickly learns, however, that creating a vision statement is the easiest step. For a vision to work, it must be shared with others whom it affects. It is one thing to cast a vision, another to be able to convince others that your vision is also their vision.

For leaders to have their visions become owned by others takes time and commitment. They must also have passion and persistence. Peter Drucker, one of our nation's most influential thinkers on management theory, once described these kinds of leaders as *monomaniacs with a mission.*[62] If we have ever learned anything about people in organizations, it is that to change anything takes time and commitment, passion and persistence.

Like most chiefs new to a department, I came with a vision that was, at first, a set of expectations as to how I wanted the men and women of my department to conduct the business of policing. These expectations came about through my own learning and experience—the things I thought important.

62. "Whenever anything is being accomplished, it is being done, I have learned, by a monomaniac with a mission." Peter Drucker. *Adventures of a Bystander.* New York: John Wiley and Sons. 1994.

From day one as a chief, I began to describe my expectations for the department at every opportunity. I was in the business of selling organizational change. I found that one of the top opportunities to do this was at the graduation of a class of new police officers. This was always a big event in Madison. I wanted my new officers to know who I was and what my expectations were—but most of all, how passionate I was about them.

- Employ your full skill at all times and to all persons.

- Prevent, manage, or intervene in situations requiring police service.

- Be open, accept change in this changing world, develop and maintain a broad perspective of your function and the society in which you work, be flexible and develop the ability to grow with the people you serve.[63]

Expectations matter. I would continue to use the same set of expectations over my years in Madison because they were what I expected of myself and from every police officer with whom I worked. These expectations would be the foundation of the Madison Vision. But before my expectations became the driving vision for the Madison department, there was a lot of work that first needed to be done.

If a vision is going to be sustainable and last beyond the leader who casts it, the process is as important as the product. First, police leaders are needed who are not only monomaniacs with a mission, but who are willing to stay around long enough and to suffer through the pain that inevitably comes with seeing an organization through the process of change.

Second, there needs to be constant and on-going support by the community, including elected officials—those outside the organization—to help make the vision a reality. Leaders must cast their vision outside the department as much as they do inside of it.

---

63. At the graduation ceremony of the Madison Police Recruit graduation, August 8, 1974.

Third, those within the organization must know their leader is willing to engage in a process with them to develop the vision. They too must be willing to participate in the work to make the vision become a reality and do all that they can to operate under its direction.

The Madison vision statement gained more traction within the department as each class of new officers took to the street. Time was on my side. And working closely with members of the department, I began to develop, with them, a more formal vision and mission statement that reflected the values that I sensed we all were beginning to share. The vision and mission statements brought out in 1986 had that support. It defined who we were, what we wished to become, and what our citizens deserved. It laid the groundwork for even bolder steps ahead.

My job in creating a shared vision from a set of my expectations would have been more difficult if corruption had been extreme within the Madison department, its internal management mechanisms were in disarray, its officers were excessively violent, or there was seething racial resentment within the minority community. This kind of situation would have set my vision back by years—perhaps so far back that nothing else could have been accomplished except to try and turn around these impediments. I could, therefore, with some confidence, say that my job in coming to Madison was to pursue excellence in policing. I did not dwell on the department's shortcomings.

A leader must be able to encourage and enlist a substantial cadre of supporters within the organization, both junior and senior, who will stand up, move out, and help make their leader's vision *their* vision. Unless that happens, a vision will never become a reality.

In Madison, a major amount of my time was spent establishing the value of an operating vision and the steps needed to make it happen—that is, its mission. The process of doing so is called *catch-ball*.[64] The term comes

---

64. The Japanese developed this concept after World War II to develop highly-efficient policy management. The term is "Hoshin Kanri;" literally translated as: "point the direction and motivate everyone to achieve the vision." The way this is done is by what we in America call "catch-ball;" that is, pass concepts, goals, objectives, and strategies back and forth throughout the entire organization—from top to bottom—to improve

from the quality improvement days of Deming. The leader is to form a vision and pass it to members throughout the organization. They look at it, consider it, talk about it, and bounce it back. The leader receives their input. They may even have added new ideas and information. The leader ponders and incorporates their feedback, and passes it back again. And so it goes until the vision becomes shared. This is an effective organizational technique in which not only visions but also ideas and methods can be passed back and forth within the hierarchy of the organization with the purpose of developing shared visions, ideas, and methods.

I continued to promote my vision whenever I had the opportunity. As chief, I was in the sales business. And selling involves knowing your product and what your customers need. But if you don't have a desired product, no matter how hard you sell, buyers will be few.

Step Two: Select

Police must encourage and select the best and the brightest to serve as police officers.

IN THE NOT-SO-DISTANT PAST, NEPOTISM was rampant within police departments. This was a protective response by police to make sure that those who joined them were just like them—reinforcing the subculture and the *status quo*. Police encouraged their friends and relatives who held the same worldview as they did to join their ranks.

The goal today is to continue to staff the ranks of the police with persons who reflect the community served. To a large extent, that has happened in our nation's bigger cities. But it didn't happen overnight. In most instances, it didn't happen through police leadership, but by the changing color and gender of the electorate in our nation's cities.

What may have been the most difficult task of police administrators came about through legal mandates and civic elections, not because they

---

and share them. See: http://cokepm.com/pmbok3/KnowledgeBase/qua litycorner/700WorkingTogetherUsingCatch-Ball.pdf, and http://www. realinnovation.com/content/c080623a.asp. January 23, 2012; 1035 hrs.

were seeking diversity in their ranks. The forces behind those court decisions and electoral politics were that of a nation weary and angry at the injustices of racial segregation and keeping women out of all-male workplaces. So it didn't take long for elected officials to see that women and racial minorities were moved into the ranks of their police departments in our nation's larger cities despite police resistance in the ranks.

During the early '70s, our nation's law and culture were rapidly changing. There is no doubt in my mind that President Johnson's adding "gender" in 1968 to the anti-discrimination list of "race, religion, and national origin" was a huge opportunity for women to serve in non-traditional jobs. This executive order assisted one of the most fundamental goals of a professional police—diversity. It enabled women as well as minorities and, eventually, those with different sexual orientations, to come to see the police as representing them and their interests—something that before had been almost unimaginable. But again, with a small number of exceptions, it didn't come about from police. Even today, most departments are sorely deficient in numbers of women police and even more so in the top ranks.

During this period, there was also opposition to raising educational standards for police because of the fear that this would make the hiring of minorities more difficult. The argument was that minority applicants didn't have equal access to higher education and, therefore, a higher educational requirement would be another barrier to diversifying the department. At the time, this was partially true.

Today, however, the argument is no longer valid, but I do remember the struggle back in the 1970s. My efforts to get the police commission to set a baccalaureate degree requirement were always thwarted by the access-to-education argument. There was fear that requiring highly educated police would shut out people of color. Looking back, even though the Madison department didn't have a formal four-year college degree requirement, I was still able to attract and select many applicants with college degrees—including many from minority backgrounds. Through aggressive recruiting and the compelling image we presented that we were a place for college graduates and the obvious visual change in the complexion and gender of our officers, we were still able to quickly integrate the department, raise the educational level, and receive praise from our community for doing so. Madison police were perceived to be educated men and women.

Assisting my commitment to hire police officers with degrees, I had a powerful educational incentive program in place. Madison's incentive program paid baccalaureate degree-holders 18 percent over and above their base pay, and master's degree-holders 22 percent. This meant that a police officer with a master's degree—and we had a number of them—was paid a salary equivalent to a lieutenant with a high school diploma. It was quite clear to all how Madison felt about the importance of education for its police.

At the time I retired, more than 25 percent of sworn officers in the department were women, and 10 percent were from racial minorities. In the years since my retirement, I'm proud to report that these numbers have increased, respectively, to 32 and 16 percent.

I'm confident that one of the more enduring things I did in Madison was to bolster the image of the police officer. It took a good 10 years before the image changed from police being narrow and uneducated to that of intelligent and highly trained.

One morning in the mid-1970s, I remember attending a briefing of senior day-shift officers, most all of whom were males older than I was. Several of them soon began complaining about the changes going on within the department—hiring women, new policies that restricted the use of deadly force, and the requirement that a supervisor call off high-speed chases if they became too dangerous to the community.

I listened as the grousing continued. Then I asked them, "When I came to the department, many of your wives told me they were embarrassed to say their husbands were police officers. They shared with me that those days of riot and turmoil took a toll on them and your children as well. Now looking back, think—is that the case now? Or are your wives and children proud that you are a Madison police officer?" It was quiet in the room. I had made a point. These senior officers knew they had gained respect under my leadership. Everyone had benefited from our effort to professionalize—to be a first-class police department. They knew they were now viewed as respected professionals in the community.

Many of our new officers had broad backgrounds. They had worked before coming to Madison as teachers, nurses, social workers, and even lawyers. Anyone who heard about the education and background of these new officers couldn't help but consider them to be not only interesting and likable but also educated and talented.

Removing the stigma of policing wasn't easy. It took time and persistence. Other police departments can learn from this—it isn't impossible to repair the damaged image of a police department. But the effort must be substantive and not just public relations work. And once it happens, the value of the effort will become clear: citizens and police both benefit from a competent, ethical, well-run police organization. There are superior relations with the community, effective problem solving, openness, good operational decisions, and a sense of safety and well-being permeating the city.

A police department in America should be, at a minimum, as good as our nation's most successful business organizations. It should develop a workplace that encourages good ideas, listens well, and is willing to receive input from both insiders and outsiders. A professional organization values the diversity of its personnel and considers it to be a strength, not a weakness. A department like this has little trouble attracting good people to join their ranks.

But how should such people be selected? And how should they be prepared and trained? I have outlined the many functions and responsibilities we should expect of police officers in a free and multicultural society such as ours. It would be foolish to think that all the functions identified earlier by the American Bar Association could be brought to a high level of competency in a shorter time than what has been done in the case of other important jobs in our society.

Nearly 50 years have passed since President Lyndon Johnson's commission recommended a standard be set that required police officers to hold a four-year baccalaureate degree. I'm sad to report today that only one *percent* of our nation's police departments have that requirement in place.[65]

---

65. See http://utsa.edu/swjcj/archives/7.1/Bruns%20Article.pdf, May 6, 2011; 1207 hrs.

Today, more than ever, our nation needs educated police. It is shameful that we don't have more.

The commission also uncovered something I never forgot. It found that most states in our nation require more training to become a barber than a police officer. At the time, I was struck by how odd that was. Are we more concerned as a society about how we look than how we are policed? I know the quality of a haircut is important, but so is the quality of decisions made by our police as they make inquiries, settle disputes, investigate crimes, arrest suspects, and give testimony in a court of law.

So I decided to check whether that observation still held true today. Using my home state of Wisconsin as an example, I found that to practice their trade, barbers and cosmetologists in my state must first graduate from a licensed school of barbering or cosmetology and then participate in an additional 1,800 training hours, all of which must be completed in not less than 10 months. On the other hand, the required training for police officers in my state is 400 hours. The observation made by the President's commission in 1967 still holds true. Wisconsin barbers and beauticians have a higher standard of training than that required of police.

The Wisconsin Law Enforcement Standards Board (LESB) requires police applicants to have either a two-year associate degree or a minimum of 60 college credits. But while it may be a standard, it isn't a *requirement*, as newly appointed police officers may practice until the end of their fifth year of service before having to meet this standard. We don't permit our barbers and cosmetologists to cut our hair without being properly trained and licensed, but we permit police officers to enforce our laws without training. This strange situation is not unique to Wisconsin.

There is something even more necessary to alter the present course of policing: how police candidates are attracted to the job. I would maintain that until policing is a job for a college graduate like it is in Madison, there will continue to be few college graduates willing to serve as police officers. As an example, I recently read this description concerning employment opportunities on a website directed at those who may be considering a police career. It stated this about police training academies:

They are usually very disciplined and regimented. You will walk in formation and line up for inspection. During the week, you are usually required to spend all your time at the academy. On Friday night, you may be granted "liberty" and allowed to leave the academy for the weekend, returning on Sunday night.[66]

Who would be attracted by the above introduction? Very few of the kind of people I was looking for. I found the most effective recruiting results were obtained by likening police work to joining a domestic Peace Corps and describing it as an essential job in our community in need of people with solid backgrounds in social work, conflict resolution, and helping professions like teaching, law, nursing, emergency medicine, psychology, and business. We must never forget that it is the people—the police officers—that make the difference in the quality of a police department.

So why would an educated person want to join the police? When I was in Madison, the first thing I would mention was the opportunity for both personal and professional growth. Second, I would tell them we were an organization that is committed to listening to and acting on the valued ideas of its employees; that is, in Madison, a police officer isn't simply a cog in the organization wheel, he or she is a player. Third, as a member of this department you will have the privilege to serve, protect others, help those who are disadvantaged in our society, and contribute to the social good.

In being committed to developing a quality, world-class department from the inside out leaders must always begin with proper selection of the best and brightest applicants to serve as police officers. The future demands no less.

---

66. http://www.policejobsinfo.com/hiring-process/training/ January 1, 2011; 1407 hrs.

Step Three: Listen

Police leaders must intently listen to their officers and members of the community.

THIS BOOK IS ABOUT MORE than change—it is about transformation. And transformation involves conversion, inside work, not just a change in appearance. The transformation of a police organization first begins inside its members. Much of what I have written here may be new and startling to some. But it shouldn't be foreign to those who are watching and listening to what is happening in the world today. The non-hierarchical pro-democracy movements around the world are really harbingers of the future. For the American police to attain the high level of professional excellence that I believe they are capable of, they will have to undergo this kind of total transformation.

By 1980, with eight years under my belt in Madison, I was getting content with how far we had come. The job seemed too easy. I had promoted the people I wanted and had them in place throughout the department. The community seemed satisfied with how the department had changed— we were more diverse and we, effectively and fairly, kept peace on the streets. The perception of citizens was that crime was under control. And I was reminded of the adage, "If it ain't broke, don't fix it."

I had stayed on message, cast a bold vision and was selecting outstanding police officers. But what about their senior leaders? Had the vision transformed them as to their leadership style? What more did I need to do?

As I noted earlier, a new and growing movement was on the American horizon. It was a movement to increase the quality of our products and services. Government was an agency that provided a service—not a product—however, taxpayers didn't seem like customers. But the American economy was in recession, and ideas like continuous improvement, reducing our costs, and increasing customer/taxpayer satisfaction looked like possible solutions to our problems.

This was the environment in which I found myself mid-career in Madison. During this time, an image came to me. It was that of the wagon trains which carried homesteaders west during the 19th century. On their journey, they had to cross oceans of virgin prairie. When approaching this sea of grass, the wagon master would intentionally stop the wagon train, stand on top of one of the wagons, then look, and listen. He would scan the horizon, then get down and put his ear on the ground. He looked and listened for signs of danger. He looked for telltale smoke of a deadly prairie fire raging through the high grass. He listened for the sound of a stampeding herd of bison that could capsize and crush the wagon train and cause injury or even death to those in his care. Good wagon masters did this because they needed information in order protect those who followed him. I found myself in the same place in 1980 when I thought about my career in Madison and the future of the department. The stress and conflict of the past eight years had hit me hard.

While things were stable within the department, everything else around me seemed to be tumbling down. A long-term marriage had broken apart, and my children were angry with me. I needed a break. I remember telling colleagues that it was my belief that most of us could handle a crisis at work or a crisis at home but not both at the same time. I now found myself with both.

Joel Skornicka was mayor at the time, and I requested a six-month leave of absence without pay. I was tired, and I think he knew it.

Thankfully, he approved. When I was asked why I requested a leave, I said it was to write a book. I even had a title: *The Consumer's Guide to Police*. But others around me knew I was hurting. The speculation was that I was done. I wouldn't return. It was a fair prediction. As an anonymous source within the police department was quoted in the newspaper as saying,

> *Couper won't be back. He has talked a lot about teaching and writing, and I don't think he'll be back.*"[67]

The article in which this quote appeared also reported that I had filed for divorce the previous week and had moved out of the family home. Assistant Chief Edward Daley would be in charge during my absence. A day later I had to defend my request to inquiring reporters.

67. *The Capital Times*, December 11, 1980.

After eight years, I think six months is a reasonable rest for a police chief in Madison… It's a question of whether the people of Madison want a police chief with a heart attack or a police chief with a lot of other problems. I need this rest to be more creative and an even better executive. I am in tune with myself enough to know when it was time to take a break.[68]

As it turned out, writing, skiing, connecting with friends I hadn't seen for a while, and meeting some new ones made all the difference in the world. It was time to recharge my batteries.

During this sabbatical time, one of the new friends I made was the woman who was to change my life. She was a new officer in the department, just out of recruit school. I ran into her one day while on leave, out walking on the Capitol Square. We talked and had coffee together. We decided to pursue a relationship. As it developed, she offered to leave the department prior to my return and continue her police career elsewhere so we could see where we were going. She did so, and a year later, we were married.

Later, I remember asking her why she agreed to have coffee with me that day. Sabine looked at me seriously.

"Because I wanted to know if you were as big a jerk as some people say you were."
"What did you find out?" I asked.
'You were," she said, smiling, "but you changed."

Three months later, I surprised everyone and returned to full duty.

Upon my return, I started thinking about leadership—my leadership. Couldn't I do better? I needed to find out. And the optimum way to find out was to ask those whom I was responsible for leading. Was I a jerk?

After I talked with Sabine, who was very familiar with the workings of the department, she suggested I hold many employee meetings in which I would be there not to talk but to *listen*. I did so and asked every member of the department in these groups what they thought the biggest problem

68. *The Wisconsin State Journal,* December 12, 1980

facing the department was. The answer was clear, direct, and unanimous—me. I was the problem, along with a lack of communication department-wide. Those small group meetings with all the employees of the department were brutal but necessary. If I had not done it, I never would have seen my vision come to fruition. And without this scanning and listening to employees, the changes I implemented never would have lasted beyond my tenure.

I began to follow up on what I had learned. I began responding to the communication problem. I did that by establishing an Officer's Advisory Council (OAC). I committed to meeting with the council once a month and thoroughly discussing with them the things they identified as important. It was to be a 10-person council with members elected throughout the department to represent both officer and civilian ranks.

After the first election, despite our growing diversity, all those elected turned out to be male and white. At the first meeting, we discussed this problem. Rather than take an attitude of "tough luck, that's the way it is," those elected officers and employees decided that until women and minority representatives were sufficient in number to be elected, we would establish two more elected seats on the council—one for a female police officer and another for an officer who was a racial minority. This was a significant step for these officers to take. I knew then that the time was right. It was a signal to me that the race and gender wars were over.

As a department, we were now ready to become more than just a good police department.

The OAC came to play a major role in the leadership and administration of the police department. Its members were given the responsibility for deciding issues like uniforms, types of weaponry, and criteria for the purchase of new patrol vehicles. Today, the OAC continues as a vital player in the Madison Police Department, and it will soon celebrate its 30th year of existence.

At the time, I considered changing my leadership style. I had to ask myself what it was that I expected from those with whom I work. I knew that I wanted to work with people who were competent and worthy of my respect. I wanted work that was interesting and challenging. I wanted to work for leaders who listened to my ideas, recognized me when I did good work, and kept me informed about what was going on. And I wanted to be able to grow and develop in my job.

I must admit that leaders on the departments in which I served as an entry-level officer did not usually meet these work expectations. This was primarily because these work desires cannot be met in a coercive, top-down organization.[69]

When I personally asked the members of my own department regarding the kind of leader that would help them in their work, they described the very same things. They wanted to work for leaders who:

- *Respected them.*
- *Cared about them.*
- *Had confidence in their ability to do their jobs.*
- *Trusted them.*
- *Spent time with them.*

They also said that those leaders needed to be:

- *Competent (knew their job).*
- *Champions (walked their talk).*
- *Fixers and improvers.*
- *Visible and involved.*
- *Willing to take risks and initiate action.*
- *In touch with them, understanding, and giving support.*
- *Open about what was going on.*

When I started to understand what I was being told, I realized that I must be the first person to be this kind of leader—to change myself and how I acted. Then I had to help other leaders in the department to do the

69. *The Wisconsin State Journal*, December 12, 1980

same thing. I knew that we were all creatures of habit, and that changing to this new way wasn't going to be easy—it would take time and would require a lot of training, patience, and hands-on coaching. It would also, at times, be painful.

In the past, I had set some things in place that were now helping me institute this new leadership style. The first was that I eliminated the military-style atmosphere of the police academy. When I was introduced to the academy class that was already in training before I was appointed, the class stood at attention when I entered the room. In fact, I found that not only did they stand at attention when I entered, but they did so for every supervisor who came into their class. I also found that their method of teaching left much to be desired. This was more like middle school than a police academy. This, I knew, wasn't how adults learn.

So I not only had to relax the training atmosphere to make it more suitable for adult learning, but also find an academy director who shared my thoughts about this. I wanted the police academy to be run like a college or university. If I was going to begin to build a new future for police officers, it had to begin with their first police experience—the training academy.

I was now in the next step. I wanted department leaders to use an adult-oriented leadership model—police officers were not children and were not to be treated as if they were. A coercive, top-down leadership model had no place within a police department that was seeking highly-educated people to come and join it. Some of the people we were trying to attract into a police career were currently in business, law, social work, or teaching. And most of them wouldn't choose to remain in a police department that ran like an 18th century British warship.

I need to clearly say that these changes were not easy for any of us.

Over the years, we all had found comfort in the old leadership model. When I began as a leader, I made a lot of mistakes—but I kept on trying to get it right. I expected the same from others. I came to learn this about organizational change: it should never be imposed by the boss on the workers but rather come from the inside out—that is, after listening, input and study from within the organization. While everyone may not agree with the final direction taken, they need to understand why it is being taken. And once the change is internalized within the department, it can be introduced to the community.

What I began to see is that if I change myself—that is, "walk my own talk"or "practice what I preach"—I teach in a most significant and lasting way. I became the lesson I wanted to teach. To do it myself, however, I had to clearly explain specifically what I was talking about: why the new approach was necessary for our future and how we would begin to practice it. Then I had to listen to their feedback—deeply and intently—learn how they understood what I was trying to communicate.

I found that the way to begin was for me to get out of my office. I had always believed in an open-door policy. But I thought the open door was to permit my employees to come in and talk with me. How wrong I was. The door to my office was open so that I could get out and listen to them.

This became one of my first experiments in what Tom Peters in the 1980s would call MBWA: Managing by Wandering Around. I started to make a weekly (and sometimes daily) habit to get out of my office and into the workplaces of the department. Each summer I booked a month on the street. I worked nights in uniform, driving a marked squad car, and took calls.[70] My job was to model the street behavior I expected from my

70.   In researching this idea, I found that I was, in fact, "managing by wandering around," a concept first championed by Tom Peters and Nancy Austin in 1985 after they saw it in operation at Hewlett-Packard. [See Peters, T. and Nancy Austin, *A Passion for Excellence: The Leadership Difference*, Collins, 1985.] It was there that Peters saw this technique used by Bill Hewlett and Dave Packard who pioneered the open style of management. See online article in *The Economist* magazine: http://www.economist.com/node/12075015;7/29/11,1149. Today it is still viewed as one of the "more influential business-management ideas." However, I first started this practice in 1980 at the urging of my wife Sabine, who was then a rank-and-file police officer. It just seemed to her that it was a good practice for anyone in a leadership position and detached from the daily and critical work done by police officers and detectives. I remember Dr. Deming once saying that if managers wait for employees to come to them, they will only bring managers small problems. The big problems, he said, need to be sought out and found. It is a leader's primary job to do so.

officers and to find out what needed improving. I was beginning to learn that transformation begins at the top. Not the other way around.

When department leaders started *listening* to their officers and avoided strong-arm tactics to get work done, change started to happen. The same thing can go on within the communities police serve—listening works.

Step Four: Train and Lead

Police leaders must implement professional training and a collaborative leadership style.

To TRAIN IS TO LEAD, and to lead is to train—the two are inextricably linked. Good leaders are good trainers and *vice versa*. When I embarked on the huge task of improving the Madison department from top to bottom, I started thinking about the valuable role rank-and-file officers could take in being an active part of this transformation.

Therefore, I had to be able to attract, hire, and promote to leadership positions the finest people I could find. I knew the kind of people I was looking for and that such high-quality people would only be attracted to serving in an organization that considered each of them to be of high value and a future leader.

To build a quality department, commanding officers—up to and including the chief—must themselves exhibit a willingness to learn and to alter their own behavior that works against change, and begin to lead by example. Police officers must listen to and respond appropriately to their communities, but the most optimal way to learn this is by what they see going on in their own departments. They can only learn to serve their communities if their own leaders *first serve them*. In this respect, there is much police can learn from the private sector and the academics who work with and define successful leaders in business and industry.

It took me years to develop a style of leadership that was based more on coaching than on compulsion. In my early years, it seemed as if coercion was the only way to get officers to do what I wanted them to do. I often wonder today whether if I had taken on the role of coach earlier, it would have reduced resistance. At the time, I feared that if I did, resistance would have been even greater. I'll never know.

Where did I learn to use coercion? It was in the Marines, and it seemed normal. Everyone else was using it. But you don't have to serve in the Marines to learn strong-arm tactics. It's all around us—in our families of origin and in our workplaces. In the Marines, I did what I was told and made sure that those for whom I was responsible did what I told them to do—or else. That was how I saw my leaders operate. But I also was learning something else: the importance of organizational history and tradition and of courage, honor, and steadfastness in the face of adversity. The Marines taught its recruits all that was noble about the Corps. We all learned the motto: *Semper fidelis*, "Always faithful." I believed I would fight just as fearlessly and ferociously as Marines in the past had done, from the Revolutionary War to the present day; that's what Marines did and who they are.

When I joined the police, I found that most of the men I worked with were veterans like I was; many were former Marines. We had a common language and a common set of leadership expectations as we came together in the police. I remember as a police officer in Minneapolis I was put in charge of training a large group of officers (including supervisors that outranked me) in civil disturbance training. One of the sergeants challenged my instruction, and I remember clearly using the leadership style I had learned as a Marine: "Knock it off! I'm in charge here. And if I were you, I wouldn't want to challenge that." He backed down, but looking back, I'm embarrassed about how I handled that situation. I already knew there were other ways to handle this than the way I did.

Today, many police departments continue to run their training academies like boot camps. These departments have training officers who look and act like Marine Corps drill instructors. They even wear the familiar Smoky Bear hats of Marine drill instructors. As I became more acquainted with police work, I couldn't understand why police were using the same training model I had been subjected to as a Marine. There was no similarity whatsoever between being a Marine infantryman and a police officer—the two job functions were as different as night and day.

Later in my career I began to understand that leadership is more than giving orders. I realized that most people, me included, don't like being subjected to pressure in their workplaces. And when we are, our reactions are far from positive. Tom Gordon taught me to reconsider my use of it as a primary leadership style. At the midpoint of my career, I was beginning to have huge doubts about the value and effectiveness of putting people under duress, that is, using coercion. Then I read Gordon's book, *Leader Effectiveness Training*. It provided me with the rationale I needed to avoid it whenever possible.[71] Gordon was widely recognized as a pioneer in teaching communication skills and conflict resolution methods to parents, teachers, youth, organizational managers, and employees.

Gordon was a licensed clinical psychologist on the faculty of the University of Chicago, and he served in the Army Air Force during World War II. His target audiences were parents, teachers, and organizational leaders; now it would be my department and me.[72] In his book, Gordon describes how people react to pressure or intimidation when their leaders use it:

> *The use of coercive power causes people to reduce their upward communication in an organization. It can also cause people to engage in rivalry and competitiveness, and to rebel and withdraw. The use of coercive power costs the leader in time, enforcement, alienation, stress and, eventually, diminishing influence with employees.*

Gordon is saying that when leaders use coercion, they are faced with two immediate problems: they must now make sure their decisions are followed (and that takes extra work), and the quality of these decisions will be less than if they had asked their employees for input. That is because workers will naturally withhold essential information from those who

71. Tom Gordon. *Leader Effectiveness Training*. New York: Bantam Books. 1978.

72. For more information on Tom Gordon and his work, see: http://www. gordontraining.com/leadershiptraining.html.

coerce them. This, of course, could be information critical to a high-quality decision. Gordon goes on:

> We can all think of situations in which we were coerced into having to accept a superior's decision without our input... [It] also has a negative impact on ideas, creativity, innovation, and motivation.

> A leader is best
> When people barely know he exists
> Not so good
> When people proclaim and obey him
> Worse when they despise him
> But of a good leader
> Who talks little
> When work is done His aim fulfilled
> They will say
> We did it ourselves

> Lao Tzu. 6th century, b.c.e.

The coercive method, nevertheless, became the way most of our industrial, governmental, and educational systems operated—including our police departments. It is the way many of us have experienced leadership in our adult lives. The historical legacy of this, as I mentioned earlier, goes back to Frederick Taylor and his *Scientific Management*.

The cumulative negative effect of using intimidation to lead our nation's workers, especially police, no doubt is incalculable. I cannot say this any clearer: the use of it to lead is wrong and shouldn't be tolerated in any organization. There are more effective ways to lead—and the finest leaders will know this. Along with avoiding using this tactic, there is being a leader who helps, coaches and develops others—a servant leader.

That brings me to Robert Greenleaf. Greenleaf first used the term "servant leadership" in 1970:[73]

---

73. For more about Robert Greenleaf's work see http://greenleaf.org.

> *The servant-leader is servant first... That person is sharply different from one who is leader first... The leader-first and the servant-first are two extreme types.*
> *Between them there are shadings and blends...*[74]

According to Greenleaf, servant leadership is primarily having a focus on *others*, not oneself. It is that focus on others that makes a talented leader. The preeminent leadership test, Greenleaf noted, is for leaders to be able to ask themselves three questions:

- *Do those under my leadership grow as persons?*

- *Do they become healthier, wiser, freer, more autonomous, more likely themselves to become servant leaders?*

- *What is the overall effect of my leadership on those who are underprivileged and will they benefit by my leadership or not?*

These three questions can, of course, be used to evaluate our leaders—but first they should be used to evaluate our own leadership style. Almost all of us will, at one time or another, be put into a position of leadership where others will be dependent upon our direction. This may be in our home, at work, or in a volunteer community group.

According to Greenleaf there are also two other serious maladies that confront our society: widespread alienation and the inability or unwillingness of persons to serve. No two attitudes could be more disastrous to any society than these two—a sense of disconnection and the avoidance of serving others. I sense that even today those two maladies continue to confront our society as our economy and our place in the world falter.

Greenleaf also foresaw the chief institutional problem of most of our public and private organizations: too high a priority on telling others

74. Robert Greenleaf. *The Servant as Leader.* An essay. 1970. Larry Spears, ed. and R.K. Greenleaf. *Servant leadership: A journey into the nature of legitimate power and greatness* (25th anniversary edition.). New York: Paulist Press. 2002.

what to do, and too low a priority on showing them how to do it; that is, modeling the behavior you wish others to practice.

I came to find that these ideas of leadership were not new. I see it today in the motto of the British officer training school at Sandhurst—*Serve to Lead.*[75] Yet the concept of a servant leader is much older than Sandhurst. It emerges cross-culturally in the writings of the ancient Chinese philosopher Lao Tzu. While some historians disagree as to whether Lao Tzu was an actual historical figure or not, the sayings attributed to him have stood the test of time.

Servant leadership, therefore, isn't a new idea. An essential aspect of the concept is that people who wish to lead must first serve—that is, they must know what it is like to serve others rather than increasing their own wealth or power. The benefit of servant leadership is that those who receive it experience personal growth as they become involved in the working and decisions of the organization, are listened to, and consulted as to what can be done to improve the work they do.

Many of today's management consultants, like Stephen Covey, build on Greenleaf's concept when they highlight the important characteristics of good leadership. These kinds of leaders:[76]

- *Inspire trust by building relationships.*

- *Clarify purpose by creating goals to be achieved.*

- *Align systems so that there is no conflict between what they say is important and what results they measure.*

- *Able to unleash talent in other people.*

- *The world is vastly different today and ever-changing. If we can develop leaders who can withstand and embrace the changing times*

---

75. Royal Military Academy at Sandhurst, UK. http://www.army.mod.uk/.

76. http://www.stephencovey.com/blog/?p=6 May 28, 2011; 1124 hrs.

> *by deeply rooting themselves in these principles of great leadership,*
> *then we can develop great people, great teams, and great results.*[77]

This brings me to the third influence on my leadership development—W. Edwards Deming.[78] In the case of Deming, his teaching was more personal because I got to know him over the years. I attended his lectures and worked with some of his closest disciples like Peter Scholtes, Brian Joiner, and Bill Hunter, and others who came with Deming to participate in the Hunter Conference, an annual quality improvement gathering in Madison.

Later, Deming invited me to a series of Saturday morning discussions he held at the University Club in Washington, DC This was a time when many of us in Madison city government were intensely involved in bringing Deming's concepts into our work in city government. I found his personal touch and coaching to be extremely helpful to my own personal growth.

Under then-Mayor Joseph Sensenbrenner's leadership (1983-89) there was a total involvement by city employees in this movement. He called it QI: Quality and Improvement. They were the golden years of quality in Madison as government, business, and educational institutions all found wisdom in Deming's methods and then worked together to make quality a lifestyle in Madison. His approach helped me see police work as a system capable of being continuously improved along with the importance of collaborating with others outside the police department. But more importantly, this changed the way I saw myself as a leader.

Deming's ideas first took root in Japanese industry after World War II. Many years later there began a growing movement in our own country to use his methods not only in American industry and business, but government as well. The Madison Police Department was a part of that movement.

How was a 90-year-old professor able to impact business both in Japan and the United States? During World War II, Deming worked as

---

77. Steven Covey. *Seven Habits of Highly Effective People.* New York: Simon and Schuster. 1992.

78. For an overview of Deming, see the W. Edwards Deming Institute website at http://deming.org.

a census statistician in Japan for General Douglas MacArthur. In Japan, Deming's expertise in statistical quality control techniques, combined with his involvement in Japanese society, caught the attention of Japanese industrialists. He was invited to join the Japanese Union of Scientists and Engineers (JUSE), whose members had studied the statistical control methods of one of Deming's former teachers, Walter Shewhart. Like Shewhart, Deming believed that a worker's lack of information profoundly hampered the process of improving products and delivering services.

Shewhart, who had worked for Bell Laboratories, developed an improvement cycle that will be familiar to anyone who has studied problem-oriented policing. The cycle contains four continuous steps: *Plan, Do, Study, Act.* Shewhart and Deming both believed that if this cycle of improvement is maintained, and if management is willing to disregard unsupported ideas, the quality of work, products, and services will consistently improve, and costs will be reduced.

As part of America's post-war reconstruction efforts in Japan, that country's industrial leaders wanted to learn more from Deming. During the 1950s, Deming trained hundreds of Japanese engineers, managers, and scholars in his methods. The message was plain and direct: if Japan improved the quality of their products, they would reduce their expenses, increasing both their productivity and market share.

Almost immediately upon hearing Deming's message and learning his methods, many Japanese manufacturers applied his techniques and soon achieved almost unheard-of levels of quality and productivity.

They not only raised the quality of their products but also did so at reduced cost—and it created an international demand for Japanese products.

Within a few short years, Japanese products moved from being considered junk to the legendary high level of quality and customer loyalty they enjoy today. These Japanese manufacturers who listened to Deming are now familiar household words around the world: Honda, Sony, Toyota, and Mitsubishi.

After the Japanese occupation ended, Deming returned to the United States and began a small consulting business out of his home in Washington, DC And without the startling first decline of the American automobile industry in the late 1980s, along with the energy crisis, Deming most likely would have spent the last years of his life quietly advising a few businesses on the East Coast and writing his memoirs. Then in 1980, he was featured prominently in a now-legendary NBC documentary titled *If Japan Can... Why Can't We?*[79]

This documentary lit a fire in America. It was a question many of us asked. And it deserved an answer. Why couldn't we? The television program that night highlighted the increasing industrial competition we were facing from Japan. It documented how Japan had gone about a process of continuously improving their products, reducing their costs, and dramatically improving the quality of their products. At the time, these were two things our huge, but failing, automobile industry was struggling to achieve.

I remember sitting at home the evening the program aired and feeling something stirring within me—a fire was being lit. Central to the NBC program was an interview with Deming about what he had taught Japanese industrialists after World War II. Because of the broadcast, the demand for Deming's services increased dramatically. Ford Motor Company was one of the first American corporations to seek help from him.

To the automaker's surprise, when Deming began teaching at Ford, he didn't start out by talking about quality, but rather about poor management at Ford—their leadership. He told them that their managers were responsible for *85 percent* of all the problems they were experiencing in developing higher-quality and lower-cost products. The problem wasn't American workers—the problem was their leaders.

Less than four years later, Ford came out with more profitable and higher-quality vehicles. Ford chairman Donald Petersen said,

We are moving toward building a quality culture at Ford, and the many changes that have been taking place here have their roots directly in Dr. Deming's teachings.[80]

79. "If Japan Can, Why Can't We?" Television special by NBC TV on June 24, 1980. See Vanderbilt University Archive: http://tvnews.vanderbilt.edu/siteindex/1980-Specials/special-1980-06-24-NBC-1.html.

80. http://www.bbh.ro/pdf/EW-Deming.pdf January 1, 2011; 1320 hrs.

Leadership cannot be separated from training. How any worker is trained is directly related to the quality of their work. If leaders don't provide quality training to their employees, how can they expect their employees to be able to deliver the high-quality services they demand?

When I came to Madison, I knew that I must immediately adopt a two-fold approach to my work. The first goal was to improve training, both pre- and in-service, within the police department. The second was to develop its leaders.

I knew that it took more than the four weeks of police training I received in 1962 to effectively prepare a new police officer; my guess was, it took at least a year. And I knew that I had to immediately put an end to the authoritarian model of leadership Madison was using to train and lead its police officers—old and new.

Top-quality leaders and competent instructors who are themselves modeling the coaching and mentoring style of thoughtful servant-like leadership must staff the academy. And an academy must be of sufficient length to be able to train officers in the basic skills necessary to be a competent and effective police officer. It must also acculturate them into a new style of policing and embrace its values. I needed to stress to Madison recruits that the most powerful weapon they had out on the beat was their brain, not their firearm.

Currently, police recruit training in the United States averages about 16 weeks in duration. Larger departments—those with more than 100 officers—train their officers only slightly longer: an average of 21 weeks. As to in-service training, while over 80 percent of our nation's police agencies report that they conduct it, it averages fewer than five days a year.

Police have argued back and forth for years about the time necessary to adequately train a police recruit and the amount of time that should be committed to in-service training after they are sent out on the beat. Many factors come into play here. On one hand, there is intense pressure from elected officials and citizens on police leaders to deploy newly-hired officers as quickly as possible. Often, political squabbling and financial restrictions within a city have delayed the police department's hiring plans, and as a result, pressure comes from within the police ranks as well to get newly-hired officers on the street as soon as possible.

Yet a clear and present danger exists, both in terms of safety and liability, if police officers are deployed who are not adequately prepared. Unfortunately, most police trainers are given a set period in which they are expected to turn out competent police officers. The inclusion of new topics in the curriculum to meet current trends, needs, or expectations—such as learning how to care for an increasing population of homeless or mentally ill people—is often neglected in favor of the traditional curriculum. And when new courses are proposed, police trainers are left with a decision as to which current courses they should be reduce or even eliminate to keep within the timeframe they have been given.

Even more unsettling is to learn that well over half of our nation's police academies train in an atmosphere police trainers themselves identify as stress-based, that is, intimidating, even bullying. This makes half of American police academies more like military boot camps or correctional facilities than places in which college-educated young men and women are prepared to be professional police practitioners.

Looking to other occupations that are like police work, from paramedic work to psychology, we find statewide requirements for their practitioners' education and training, methods of examination and licensing, independent reviews of their conduct, and required continuing education. In comparison, what is required of the police seems grossly inadequate.

In recent years, police have learned the benefits derived from a supervised field training experience for their new officers. Such a program enables a department to continue the training and evaluation of their recruits in the actual environment in which they will work. Coupled with an 18-month probationary period, a structured field training experience with a senior officer helps ensure that new officers are not only well-coached but also capable of making the crucial day-to-day decisions required of them. But for that to work takes well trained and prepared field trainers who are also able to be effective trainers and leaders.

In-service training—or continuing education—is necessary for veteran police officers, and the need can be met in several ways. There should be a formal annual in-service training for all police officers for at least a period of two weeks. There should also be various short roll-call training topics supervisors can cover before officers go on duty; this sort of on-going training will also model leaders as teachers. And there can be formal coaching programs, specialized schools outside the department, and encouragement of police officers to increase their formal academic education in related fields such as criminology, public administration, psychology, counseling, and law.

Given what other professions in America are doing, primarily through their governing bodies and state licensing boards, it wouldn't be unreasonable to expect police officers, including those in supervisory and command positions, to meet an annual two-week training requirement of at least 80 hours of continuing education credits.

When citizens in our society have contact with most vocational practitioners, from physicians to plumbers, they have a set of expectations. They expect the practitioners to be competent and to solve their problem to the best of their ability, and to do so at a fair and reasonable price. They also expect that practitioners will behave respectfully and competently.

And when it comes to police, these expectations should be no different. In fact, given the authority given to police in our society, citizens have the right to expect even more—the very highest level of respectful treatment and competent practice.

While the improper practice of some professions may result in inconvenience or monetary loss, improper practice on the part of police may result in the loss of not only one's liberty, but also life. With so much at stake, it shouldn't be unreasonable to expect that each state has a politically independent police standards board with the authority to set minimum standards for police selection and training. Equally reasonable would be a requirement that police be licensed by the state and their conduct subject to review like other licensed professionals as some forward-thinking states are now doing.

Historically, trying to make police be more accountable to their communities through the courts has been unsuccessful. Any change that is court-ordered usually isn't sustainable. Therefore, it can in no way be considered an effective method for organizational transformation. I would also place on the ineffective list training curricula or programs like community and problem-oriented policing that are implemented top-down, without officer input or without consideration to the other organization-wide changes that also need to be put in place.

More recently, two American criminology professors, Allison Chappell and Lonn Lanza-Kaduce, studied a police academy in Florida. They looked specifically at storytelling as a way for leaders to help implement community-oriented policing. I found it to be very interesting because storytelling was one of the primary leadership tools I had used in Madison years earlier. There is power in a story.

When I began to teach other police leaders around the country what we were doing in Madison, the stories I told seemed to be the most effective way I had to get my points across. Those who attended my classes wanted to hear the stories. In effect, the stories that are told within a police academy or department are usually the real things that an organization values. That's why they are so essential; through story, police officers begin to understand the nature of policing, how they are supposed to act, and what seems to be important.[81]

Unfortunately, in most police organizations there are more stories about the successes of traditional practices than of community policing. In fact, the culture of traditional policing is full of stories that range from high-speed pursuits to drug busts and shoot-outs. Stories are effective; they capture a listener's attention and, regarding traditional policing, invariably involve the physical, not the service-oriented, side of policing. Chappell and Lanza-Kaduce found out that police called those traditionally-oriented stories "war stories:"

The context of war stories shifted the setting; it became informal and relaxed—both for the storyteller and the listeners. War stories were

---

81. Chappell, Allison T. and Lonn Lanza-Kaduce. "Police Academy Socialization: Understanding the Lessons Learned in a Paramilitary-Bureaucratic Organization." *Journal of Contemporary Ethnography*. Sage Publications, December 2009.

"times out" from the usual discipline that was expected. The recruits were allowed to laugh and enjoy themselves. The relaxed storytelling defined what was truly valued in police work and in the police culture.[82]

I found, however, that a department transforming to a more community- and problem-oriented culture can find just as many interesting and captivating war stories as those told about traditional policing.

A case in point comes from a neighborhood foot patrol officer in my department who worked very closely with her community. In the process of doing this, she found that quite many residents on her beat had outstanding warrants for a variety of offenses. She went back to the office and developed a list of those in her neighborhood with outstanding warrants with their home addresses, mug shots, and phone numbers. Rather than forming a traditional task force to go out in the early morning hours and raid their residences, she did something different. She started making phone calls. "Hello, this is your neighborhood police officer. I work in your neighborhood, and I understand you have an outstanding warrant. It is necessary that you get this cleared up, so I expect you to satisfy this warrant within 10 days. Can you do that?"

When she started this, the number of open warrants in her neighborhood diminished significantly. People came in and took care of them in ways a traditional police crackdown could never have accomplished. Of course, there was criticism from some of her peers. "She has no authority to do this. Only the court can grant an extension, and her job was to go out and arrest these criminals." But the proof of the pudding is always in the eating, and the power of this story is that she cleared up more warrants than anyone else or any special task force had. And she did it in a very creative and effective way.

Another officer in another neighborhood across town (who is now Madison's chief of police) put together a computer skills class for unemployed, low-income women in his neighborhood. These women had lost their jobs because their clerical skills didn't include computerized word

---

82. *Ibid.*

processing. His efforts resulted in many of these women finding employment again.

Still another officer found empirical data to support placing highly-visible traffic cones in restricted-speed school zones. As part of this experiment, he clocked the speeds of vehicles in zones that had the more visible warning cones versus those that didn't.

There was a significant reduction in the speed of traffic in school zones with the traffic warning cones present. This officer took a chance in doing this because one of the city attorneys had previously stated the police had no authority to put objects like traffic cones into the roadway so we couldn't do this.

Since that time, however, the practice he recommended has become standard not only in Madison but throughout the state. He, too, suffered some peer criticism, "How could he not have ticketed those speeders? His job is to write tickets, not do speed studies."

Perhaps, but this officer saw his job as more: ensuring a lasting method of safety for children in the community. To him, the most effective way was to develop a method to reduce the speed of automobiles in school zones throughout the city. And he could prove that his system worked.

Another officer responded to complaints that cars were speeding in his district another way. The traditional approach was to run radar, write a bunch of tickets, and then go on to other business. This officer, however, thought there might be a better way. He decided he would work with the neighborhood association. He called neighborhood leaders together and asked for help. Together, they developed a plan.

After notifying the media about what they were about to do, they set up radar and waved those who were speeding into a large parking lot off the street. It was there that neighborhood residents approached the speeders and requested that they slow down for their children's sake.

The officer was present in the parking lot but didn't make the initial contact after he stopped the vehicle. No tickets were issued. The entire city heard of the traffic safety project in the local news, and people began not only to slow down at that school crossing zone, but it was reported that speeding was reduced throughout the city.

Yet another neighborhood officer, assigned to an area with a high concentration of Hmong people, took the time to learn their language so she could be a more effective police officer in their neighborhood. This skill was critical when she had to inform community leaders that cultural practices like abducting underage women for purposes of marriage weren't permitted here. She paved the way for our first Hmong officer, who was hired in 1991.

For new police, these can be powerful stories because in each case the officers involved stepped outside the traditional policing box to alter an established practice of the department. In each case, what they did resulted in sturdier bonds with the community. In each project, officers were willing to work informally and outside established hierarchies to get the job done. These stories soon became the new stories, stories that could reinforce principles of community policing and compete with the old war stories.

In concluding their study, Chappell and Lanza-Kaduce made some specific recommendations to integrate community or problem-oriented policing within a police organization. They suggested three crucial changes:

The academy should re-examine its paramilitary structure (marching, posting, dress, discipline, war stories); especially consider introducing the horizontal and less-formal relationships that occur in many community-policing activities.

The academy must find ways to align informal instruction with the formal curriculum (blending traditional and community-oriented policing).

The academy should re-examine its culture in terms of how it defines police work and in regards to the us vs. them mentality... all members of the public, including the suspects and the perps, should be dealt with professionally. [83]

Department leaders must know, experience and be able to relate stories that support the new direction the department is going. And this

83. *Ibid.*

storytelling must not only be done within the department but within the community as well.

As I have sharply argued, the education and training of police isn't a subject that can be discussed separately from the structure and style of leadership of the police department (including storytelling). The practice of educating and training employees is part and parcel of an effective city government—a government that will also make sure that the chief of police of their city is also able to meet specific professional expectations.[84]

The following story comes from a time when I was teaching three-day leadership courses for police chiefs and their staffs across the country. I developed this course to share what I had learned about leadership and community-oriented policing in Madison.

One morning I was at a large urban police department in Nevada. As I was setting up my classroom at their training academy, I looked out the window and observed a formation of their new police recruits. I decided to go outside and get a closer look. The recruits were standing in three ranks—it was an inspection, a situation I could easily relate to from my days as a Marine.

Suddenly, the training instructors started yelling at the new officers. Some were ordered to do push-ups by way of the familiar military command: "Drop and give me ten." In addition, I heard the instructors calling the young officers "assholes." I returned to the classroom in time to greet the chief and his command staff. I introduced myself and the curriculum for the next three days, and then asked, "Are your officers permitted to call citizens names?"

They seem shocked. "We have rules against doing that. Why do you ask?" "Well," I replied, "I was watching your new officers outside this window and observed your trainers calling them very derogatory names. You know, it really doesn't matter if you have rules against such conduct because when their teachers call them names, they will think that it's okay for them to do the same to citizens. And if you ever try to discipline them, their defense will simply be 'That's what the department taught me.'"

84. See Appendices E and F.

I recently learned that the department never did change. Their academy remains stress-based, military, and intimidating. I don't know if their training officers ever stopped calling recruit officers names. But one thing I do know is that if they don't stop, I predict they will continue to have problems with officers disrespecting citizens. How could they expect any different kind of an outcome? [85]

From insights like this, I developed a new style of leadership in the early 1980s that was closely aligned with the teachings of Gordon, Greenleaf, and Deming. I called "quality leadership." Now I had to start walking my talk. It had to start with me, but it also needed to be practiced by other leaders in the department. Not every leader in the department was enthusiastic about changing their leadership style.

But I stayed on message, trying to demonstrate that those of us who were the leaders of the department were the first people who had to start. In police work, senior leaders didn't (and still don't) typically rise to a level of authority by being more open, good listeners or supportive of the men and women they are responsible to lead. Instead, traditional police leadership was and is more known for being closed, not taking input from subordinates, and not being supportive of them—coercive—more about controlling than coaching.

After I trained department leaders, the next step was to conduct something I called the *Four-Way Check*. It required every department leader, including myself, to participate.

Briefly, the check required leaders to get feedback on their performance from four directions—1) those whom they supervised, 2) peers with whom they worked, 3) the person to whom they reported, and finally 4) an in-depth self-evaluation and meeting with me.

As you might expect, all this aroused and stirred up headquarters. I had

---

85. That department recently was identified as using "harsh" recruit training methods in the *Las Vegas Review Journal*, "Police Academy Recruits Endure Harsh Road," http://www.lvrj.com/news/a-new-day-a-new-life-112139069.html, January 1, 2011; 1151 hrs. It didn't note whether recruit officers were still called "assholes" or other derogatory names during their training.

some people on my top command staff that were digging in their heels. They had supported me and been with me since the early days of the 1970s.

Many of them felt they didn't need to change, and they didn't particularly want to do this. Some of them were not interested in asking their employees how they were doing as a leader. They were quite comfortable with the control style of leadership we had all invariably used for years.

The reluctance of my command staff (all of whom had tenure) was troubling, but I knew this was a noteworthy moment of truth for me and for the future of the department. Was I really committed to this new process, or would I back off when the people who reported to me showed reluctance?

At a meeting of the department's highest commanders I talked about why I thought the new process was crucial for us and why the future of the department was dependent upon it. I wanted them to reach a consensus before I went further. But as we went around the table that day, I knew I didn't have one—in fact, only a few were in favor of what I was proposing.

What was I to do? Well, I had learned that one of the major benefits of following Deming's teachings was that it would help us build relationships with leaders in other fields who were trying to do the same things we were. And at a quality training session a year or so earlier, I had met a man from Milwaukee who was in the manufacturing business.[86] I remember him saying that he had struggled with getting buy-in from his managers. So I gave him a call and went to visit him.

He turned out to be extremely helpful. He said that in his experience, if the principal leaders in an organization waited until everyone got on board, they would never get to where they needed to go. Instead, he suggested, if I could get 25 percent of my staff willing to move with me, I should do so.

At first that sounded dangerous. Just 25 percent? Didn't I need to have a majority? Would I dare move with less and leave a lot of my people behind? Even those who had been my stalwarts?

He replied, "No, you don't leave them behind. You tell them you are

---

86. I can't remember the date, though it was quite early in our change efforts, probably the early 1980s. I only remember his name was "Bill" and that he was the quality person for Falk Gear in Milwaukee.

leaving, going to a new place, because you intensely believe it is the right thing to do. You need them. You want them to come with you—but you can't allow them to stay back. They have to come along now."

He went on to share with me a compelling image:

> *Your boat is about to cross a wide river and land at a new place. When the boat leaves, it won't return. It's a one-way trip. You want your whole team to come with you, but you won't be able to come back later for them. You want everyone to come on board with you because you value them and their contributions, even if they are not fully committed to making the trip. Later, you tell them, they will become more comfortable with what you are asking of them and willing to do yourself. You commit to helping, coaching, and teaching them so they will be successful in this new way. You won't leave them hanging out. You remind them this is also a new and difficult way for you. But you need them to come with you—now.*

So when I determined that I had at least a quarter of my topmost commanders on board, I gave the boat speech. I could tell it was very uncomfortable for some to hear, but for others it was a sign that I was really committed to the direction we were about to go. There was electricity in the air—invigoration for some and shock for others.

As the boat left the dock, it was a stormy journey—but what my friend in Milwaukee told me that day turned out to be excellent advice. And eventually, it worked.

But when leaders who reported directly to me were not seen as supporting this effort or were unwilling to make personal changes, I had a big problem on my hands. Remember, I worked within a civil service system of tenured leaders. Would I formally discipline them? What was I going to do? These were my team members, men and women I had promoted and worked with over the years. Now some were refusing to change.

All in all, this era became the second major transformation I introduced in the department. We all had survived the first, but would we survive this one? The first transformation was to address our training needs, recruit more educated and talented personnel, and alter the way in which we were responding to public protest. Now, almost 10 years into the job, I made the decision that we must develop a work environment that was able to listen and tap into the intelligence and experience of our officers and other employees. It was a difficult time.

As it turned out, most tried. And even though their employees didn't consider them as true leaders or as adopting the new leadership style, they were given credit for trying.

Other command officers simply waited me out. Waited for retirement eligibility and left. The officers who replaced them, however, were those who not only adopted the new leadership but also were enthusiastic about it. These new leaders were viewed by department employees as being honest practitioners—they practiced what they preached. We now were into the second transformation.

One of the more effective steps I took to get reluctant command officers on board was to have them identify three to five things under their command that needed improvement, for which they would take personal responsibility, and then work on them. They were to submit their list to me for approval, then share it with their officers.

Periodically, they would report to me as to how their efforts were progressing.

The main factor, of course, was that they were to use our new methods of leadership to do so. And when members of the department saw the department's highest commanders working to improve the things for which they were responsible and using the new methods, it made a big difference. They became more effective leaders. Leaders were now teaching by doing. This is the crucial relationship between leadership and training in operation. The two are not separate. Leaders train and trainers lead.

Step Five: Improve Continuously

Police must unceasingly improve the systems in which they work—everything they do.

IMPROVEMENT OF OUR NATION'S POLICE is possible, but it has got to be constant and not a sporadic occurrence. It is going to take some work from every one of us. It is possible to engage police officers in a pursuit of excellence, which is essentially what this is. In the long run, this commitment to improving the systems in which police work is good for them and all of us: police will have more support from their community, they will feel nobler about themselves and the work they do, and their workplaces will be more comfortable, gratifying, and engaging.

It will be so for citizens too, because police themselves will be treated with dignity and worth within their own workplaces, and have leaders who respect and listen to them.

The method I used was that which Deming proposed—all work is a system; all systems can be improved.

While this isn't the only method available, it was one that found persuasive resonance with me. But one thing must be clear: whatever system is used in the organization, it must always exist to help them excel and excel *incessantly*. What is isn't good enough because what is can and should be done better, whether it is processing traffic tickets or responding to public protest.

An organization that is committed to and engages in making things better is a more effective and exciting place to work. Citizens will feel safer and more in control of their problems when they have a department like this in their community.

Additionally, citizens will benefit by being policed by men and women who are committed to protecting their rights. There will be more ease in the minority community as many of the police officers will be themselves people of color. But most significant of all these characteristics, officers will treat everyone fairly and respectfully and will be willing to work with community members in solving problems.

The reality, however, is that even if you begin today, it will take years to do this. The first place to start is in your city, county, town, or village, and the time is now. For the most part, good police departments come from having people working inside of them who hold the values I have identified in this book. It is a truth that good policing, on the way to being distinguished policing, happens not so much because of the techniques, tools, or structures of a police department but because of the values held by the men and women who do the work. Those police departments are found in communities that hold dear the basic values of our society: liberty, justice, fairness, equality, and participation.

I have always said that I could pick first-rate officers and leaders if I knew whether they thought people were basically good or bad. If they believed people were essentially good, then they could be trained and developed to be good police officers and leaders of police. If they believed otherwise—that people were essentially bad or evil—it was a very difficult task to train and develop them into the kind of police and leaders I wanted in my department and you want to police your community.

Officers who believe everyone is just waiting for a chance to do evil are not able to be caring or compassionate. I say this not to deny the existence of evil, for there surely are terribly evil people out there, but rather to say we must see things in balance: there *are* evil people in the world, but they are small in number compared with those of us who try to follow society's rules and help others.

As these critical steps—casting a bold vision, selecting the finest, focusing on training, listening, collaboratively leading, and working to continuously improve—are taken they will begin to show results both inside the police department and outside in the community.

The next step is to evaluate and to measure what has been done— are there data to show that things have, in fact, turned around? Can the department measure its stated achievements?

Step Six: Evaluate

Police must be able to critically assess, or have assessed, the crucial tasks and functions they are expected to perform.

My first efforts to evaluate how we were doing were rudimentary. I knew I had to have frequent and on-going contact with the Madison community I was hired to serve and protect. I should say its *communities* because no city is just a community by itself; a city today consists of many diverse communities. But for the most part, I became the sounding board for the department. Listening was my first attempt to try and determine how we were doing in realizing our vision and staying on mission.

This caused me to always be willing to talk to just about any group in the city or journalist from the media and tell my story—my vision for our police department—and listen to what they had to say in response.

Another effort came about as we evolved into a community-oriented organization. I came to understand that I needed a more official and systematic way to find out how we were doing. To find a way beyond just listening at community meetings, receiving comments from elected officials, or reading letters to the editor in our daily newspapers. I needed to find some way to ask citizens directly about their level of satisfaction with our services.

From my own experience, I knew this: citizens who have had no contact with their police tend to rate us quite high; out of sight, out of mind. Conversely, those who have had contact with us don't rate us quite as high as those who have not. And, disturbingly, the more contact citizens have with us, the lower they tend to rate us (remember what Nicholas Peart said earlier about what he thought about repetitive stop and frisk tactics by police in his community).

What I intended to do was create a survey of people who had contact with us—I called it a customer survey. A contact could be, for instance, making a verbal complaint, being the victim of a crime, or even being arrested. As it turned out, the results of this monthly survey became a valuable source of information. It helped me to more realistically evaluate how we were really doing.

Think about it: without an ongoing survey, how will any police department know how it is doing? In the business world, customer feedback is essential. It should be no different in a police agency. How else will police know what their citizens think of their services? But more critically, how else will police know what services or functions need to be improved?

I decided I needed to have this kind of feedback. I wanted to hear from those with whom we had actual contact, not those who just have an opinion about us. I wanted to know how we were doing from those with whom we had dealt face to face. If I was requiring department leaders to get feedback from each other and their employees, why not from those who used our services?

After several things were considered such as cost, the number of surveys we needed to send out, and to whom we'd send them, I began to mail out a survey form with a self-addressed, stamped envelope. It was sent from me to the people identified in every 50th police incident (as determined by randomly-selected case numbers). Each survey was enclosed with a personal letter explaining why I was doing this, why I thought it was necessary, and it asked for their feedback.[87] The survey asked them to rate their experience with us on a scale from one to five (one being poor and five being excellent) in seven categories:

- *Concern*
- *Helpfulness*
- *Knowledge*
- *Quality of service*
- *Solving the problem*
- *Putting you at ease*
- *Professional conduct*

---

87. At that time, we were assigning about 100,000 case numbers each year; therefore, a 1-in-50 sampling meant we mailed out an average of 160 surveys each month.

At the end of the survey, I asked the critical question: how can we improve? And those who answered were not hesitant to tell me.

The survey also asked respondents for personal information about where they live, their age, race, gender, and income level. I made a commitment in the letter I sent out to read *every* returned survey and publish the results in our newsletter, whether the commentary was good or bad. I also made it clear to both officers and the citizens who received the surveys that they wouldn't be used to initiate disciplinary action against any officer. There was another way to do that. If a citizen had a complaint against an officer, they were directed to contact our Internal Affairs Unit. I had to make it clear this survey wasn't about discipline but about gathering important information as to how we were doing.

We had a very respectable return rate of 35 to 40 percent. I used the results to report to the mayor and city council how the department was doing in personal hands-on contacts. During the seven years I used the survey, we made steady progress in improving overall citizen satisfaction every year. I put together and published a line graph showing the rate of citizen satisfaction officers were achieving. It was a clear, visual indication that Madison officers were continuously improving. And they did it on the street with all types of people and in all kinds of situations.

Traditionally, police departments have learned how they are doing by paying attention to the wrong things. Police leaders gathered information by reading newspapers, watching television news, attending city council meetings, civic gatherings, reviewing formal complaints, and talking with community leaders, just as I had done for years.

These things need to be done, but they won't tell a police chief how his or her department is *really* doing. Only a broad survey that pays attention to age, gender, race, and socioeconomic level can do that. The only effective way to know whether the people who use police services feel their police department is doing a good job is to ask those who have had *direct* contact with its officers and employees.

My next step was to seek an outside evaluation of our efforts. Were they effective? Did continuous improvement really happen? I needed to know the answers to these questions as well, not just from my gut or from a survey, but from empirical data. I decided to ask the National Institute of Justice to formally evaluate us. A research proposal was developed, and the contract awarded to the Police Foundation in Washington, DC. After a three-year study, this is what they found:

- *Job satisfaction among police employees was high.*

- *Teamwork went on between shifts, especially in officers' approach to problem solving; it also included detectives and neighborhood officers.*

- *The burglary rate in the community was lowered.*

- *There were reduced sick leave and use of overtime.*

- *There was high citizen satisfaction with police services.*

- *A work environment was established that empowered police employees to be creative in their duties.*[88]

The findings were significant. A transformation had occurred.

They found that our new style of leadership was apparent throughout the department as well as in the experimental police district (EPD). (The mission of the EPD was to experiment with new patrol and investigative strategies including an intense experiment with quality leadership.)

An interesting additional finding was that even though the number of officers in the department had not increased during the four-year research period, citizens reported seeing *more* police all over the city; an outcome, perhaps, of getting closer to the community and encouraging motor patrol officers to get out and walk their neighborhoods.

The three-year study examined the efforts undertaken by us to create a new organizational design—both structural and managerial, built to support community- and problem-oriented policing. Notably, researchers

---

88. *Community Policing in Madison: Quality from the Inside, Out. Technical Report*, Mary Ann Wycoff and Wesley G. Skogan. Washington: Police Foundation. 1993.

found the department's attempt to bring progressive, comprehensive change to our operations was successful:

- *Employee attitudes toward work and the organization improved.*

- *Physical decentralization was achieved.*

- *Residents believed crime had become less of a problem.*

- *Residents believed police were working to resolve issues of importance to the neighborhood.*

In the conclusion of their report they made a statement that I believe captures Madison's 12-year effort to raise the fairness and effectiveness of the police function in their community; a second major effort during my 20-year tenure.

> *[I]t is possible to change a traditional, control-oriented police organization into one in which employees become members of work teams and participants in decision-making processes… This research suggests that associated with these internal changes are external benefits for citizens, including indications of reductions in crime and reduced levels of concern about crime.*

All the above methods of evaluation are ways that communities and their leaders can attempt to determine how well their police are doing. But no matter what I did, the methods I devised to measure and evaluate how my department was doing paled in comparison to the public influence created by publication of *Crime in the United States*, the annual report of the FBI as part of the national system of Uniform Crime Reporting (UCR).[89] I vowed early on in my career that I wasn't going to allow this to be the sole measure by which my department and my leadership were going to be evaluated.

In a recent interview, veteran journalist Bill Moyers talked with David

---

89. http://www.fbi.gov/about-us/cjis/ucr/ucr; December 13, 2011; 0932 hrs.

Simon, creator of the popular HBO series *The Wire*, Simon, a former journalist and police reporter, talked about evaluation. Simon mentioned the propensity of corporations, governments, and their agencies to "juke their stats"—that is, to alter data so that it appeared that they were doing well even when they weren't. The following dialogue is from an episode from *The Wire*, in which "Prez" Pryzbylewski, a cop turned teacher, has an exchange with the school principal about numbers and teacher evaluation:

Principal: So, for the time being, all teachers will devote class time to teaching language arts sample questions. Now, if you turn to page eleven, please, I have some things I want to go over with you.

Prez: I don't get it—all this so we score higher on the state tests? If we're teaching the kids the test questions, what is it assessing in them?

Teacher: Nothing—it assesses us. The test scores go up, they can say the schools are improving. The scores stay down, they can't.

Prez: Juking the stats.

Teacher: Excuse me?

Prez: Making robberies into larcenies, making rapes disappear. You juke the stats, and majors become colonels. I've been here before.[90]

In his interview with Moyers, Simon further reflects on his life as a journalist and police reporter:

You show me anything that depicts institutional progress in America, school test scores, crime stats, arrest reports, arrest stats, anything that a politician can run on, anything that somebody can get a promotion on. And as soon as you invent that statistical category, 50 people in that institution will be at work trying to figure out a way to make it

90. *The Wire.* Home Box Office miniseries, Season 4. 2006.

look as if progress is actually occurring when actually no progress is… a police commissioner or a deputy commissioner can get promoted, and a major can become a colonel, and an assistant school superintendent can become a school superintendent, if they make it look like the kids are learning, and that they're solving crime. And that was a front-row seat for me as a reporter. Getting to figure out how the crime stats actually didn't represent anything, once they got done with them.[91]

I spent a good deal of my time as police chief trying to teach members of the media, as well as elected officials and community members, what exactly crime was and what it meant. To remind them that a numerical increase or decrease didn't necessarily mean that crime was *actually* up or down. I didn't juke the stats nor pressure my officers about reducing these imaginary numbers.

A reported numerical increase (as the UCR shows) could instead mean citizens have more confidence in the police to solve crime, and therefore are now reporting it. On the other hand, a decrease in the rate of reporting could indicate not that crime is down but that police are underreporting various crimes by labeling them as lesser offenses, a practice that many believe to be standard operating procedure in most American cities today.

For example, an attempted burglary might be classified as a vandalism, a forcible rape as an assault, a homicide as a sudden death. Each of these instances of downgrading would move a crime from the UCR's closely watched eight Part I Offenses category to the lower category of Part II Offenses.[92] A decrease in reported crime could also mean that citizens have less confidence in the police to do anything about it and, therefore, simply don't bother to report it.

The fact is that none of us can make a valid judgment one way or another when it comes to analyzing *reported* crime as the data are presently collected. However, there are more valid statistical methods in existence to

91. Bill Moyers. PBS interview with David Simon (producer of the critically acclaimed HBO series *The Wire.*) April 17, 2009.

92. Federal Bureau of Investigation. Annual Uniform Crime Report.

determine *actual*, not simply reported, rates of crime. This method uses a statistical sampling of citizens rather than relying on offenses that are reported to the police and that the police in turn report. Yet America and their police still are wedded to this archaic method of data collection and evaluation despite the existence of more effective and truer methods of measurement.

That said, and despite my years of educating the media, I don't think many of them wanted to abandon the simplistic aspect of being able to report crime being either up or down—the data released by the UCR. Remember, when you hear crime is either up or down, it really isn't a very good way to evaluate how your police are doing. You need to ask more questions.

Social and economic factors have an enormous influence on the nature and levels of crime in any community.[93] In fact, even the UCR lists factors that can influence crime: the size of the community, how crowded an area is, the composition of the population, with particular regard to age, the stability of a community, economic conditions, job availability, climate, and various emphases of local law enforcement agencies.[94] What wasn't anticipated at the time the UCR was created was that police agencies themselves would manipulate the data for their own purposes—that is, juke the stats, to show the supposed effectiveness of a particular mayor or police chief.

But, of course, we should have. The problem of how we count things isn't a new one. Nearly a century ago, a British public servant had this to say about reporting statistics:

The governments are very keen on amassing statistics. They collect them, add them, raise them to the nth power, take the cube root, and prepare wonderful diagrams. But you must never forget that every one of these

93. David Couper. *How to Rate Your Local Police*. Washington: Police Executive Research Forum. 1983.

94. http://www2.fbi.gov/ucr/cius2009/about/variables_affecting_crime.html, May 25, 2011; 0907 hrs.

figures comes in the first instance from the [village watchman], who just puts down what he damn pleases.[95]

It is true that citizens who live in a community where the police are respected and responsive are more willing to report crimes than those who live in communities where police are not respected or not thought to be effective. The result can be that a police department that is negatively viewed by the community will have a *low* incidence of crime reporting and therefore a low crime rate, while a police department thought to be highly effective and responsive would experience a high reporting rate. In these cases, reported crime will be up because citizens believe their police can and will do something about it.

Additionally, the *kind* of criminal activity that often threatens a community and causes widespread fear isn't often captured by many of the eight Part I UCR Crimes. These are criminal activities that affect the quality of life in our cities such as street drug dealing, weapons offenses, littering, graffiti, noise violations, and other alarming and unsettling events. Simply stated, the current system isn't a good method either to know the amount and extent of crime in your community or to evaluate your police department. There are other ways to do this.

One way would be to expand the National Crime Victimization Survey (NCVS), which has been collecting data on personal and household victimization in America since 1973. It provides an ongoing, statistically-sound sample of residential addresses. Twice each year, data are obtained from a nationally-representative sample of roughly 49,000 households, comprising about 100,000 people, as to the frequency, characteristics, and consequences of criminal victimization in the United States. The U.S. Census Bureau administers it on behalf of the Bureau of Justice Statistics.

The NCVS provides the largest national forum for victims to describe the impact of crime on them and the characteristics of violent offenders. It was designed with four primary objectives in mind.

---

95. Josiah Stamp. *Some Economic Factors in Modern Life*. London: King and Sons. 1929.

- *To develop detailed information about the victims and consequences of crime.*

- *To estimate the number and types of crimes not reported to the police.*

- *To provide uniform measures of selected types of crimes.*

- *To permit comparisons of crime over time and types of areas.96*

The survey categorizes crimes as personal or property crimes. Personal crimes are rapes and sexual attacks, robberies, and aggravated and simple assaults, including purse-snatchings and pocket-picking. Property crimes are burglaries, thefts, auto thefts, and vandalism.

We also must remember that even though we have a statistical method to more effectively uncover unreported crime through the NCVS, a substantial number of crimes still take place that will remain unknown to either police or those who conduct the surveys. It is crime that neither reporting nor surveying discovers.

Victimization studies frequently reveal that *less than one-half* of the crimes that occur are reported to the police. The reason for this is that victims often feel there is little the police can do about a crime or the crime involved an activity they don't wish others to know about such as a man who gets robbed in a park known for being frequented by homosexuals.

Because his family and co-workers don't know of his sexual orientation, he may choose *not* to report the crime. This can also be true in other assaults, including forcible rapes after which the victim does not wish to either be identified or testify as a witness against his or her offender.

Victims often do not report certain crimes to police because they are ashamed, embarrassed, or feel that they somehow caused their victimization.

Here are some things we have learned about crime from studies like the NCVS:

- *Most crimes go unreported to the police.*

- *Most are not serious.*

---

96. *Ibid.*

- *Most are thefts.*

- *Most victims of serious offenses know their attacker.*

- *Most rapes happen indoors between people who know each other.*

- *Most crime is between persons of the same race.*

- *Most crimes are unsolved.*

- *Children (people under 18 years of age) are responsible for almost one-half of all arrests for serious crimes.*

- *Crime may or may not be increasing. (We cannot tell unless we know the actual amount of crime.)*

- *The reduction of crime will primarily be a function of demographics. As the percentage of people under age 25 rises or falls in the overall population, so will crime rise or fall.*

- *The reduction of crime is not largely dependent upon governmental techniques to control it.*

With the rise or fall of reported crime often being the major issue impacting the leadership of police departments in most American cities, it isn't difficult to understand why police would try to underreport crime.

This is often done by redefining a criminal incident—labeling an attempted burglary as a broken window—therefore putting it in the "damage to property" category so that it no longer counts as a major offense. This means the declassified incident will not add to the city's formal crime rate.

So, is crime increasing or decreasing in your community? Without knowing the results of a victimization study, you cannot know. You cannot take the UCR as an indicator. If you read in tomorrow's newspaper, see on television, or hear on the radio that the number of rapes in your city is rising, you must first ask: is the seeming increase in rape due to an increase in the reporting of these crimes to the police because victims have more confidence in the ability of the police to do something about them? And might such confidence in the police department be due to training and hiring practices that have placed female police officers in patrol and investigatory roles? If so, the increase in the number of reported rapes would be a positive indicator of police competence, not negligence.

Or, on the other hand, is a decrease in the number of reported rapes due to the reluctance of victims to report these offenses to the police because they see the police as not being caring or sensitive in these matters? In this case, a seeming decrease in the incidence of rape would be an indicator of police incompetence.[97]

The way out of this confusion is for the nation's police leaders to refuse to participate in the UCR program and, in lieu of participation, to call for a victim-based survey in their city. Local departments can supplement these data by partnering with local colleges and universities to gather these data, which would provide more accurate crime statistics to the police and the community. Currently, one of the major problems with the NCVS data is that it is collected from a national sample and cannot now be broken down city by city. If it could be, American police and citizens would know the actual amount and extent of crime in their communities.

In addition, there are several other surveys that should be conducted on an ongoing basis, such as surveys of people who have contacted police either as a complainant or a victim, or who have been stopped and frisked or arrested by police. Communities and their police departments need to have an idea of how these recipients of police action have been treated, especially regarding their age, race, ethnicity, immigration status, or sexual orientation. Surveying community members as to how fair and effective they believe their police to be is vitally necessary in a democracy and would provide police leaders and citizens with critical information.

---

97. An internet search of "manipulating crime statistics" reveals several sources to emphasize this point. See http://www.huffingtonpost.com/len-levitt/ adrian-schoolcraft-enter- b 714484.html?ref=email share December 5, 2011; 0243. Also, listen to an interview with Officer Schoolcraft at: http:// www.thisamericanlife.org/radio-archives/episode/414/right-to-remain-silent; December 5, 2011; 0250. Of course, the New York City Police Department is not the only department that has struggled with charges of "jukin' the stats."

Step Seven: Sustain

Police leaders must be able to maintain and continue improvements to their organizations.

As I mentioned, a leader should always be thinking ahead, scanning and listening. And this should be with the intent to sustain the good work and improvements that the organization has accomplished. It turned out that what I was developing almost unknowingly in Madison was something Peter Senge later came to identify in his book *The Fifth Discipline: The Art and Practice of the Learning Organization.* When I first read Senge's excellent definition of the learning organization, it made clear that what we were attempting to do was just that:

> *Organizations where people continually expand their capacity to create the results they truly desire, where new and expansive patterns of thinking are nurtured, where collective aspiration is set free, and where people are continually learning to learn together.*[98]

An organization that is learning together can sustain itself. It is also an organization that should be practicing the new leadership because that's what the leadership I have described in this book does. It frees people to learn together. While there are varying definitions of a learning organization, there remains a core principle in all of them.

They are organizations that facilitate the *growth* of all their members and continuously work to transform themselves.[99]

My experience taught me the benefits of such an organization. This kind of organization can learn from its successes as well as its mistakes. It can innovate, be competitive, respond to external pressures, link and

98. Peter Senge. *The Fifth Discipline: The Art and Practice of the Learning Organization.* New York: Bantam-Doubleday. 1990.

99. The Learning Company: A strategy for sustainable development, M. Pedler, J. Burgoyne, and T. Boydell (1997) and "Managing Learning: what do we learn from a Learning Organization?" *The Learning Organization,* D. McHugh, D. Groves and A. Alker (1998).

adjust its resources to meet customer needs, continue the pace of change, and bolster its image in the community, that is, it can sustain itself. I can say this was our experience, and that every one of the characteristics of a learning organization should be present in all the places in which we work—in factories, corporate offices, schools, churches, etc., not just police departments.

One of the many outcomes of the quality movement in Madison was developing teamwork and organizational skills in group facilitation. This gave us a tremendous edge. Within a few years, no one in the police department wanted to attend a meeting that didn't have a trained facilitator present. Meetings went so much more smoothly when trained facilitators were present. They assisted not only decision-making but also relational processes—how the group works together. By having trained group facilitators within the ranks of the department, we could more effectively conduct the business of committees and work groups within the department.

The job of a team leader is to help the group accomplish its agreed-upon tasks and to make the necessary decisions. The job of a facilitator, on the other hand, is to work in concert with everyone in the group, including the team leader, but primarily be concerned with process, how the group works together—practicing its values, ensuring participation of everyone regardless of rank, making sure all information is shared, and helping members of the group grow.

The powerful concept at work here is that *everyone* in the group is responsible for the group's success and growth. This means that anyone in the group has the authority to call the group back on subject, identify and interrupt patterns of conflict, offer clarifying comments, summarize activities, and provide feedback.

The other big step was identifying our future. Within a year or two after launching the Officer's Advisory Council (OAC), I decided we needed to look ahead toward the future—to stop, look, and listen like the old wagon masters did, scanning for dangers and challenges. We needed to think about the kind of department in which we wanted to work and the kind of department the community wanted. This was the direction I was going. Now I needed people to help me look to the future. It became the Committee on the Future of the Department.

The requirement for participation on the committee was that members had to have at least 15 years left to serve before retirement. I wanted those who were to do this futuring work to have not only experience but also time left to participate in making that future real—to be a stakeholder in that future.

The officers who served on the committee met two to four times a month for a year before they issued their report. This kind of work is immensely significant for the success of sustaining any organization. For us, it set in motion the energy to think about tomorrow, how we might need to alter or change the organization, and how we might keep our effort going. In their report, the committee made three formidable recommendations, backed up with supportive material:

- *Move closer to the community.*
- *Make better use of technology*
- *Improve workplace wellness.*[100]

Those recommendations gave substance to my dream for decentralized neighborhood patrol districts, which I had envisioned when I first came to Madison. This now would move our officers closer to the people they served more effectively.

Very soon, construction was begun on our first decentralized police station—the Experimental Police District. The EPD was to be our field laboratory. Their recommendations also caused us to examine our structure, internal practices, and the overall direction in which the department was moving.

Ultimately, that early effort to create a future vision for the department resulted in complete decentralization of patrol and investigative services

---

100. *The Learning Company: A strategy for sustainable development*, M. Pedler, J. Burgoyne, and T. Boydell (1997) and "Managing Learning: what do we learn from a Learning Organization?" *The Learning Organization*, D. McHugh, D. Groves and A. Alker (1998).

into four standalone district stations that serve the City of Madison. The origins of this idea first began with my vision back in 1973 and the creation of a neighborhood patrol unit in the early 1980s, which assigned foot patrol officers to several of our city's key residential and business areas.

This was a new idea for Madison. Our department had always operated out of one centralized building in the downtown area. The EPD, however, was located on the far south side, in one of the most active policing areas of the city. The officers who volunteered to work out of it had a hand in not only deciding the location but also the new station's building design and cost.

But the most remarkable move made was to let officers who volunteered to work there select their leaders. This would be the place where the new leadership style and problem-oriented policing methods would be solidly exercised. Years later, the ability of the Madison department to sustain a number of changes made nearly two decades earlier was highlighted in a national publication of the Police Executive Research Forum (PERF).[101] The document surveyed the application of business management principles to the public sector, particularly police departments. In it, Chief Noble Wray and Captain Sue Williams of the Madison department highlighted the leadership academy, which was still operating nearly 20 years after its inception. They wrote:

> *In the 1980s, then-Chief David Couper instituted the Leadership Promotional Academy in the Madison, Wisconsin Police Department. The academy was initially open to anyone who wished to compete for promotion, with the approval of the individual's supervisor. Work performance during the previous 12 months must be judged satisfactory. A person wishing to be promoted is required to have attended an Academy within the five years prior to the current promotional process.*[102]

101. Chuck Wexler, Mary Ann Wycoff, and Craig Fischer. *Good to Great Policing: Application of Business Management Principles in the Public Sector.* U.S. Department of Justice, Office of Community Oriented Policing Services: Washington, D.C. 2007.

102. "Good to Great Leadership Summit" conference, Washington, DC, sponsored by the Police Executive Research Forum, March 29, 2005.

The publication went on to describe the process in which each attendee was expected to identify, analyze, and suggest the improvement of a current practice or function of the department. In doing this, attendees learn about the direction of the department from the chief and meet leaders they might not previously have known. Moreover, the department gains by ensuring all aspiring leaders acquire basic leadership skills and gain knowledge of, and strategies for, improving department work systems. The result was that the Madison Police Department learned how to sustain itself and its effective practices.

Chapter 7
2011: Year of Protest

The proper handling of public protest is a unique and special requirement for police in a democracy.

IN MY EXPERIENCE, ONE OF the biggest transformations I made in Madison was to move the department into a professional stance about handling public protest. The way in which police in a democracy respond to public protest is often a defining moment for them and the community. At the end of 2011 *Time Magazine* named the protester as its "Person of the Year." Doing so not only highlighted the centrality of protest today in America, but the important role it is taking throughout the world.

In the long run, police will ultimately be judged by how well they handle protest—how they do it fairly and effectively, without regard to whether or not they agree with the people in those crowds. Overall, police officers should always treat everyone they encounter respectfully, with courtesy, and without regard to their race, gender, national origin, political beliefs, religious practice, sexual orientation, or economic status—and that goes for people in crowds, too. It's a big job, but the primary function of police is always *relational*, whether they are responding to a domestic dispute, investigating a crime, enforcing a traffic regulation, helping an elderly person cross a busy street, or handling a crowd. Once this is understood, it is a lot easier to figure out what it is police need to do and how they should do it when it comes to handling public protest.

Early on, I envisioned a police department in which the officers would become experts in human behavior because much of what goes wrong in policing happens when police are unable to effectively respond to people. Therefore, it is vital that police have access to and understand current research regarding the field of human psychology and established methods to deal with people who are disturbed, angry, grief-stricken, or intoxicated, without having to resort to physical force—or, if physical force is necessary, to use it wisely and humanely.

Robert Peel knew this 150 years ago when the field of psychology was in its infancy. He knew that the proper handling of people by police resulted in public approval of their actions and cooperation. He also knew that when police don't do this well, it works against them. The proper handling of people simply made the job of policing a lot easier. Peel believed that police in a democracy should exercise absolute impartiality and develop a relationship with the public that gives reality to the historic tradition that, within a democracy, the police are the public and the public are the police. This is also something I have believed since my earliest days in policing.

For police to become experts in human behavior, they need to cultivate an ongoing and formal relationship with academics in this area and should be eager and willing partners with them. In the past, this has not been the case—new information and research seldom trickled down to police, and police tended not to seek it out. It is precisely the lack of these kinds of connections with academia that has severely limited the growth and ability of police in this crucial area of their work life. In fact, it is one of primary things that has arrested their development.

A good example of how police methods can be made more effective can be found in how they have tended to handle hostage and barricaded-suspect situations over the years. I use this as an example because there are few instances of the method of continuous improvement being used regarding protests. Perhaps it is because protests have tended to be less frequent in occurrence.

Nevertheless, in the 1960s, I recall police were all over the response chart regarding hostage-taking situations and barricaded suspects. At first, whoever arrived first at the scene just charged in. Shortly after I became a police officer, I assisted the Minneapolis police at a tense situation in which two officers had been shot. Thankfully, their wounds were not life-threatening. We weren't organized. No one seemed in charge as I took up a position at the rear of the building where the suspect was holed up. We exchanged gunfire, and later I found that the round I had fired from my shotgun had driven the suspect into the basement of the building. I didn't have radio communications with the Minneapolis dispatcher and knew little of what was happening. I saw the suspect, fired, and later went home. No questioning. No reports.

When catch-as-catch-can situations like this didn't work very well, police responded by training a special team of officers to do this work.

This was how the concept of SWAT—Special Weapons and Tactics— came about in the late 1960s in the Los Angeles Police Department. This only happened after scores of officers throughout the country were shot while operating independently and without a plan or training.

The next development was to bring in special hostage negotiation teams (HNT). These were officers trained to contact the hostage taker (s) and, if possible, negotiate—talk suspects into surrendering without harming their hostages. Police chiefs quickly learned that the objectives of SWAT and HNT units could conflict when a SWAT team commander argued for action and an HNT leader wanted more time to negotiate. This tension worked well for police and citizens as police became more deliberate in their actions. Tacticians and negotiators could effectively work together.

None of these strategies were developed through the social sciences; instead, they arose through trial and error. In one situation, something worked. Another time, it didn't. Why not? What were the different factors? What should we do next time? Finally, police settled upon a strategy that bought time. It slowed things down.

That worked until what appeared to be a hostage situation at Columbine High School in Colorado in April 1999, turned into a mass killing spree, and the killers were willing to die. After the shootings at Columbine, which resulted in the deaths of over a dozen students and a teacher and two dozen more being injured, a new strategy had to be developed. Officers could no longer wait and get organized but had to take immediate action to save lives that could be in jeopardy.

The new strategy was that if there was shooting going on at the scene, the first four officers who arrived were to enter and stop the shooter. Again, this strategy was developed more through trial and error than intensive study and incident research. This is strategy by trial and error. Police learned that if they were willing to be flexible and open, evaluate their actions, and make the necessary changes, things could be made better. If there were as much effort placed in developing protest response strategies as there has been regarding hostage-takers and barricaded suspects, our nation's police would be far more capable today in handling protest.

Of course, that wasn't the atmosphere I worked in as a young police officer. Those readers who are in or beyond the baby-boomer generation might remember the lyrics of a song from the late 1960s called "For What It's Worth," that I found so unsettling. The rock band Buffalo Springfield sang it. For me, these lyrics capture the protest movement that I found myself in in the '60s and '70s.[103]

There's something happening here.
What it is ain't exactly clear.
There's a man with a gun over there
Telling me I got to beware.
I think it's time we stop, children, what's that sound?
Everybody look what's going down.[104]

This song reflects the chaos and craziness of that era. At the time, I worked on that street and *was* the man who would come and take them away. Stephen Stills wrote the song not, as some assume, in response to the shootings at Kent State (which took place later in 1970), but in reaction to the growing tension he saw between police and street people on the West Coast. The song has come to symbolize that challenging time in our nation when many young people questioned the behavior of their government and the police, took to the streets in protest, and began to view police no

---

103. The rest of the song: "There's battle lines being drawn/Nobody's right if everybody's wrong/Young people speaking their minds/Getting so much resistance from behind/I think it's time we stop, hey, what's that sound/ Everybody look what's going down.

104. *Ibid.*

longer as friendly public servants but as the enemy—stop, everybody look what's going down!

Now fast-forward to the present day. The British Home Office has been concerned about the behavior of their passionate football (soccer) crowds: a thousand people in the street and the confrontations that frequently occur between those crowds and police.

In this case, the British police consulted academia for some help and found Dr. Clifford Stott, a social psychologist who studied crowd behavior.

Stott is one of Europe's leading researchers regarding crowd behavior. But he advocates a different approach for police to use when handling crowds. His studies found that:

> *[L]arge-scale disorder tended to emerge and escalate because indis-criminate, heavy-handed policing generated a group mentality among large numbers of fans that was based on shared perceptions that the police action was illegitimate. This had the effect of drawing ordinary fans into conflict with the police.*[105]

When a crowd perceives the police as overreacting or being heavy-handed, its members tend to stop observing and start taking action. It is exactly what I had experienced early in my observational studies in Berkeley and Minneapolis. To prevent this from happening, Stott advocates what he calls a "softly-softly" approach—a low-key approach in which officers mix with and relate to crowd members based on their behavior rather than their reputation.

If police approach a crowd with the *expectation* that its members are going to make trouble, it often turns out that way. Even so, most police around the world have continued to use the traditional hard methods of

---

105. Clifford Stott. "Crowd Psychology & Public Order Policing: An Overview of Scientific Theory and Evidence" in a submission to the HMIC Policing. Public Protest Review Team. September 14, 2009 and http://www.timeshighereducation.co.uk/story.asp?storyCode=189237&sectioncode=26. December 27, 2010; 1101 hrs.

the past when responding to crowds.[106] For the most part today, communicating, relating, or dialoguing with people who are protesting isn't what police do. The soft approach is precisely what I developed and used years before during my time in Madison. It worked then and, as Stott suggests, it works now.

However, in many cities, and for a short while in Madison after I left, the soft approach has for the most part been neglected if not abandoned. Instead, protesters, and others assembling in crowds, are met by large numbers of police organized into crowd-control teams, outfitted with full body armor, shields, batons, gas masks, and large amounts of liquid pepper spray at the ready. What do you think the expectations are here? Of the police? Of protesters?

Whatever soft approaches police had been willing to use in the past were quickly abandoned soon after 9/11. At that time, our nation entered a new era in which police wore soft body armor like medieval knights, carried shields and sword-like batons, but used 21st-century chemical technology—the hard approach. The result of that approach is that today almost every public protest police arrive outfitted and with the expectation of violence, and—as if it were a self-fulfilling prophecy—it happens.

In the spring of 2009, *The New York Times* reported the aggressive actions of crowd control police at that year's London G-20 meeting:

> *The police say they acted appropriately in a chaotic situation, despite having officers with little experience in crowd control. But the circulation of videotape taken by protesters and passersby does not help their arguments.*
>
> *The images—of police officers charging at and striking apparently peaceful protesters, among other things—have horrified lawmakers*

---

106. This is most likely because of how Seattle police were caught off guard by protesters at the meeting of the World Trade Organization in Seattle in 1999. This seems to be the point in time when American police started to shy away from a "soft" approach.

and members of the public and prompted demands for a review of police policy.[107]

The actions of the police in London that year prompted David Gilbertson, who once formulated national policing policy in the U.K., to remark about hard crowd-control tactics:

> The attitude used to be that the British police acted more or less with the sanction of the public. That attitude has been abandoned. The public is regarded as the enemy.[108]

This is precisely what Sir Robert Peel didn't want to have happen when he developed his principles of policing over 150 years ago. Police need to operate with the permission and approval of the public, and the public should never be regarded as the enemy.

The harsh tactics our nation's police have recently used have created a psychological and physical chasm between them and protesters. The distance between police and protesters is a critical factor: as I mentioned earlier, closer is more effective. When police are physically near protesters, the tendency will be for the crowd not to depersonalize them. When police are not depersonalized, it becomes much easier, and safer, for them to enter a crowd of people and dialogue with them.

It appears today that with the new equipment police have received, the balance of power has shifted to them. In crowd situations today, police no longer see any need to negotiate or make compromises with protesters.

They no longer must wait to see how a crowd will behave; instead, they can suit up for battle expecting one to occur and knowing they will ultimately win. These are dangerous practices.

There were four events in my career that profoundly influenced me about how police should behave in crowds. They happened many years

107. "Critics Assail British Police for Harsh Tactics During the G-20 Summit Meeting," *New York Times*, May 30, 2009.

108. https://www.nytimes.com/2009/05/31/world/europe/31police.html

ago, but as I now reflect, they were pivotal points. They changed the way I would later come to approach crowds and protesters in Madison.

The first event happened nearly four decades ago in Sproul Plaza on the campus of the University of California at Berkeley. This was at the height of the free speech movement and antiwar protest on campus. In Minneapolis, we had correctly assumed that we would soon be experiencing this on our own campus. Berkeley was the place where it was all beginning to happen. I was to train police officers in my department about what I had learned on my return.

As it turned out, I didn't learn what to do there but rather what *not* to do. I saw questionable police tactics and behavior that were very upsetting. After a few days of observation, riding with police, witnessing arrests, monitoring demonstrations, and attending police debriefings, I vowed afterward that if I ever became a police leader, I would do things very differently.

The second event was the antiwar protests that soon came to my own campus, organized by my friends from the SDS and other campus protest groups. Those protests suspended my classes at the University of Minnesota for several days until the governor sent in National Guard troops to restore order. Rather than being on the street as a police officer at the time, I was on a leave from my department finishing up my graduate work. I now found myself again as an observer of police tactics. But this time it was from the perspective of being a student.

What I saw during those days caused me to revisit that vow again—if I ever became a police leader, I would do things a lot differently. I saw no dialogue, no negotiation, and little creativity beyond a massive show of force by police and military that included the presence of armored vehicles. It seemed strange to be on the receiving end for the first time. The attitude from the police and military that were present was clear: "Shut up. We are not going to listen to you. We are in charge, and we have the power to make you stop and go home."

Remarkably, no one was killed or injured during this strike. Only a year or so later, in May 1970, a similar strike at Kent State led to the deaths of four students after National Guard troops who were on campus shot at unarmed student protesters.

I came to understand more that there were a variety of ways to effectively—as well as morally and legally—police a city and properly handle people. In each case, the argument for relationship could be made: relationships between police and their communities, relationships between individual police officers and citizens (including those who are angry, victimized, mentally ill, or impaired by alcohol or other drugs), relationships between police officers and their leaders, and, finally, relationships between police and protesters—those who are unhappy with the government.

I also began to study research concerning crowds and their behavior. It was and is quite limited. I learned that Sigmund Freud believed that people in crowds behaved differently from individuals.

Gustav LeBon, a 19th century social psychologist noted for his work on crowd psychology, observed that a crowd fosters a feeling of anonymity in people and can generate collective emotions. Elias Canetti, a 20th-century Nobel Prize-winning author, classified crowd behaviors ranging from mob violence to religious assemblies. What I found was that effective methods of crowd control were not only about force and tactical maneuvers, but also about dialogue, negotiation, and reduction of fear.

The last influential event took place after my retirement from the police. Again, I'm observing police from the outside. Like most people in the United States, I witnessed the tragic day of September 11, 2001. But unlike many other citizens, I was paying close attention to the effect it had on our nation's police. All of us in America have lived in fear since that fateful day. And our police, for the most part, have done so as well.

Our nation's police have been unable or slow to return to the community-oriented role they were in the process of working through—such as soft methods of crowd control, neighborhood policing, and focusing on solving community problems. Too many of our nation's police are busy looking instead for terrorists in the community rather than support from it.

This new militarism has gripped police and turned them away from the pursuit of community policing to focus on technology to solve their problems and on anti-terrorism. It isn't that the threat of urban terrorism should be ignored, but rather, who should have the primary responsibility? I see the police as community workers—not urban commandos.

Police officers, working closely with their communities in our nation's cities, should take advantage of their unique role to guarantee fairness and effectiveness in their practices. This is the paramount local strategy to prevent domestic terrorism. I have often thought that negative contacts, day in and day out, with the poor and people of color have done more to erode our nation's security than any international threat.

The state National Guard, not the police, should be the primary organization to respond to situations that are beyond the capability of local police departments. They have the logistics, intelligence, and weaponry to do so. The Guard is local and has the equipment and support systems to do this. While our local Guard units have been deployed to Iraq and Afghanistan, police in many cities have had to fill the gap. It will be difficult for police to give up that role when they return. In the meantime, there has been a substantial regression in their progress toward community policing.

My tenure as chief in Burnsville, MN, from 1969 to 1972, gave me the time to integrate what I had learned in the academic world and what I had experienced as a city police officer. With few opportunities for handling crowds in Burnsville, I was given the chance to think about and develop my ideas about crowd control when I interviewed for the chief's jobs at the University of Minnesota and in Madison. Handling crowds and protest was one of the major, and most controversial, tasks police had to do in that day. And to many observers, the police in Minneapolis and on the campus of the University of Minnesota had not done it skillfully. My approach as to how I would handle protest became a defining strength for me in becoming the top candidate for these positions. It is no less important today.

I had newer and more effective ways in mind regarding how to handle people other than beating them up. These ideas didn't just come from the classroom but were a blend of academic and direct experience. Every good street cop knows that communication matters—you talk *with* the person or people you're dealing with, not *at* them. Good police officers always exercise their verbal skills more than their physical ones. What was different is that I believed you could also do this with people in crowds.

One of the primary reasons I survived in Madison was that the new (soft) crowd-control measures I brought in worked. During the next 20 years, we never lost control of a crowd, and that included hundreds of protests and demonstrations at the State Capitol building, and on the campus of the university, as well as strikes by state workers, teaching assistants at the university, and local meat-packers.[109] The method we used has recently been called *The Madison Method* by police officers outside of the city.[110]

This method is just as noteworthy today because of the Occupy Movement and the varieties of police response we have seen. What is it we should expect police to do in these situations? What is the role of the community and elected officials? Are the police to be mere instruments in the arm of government or not?

All things aside, how police handle public protest in our nation is one of the most noteworthy measures of the quality of a department's policing. When police do this well and without violence, they move from good to great.

---

109. For a general listing of those protests and demonstrations see references regarding the history of protests and social action from the 1970s to '90s at: http://archives.library.wisc.edu/uw-archives/exhibits/protests/1970s. html.

110. In March and April 2011, government officials in Madison effectively used many of these techniques in handling a multi-week demonstration and occupation of the state capitol building because of the governor-elect proposing to end collective bargaining in Wisconsin for most public employees. See: http://www.policeone.com/Crowd-Control/ articles/3361291-The-Madison-Method-for-crowd-control/and http:// www.cityofmadison.com/police/specialunits/specialEvents.cfm; January 26, 1750 hrs.

Three Examples of Effective Protest Management in Madison

1. Student Block Party with a History of Violent Conflict with Police

Less than five months after my appointment, newly-elected Mayor Soglin and I were confronted with a request from the residents of Mifflin Street for a street use permit. Mifflin Street was close to the university campus and was the preferred residential neighborhood for many students and activists. The residents wanted to hold their traditional annual spring party again. But two years before I came to Madison, the gathering had resulted in a drawn-out battle between residents and police.

Though two years had passed since that blow-up, there still was lingering resentment in the community of how the police had responded to the previous gathering. It ended with arrests, use of tear gas, and liberal application of nightsticks. When the permit came before the city council, the community wondered what the new mayor and I were going to do. Were things going to be different? This was my first test and much was at stake. I knew I needed help with training, planning, and staffing.

I wisely looked inside the department and asked my officers for help in creating a new, and intensively trained, unit called the Special Operations Section (SOS). The SOS would now have primary responsibility for crowd management. This unit would model the new behaviors I was seeking to instill among all my police. Fortunately, many junior officers jumped at the chance. It would be an opportunity to try something new and creative. To this day, I don't know what I would have done had not so many officers volunteered for my experiment.

Many of them already knew the old ways had not worked very well and had generated considerable animosity and disrespect toward them and the police department. Looking back, my request enabled officers within the department to stand up and define themselves as being open to change and willing to progress. Many of them went on to be department leaders.

My plan was to put together a training experience for them on conflict management. I found help from Prof. Robert Shellow of Carnegie Mellon University, through a grant from the Police Foundation. Shellow had studied the soft methods in which I was interested. Dr. Morton Bard, a licensed psychologist and former New York City police officer, who had also done considerable work in crisis management, joined him.

At the end of the training, officers in the new unit developed their own crowd-control strategy based on the new information they had just learned. The approach was: "Here's what we know. Now what would you do?" All the officers had had experience using traditional methods of crowd control—declare an unlawful assembly, make a show of force, display batons, disperse tear gas, move the crowd, and arrest those who remained. Now they were being pressed to think of other ways.

Surprisingly, the officers chose to use none of the old methods; instead, they decided to use techniques of low-key action, increased visibility, and dialogue with residents and those coming to the event. The plan they presented to manage this potentially explosive gathering was to assign themselves, individually, as single officers, on the perimeter of the area in which the block party was to occur. They would be on-site early in the day to greet and speak with those coming to the party.

They chose to wear uniforms for identification but not hats. This was more of a change than it might appear—Madison police officers had always been required to wear their hats when on duty and were disciplined when they didn't. The young people coming to the block party would quickly see that the police department wasn't conducting business as usual; something was different. And we, of course, wanted them to know this wasn't business-as-usual.

The volunteer officers also requested permission from me *not* to wear firearms during the event. This recommendation set me back. This was the one recommendation from the unit that I had to veto—it would have generated tremendous pushback from the rest of the department. It would have made headlines around the country, but I had to think about bringing the rest of the police department along with me. I thanked the officers for their creative thinking, which was commendable and courageous, but it was simply too early in my tenure as chief to approve it, too risky. If I had sent unarmed officers to the block party, and one of them had been injured, I would have lost whatever support I had from the rest of the department and the community.

This early experiment in sharing decision-making with rank-and-file officers proved to me that they, given information and responsibility, could make good decisions. This was a lesson I wouldn't forget. When the backlash happened within the department, I put this lesson on hold. But I didn't forget it, and in later years it was what helped me and the department make that quantum leap in the early 1980s.

The day of the block party was tense as we gathered early on that Saturday morning for briefing. The media and the community were expecting another confrontation between police and students. Some were anticipating this happening. But it didn't.

It turned out that the officers were outstanding—they talked and joked with those who came to the party and were quickly seen as being at the party to help and not hinder the day's events. They were peacemakers, not agitators. I don't think we made any arrests that day. The party ended late that night, and groups of young people were seen cleaning up the day's trash from the streets and bagging it for pickup by city crews.

This was my first real test using a soft style of crowd management, and it worked. It would serve me well during the coming years.

Not everyone, of course, saw what we did as a good thing. Within the department there were several officers, including those in command, who were casualties at the Dow protests and the earlier Mifflin Block Parties. They saw this in a much different way. They saw my strategy as giving in to the students—even capitulating to them—and being weak. Many of those officers had old scores to settle. And while their injuries had healed on the outside, there remained deep, unhealed wounds inside.

2. Large Protest Regarding Public Policy at the State Capitol Building

The second major example of the department's new and evolving crowd-control methods occurred years later in April 1986, when a large, organized protest was held on the grounds of the Capitol protesting public investments in South Africa. In the years since the Mifflin block party, we had handled hundreds of protests, demonstrations, and large crowds such as the annual Halloween celebration downtown that at its height had more than 100,000 revelers in attendance without noteworthy incidents.

This protest was against also the apartheid policies of South Africa. While the Madison police normally don't have jurisdiction over state property, we were called in to assist the Capitol police. Governor Tony Earl had called Mayor Joel Skornicka for aid, who then called me. By the time I arrived on the scene to make an assessment, many of the demonstrators who now filled the Capitol grounds had begun constructing wooden shanties, symbols of the segregated townships outside the larger cities in South Africa.

I saw that many the demonstrators were not from Madison but had come from other cities in Wisconsin and throughout the Midwest. The initial attitude of the demonstrators wasn't friendly toward the presence of police. They were not the usual protest people we had worked with over the years. At first, neither of us knew what to expect from the other.

I needed to talk to the governor before we got involved in this emotionally charged situation. I told him that it would be preferable if we kept things low-key and didn't make any immediate demands on the protesters. I asked that my department be the lead agency in handling the situation. The governor agreed.

I wanted to avoid a confrontation for as long as possible, but even as I spoke, protesters had entered the Capitol building and staged a sit-in in the central rotunda. The Capitol chief and I had agreed that his officers would handle the inside of the building and we would handle the outside. At the end of the day, the Capitol police would follow their standard practice of locking down the building. When that happened, the demonstrators would be asked to leave. And some did. Those remaining were carefully escorted outside and the doors locked behind them. This happened without incident or arrests.

While we had used our soft strategy effectively during numerous demonstrations and sit-ins during the past decade, this crowd was by far one of the largest and most diverse we'd ever dealt with. I saw this as another opportunity for us to put into practice and highlight what we had learned about handling crowds and how police in a democracy operate.

I presented our plan to the governor. We would assign uniformed police officers, without hats, batons, or any riot control gear, to enter the crowd and dialogue with the protesters. But this time we went beyond merely talking with them and calming them down—we instructed these officers in some of the alternatives to divestment and how divesting might severely impact everyone in South Africa, blacks and whites. We encouraged protesters to form discussion groups in the crowd. Those assembled came to see the police as not trying to prevent protest but rather to facilitate it; they soon realized that the police who present were informed, smart, and willing to engage in political discussions.

This protest was an occupation and, literally, a massive sit-in and camp-out on the Capitol grounds. This meant that many of the protesters were doing more sitting than protesting. The point of contention, I knew, would be when some legislators got tired of all this and ordered us to expel the protesters from state property. If that happened, the businesses and government buildings on the Capitol Square and downtown area would be vulnerable to damage and vandalism. It was a waiting game on both sides.

We briefed our officers on these issues and reasserted to the protesters that our role was to *facilitate* the protest, not prevent it. We also let them know that we too were against racism and any system of discrimination. The presence of our diverse workforce in terms of gender and race also spoke a clear message that day. The protesters knew we were here to stay and not in any hurry to end things.

Our strategy was always to keep *us* from becoming the issue, and to keep talking.

The protest went on for six days. As time went on, we started negotiations with the leaders concerning dismantling the scores of illegal shanties that had been constructed on the lawn of the Capitol building. The presence of the shanties was, of course, an issue of enormous contention, as people are not generally allowed to build structures on the grounds of a state capitol and many members of the community believed the police needed to do something about it. We often heard, "Look at this mess. Who's going to clean it up?"

Everyone expected that if we moved to dismantle the shanties, it would create the issue that could ignite the crowd. It never happened. We could negotiate a smooth withdrawal, and we permitted a few symbolic shanties to remain standing for a few more days. It was a win-win ending. A positive ending brought about by police willing to be patient and withhold action.

I believe the overwhelming majority of the demonstrators went home feeling that they had made a powerful and well-heard protest against apartheid, petitioned their government for redress, been heard by that government, and witnessed democratic police in action: police who served as facilitators and protectors, who acknowledged their right to assemble and protest the actions of their government.

Now, you may ask how you get police officers to enter a potentially hostile crowd without protective gear. One of the strategies we used was having a reserve force in readiness. A few blocks away, out of the view of the public and media, was a team of police officers kept in reserve with helmets, batons, and tear gas. They were on standby in case any person, including police officers, in the crowd was in danger of harm. That was how I could justify asking officers to enter such a large crowd. Again, speaking softly and carrying a big stick works effectively for police when the stick is out of sight. The difference here was that our big stick wasn't our first or only strategy. It was only one of our strategies—and only one of last resort.

3. Protest Regarding Foreign Military Intervention

Over the years, we had gained a lot of experience in handling people in large groups—it demonstrated that our soft methods of crowd control and conflict management worked, and we continued to hone our skills. We handled many more block parties, celebrations, labor strikes, protests, and attacks on medical clinics during anti-abortion actions, more demonstrations at the Capitol and in the campus area, and a host of other gatherings, and assemblies—one of which resulted in 100,000 motorcyclists descending into our city to protest a proposed law which would require them to wear safety helmets.

After the spring of 1975, when the Vietnam War ended, we didn't have any more antiwar protests. That lull ended in 1990 when the first Gulf War broke out, and Madison citizens and university students again took to the streets in protest. We wondered if we'd be able to use the same tactics we had used for nearly two decades. Would the fact that this was a war with a potential for a draft, like Vietnam, make it a different kind of protest? I again remembered what Stuart Becker had told me about Dow Chemical. I didn't want this event to be about the police.

The atmosphere in the city was very tense as the war began. We still had some officers working in the department who had been at the Dow protests. We saw many of the antiwar folks from the 1970s back on the street again—years older and now with their children in tow.

As expected, there was also a very intense pro-war attitude in the community and a feeling that we all needed to support our troops and reservists. This attitude was also sharply prevalent in the ranks of the police department. We had veterans like myself in the department and officers who were members of local military reserve units. I had to make sure that a Dow situation didn't happen again. I wanted any protest that occurred to be about governmental policies and not the police.

As was our practice, we gave the SOS the initial responsibility to work with the community organizers who were planning the protests. Like almost every group we had worked with over the years, they agreed to meet with us. I also called a meeting of my management team and suggested we develop a statement of expectations regarding what citizens could expect from us. The statement was printed on pocket-size cards, which we distributed to those who showed up at the scenes of the protests. It was, of course, also given to the media, who gave it front-page play.

A problem that occurs at most protests is that citizens don't know what to expect from their police. That situation causes a tremendous amount of tension. So why not tell them?

At the first protest, I walked with my officers through the crowd of a hundred or more protesters and distributed the cards to those who had assembled for the march. Throughout the various Gulf conflicts, the issues stayed focused on what Washington was doing and not on us. We had learned much about handling people, applied what we had learned, continually tried to enhance and fine-tune our method, and shared what we had learned with the community and other police departments.[111]

The proper handling of public protest was a major goal of mine before and during my time in Madison. What we did in Madison is illustrative of the process police are to use in responding to any community problem. It is what professional police do.

---

111. In February 2011, protesters again occupied the state capitol in Madison to protest Governor-elect Scott Walker's proposed budget legislation that, if implemented, would effectively eliminate collective bargaining for all public employees except police and firefighters. The protest went on for several weeks in February and into April. Crowds approaching 80,000 to 100,000 filled the Capitol Square and building. Republican officials used a "soft" approach by not forcing the demonstrators out of the Capitol building and were very tolerant of crowd behavior. The tactic worked as the crowds eventually diminished and the protesters left the Capitol building. (For further information see *Wisconsin State Journal* article at: http://host. madison.com/wsj/news/local/govt-and-politics/article_9f189108-4cbc-11e0-b9b8-001cc4c002e0.html, May 9, 2011; 1555 hrs.

Chapter 8
Stop, Don't Shoot!

WHEN THE FIRST EDITION OF this book was published in 2012, the national issue regarding police was their handling of public protest, namely, the Occupy Wall Street Movement which began September 2011. Since that time, another issue of national concern has come to the forefront—police use of deadly force.

Most will agree that the tipping point occurred after the death of Michael Brown, Jr. by police in Ferguson, Missouri in August 2014. While Brown's death was not captured on video and posted on the Internet, the protest that followed Brown's death certainly was. This was the moment in our nation's history when citizens began using cell phones to video police actions. Rather than welcoming an exercise of the First Amendment, many police threatened these amateur videographers with arrest rather than changing their own behavior.

Since that time, there has been a virtual flood of these graphic accounts. The posted videos often have hundreds of thousands of viewings within a very short time. The names of those black men killed by police, in addition to Brown, are now familiar to most Americans: Eric Garner, Alton Sterling, Walter Scott, Tamir Rice, Laquan McDonald, and Philando Castile, to name a few of the nearly 1,000 Americans killed each year by their police.

The public outcry from Black Americans was loud and often destructive. In response, "Black Lives Matter" was formed and became a national movement. Police officers and their unions pushed back with "Blue Lives Matter." Public prosecutors charged some police officers involved in these shootings, but few were convicted by the jurors who heard their defenses. And, tragically, well-meaning police officers were assassinated while going about their duties as happened to five Dallas police officers shot by a sniper while monitoring a peaceful protest in their city. More recently, NYPD Police Officer Miosotis Familia, a popular officer in the neighborhood in which she worked, was gunned down simply because she was wearing a blue uniform.

Much discussion continues to surround the U.S. Supreme Court's 1989 decision in *Graham v. Connor*.[112] While it was not a case involving police deadly force and was handed down over 25 years ago, it became the standard for police training and on how deadly force was to be used. The driving words of *Graham* were "objective reasonableness." If an officer's perception of danger was reasonable and objective, the use of deadly force was legal. Opponents called the decision "lawful, but awful," while police, holding the line, stressed the danger of their work and their need to make immediate life-saving decisions—even if they may be unpopular.

Within a few months of Brown's death in Ferguson, after days of anger, property damage, and arrests, Barack Obama ordered the creation of "The President's Task Force on 21st Century Policing."[113] Its membership consisted of police and community leaders, academics, and legal scholars. Within a year, they issued their final report which addressed six vital areas, or "pillars," of policing: 1) Building Trust and Legitimacy, 2) Policy and Oversight, 3) Technology and Social Media, 4) Community Policing and Crime Reduction, 5) Training and Education, and 6) Officer Wellness and Safety. Within these six important areas they made 59 recommendations for improvement.[114]

I am listing the recommendations which I believe to be the most important:

1. Law enforcement culture should embrace a guardian mindset to build public trust and legitimacy. Toward that end, police and

112. https://supreme.justia.com/cases/federal/us/490/386/. 07/14/2017.

113. http://www.cops.usdoj.gov/pdf/taskforce/taskforce_finalreport.pdf. 07/14/2017.

114. http://www.policeforum.org/assets/guidingprinciples1.pdf. 07/14/2017.

sheriffs' departments should adopt procedural justice[115] as the guiding principle for internal and external policies and practices to guide their interactions with the citizens they serve.

2. To achieve internal legitimacy, law enforcement agencies should involve employees in the process of developing policies and procedures.

3. Use of physical control equipment and techniques against vulnerable populations—including children, elderly persons, pregnant women, people with physical and mental disabilities, limited English proficiency, and others—can undermine public trust and should be used as a last resort. Law enforcement agencies should carefully consider and review their policies towards these populations and adopt policies if none are in place.

4. Law enforcement agencies should strive to create a workforce that contains a broad range of diversity including race, gender, language, life experience, and cultural background to improve understanding and effectiveness in dealing with all communities.

5. Law enforcement agency policies for training on use of force should emphasize de-escalation and alternatives to arrest or summons in situations where appropriate.

6. These policies should also mandate external and independent criminal investigations in cases of police use of force resulting in death, officer-involved shootings resulting in injury or death, or in-custody deaths.

7. Law enforcement agencies should create policies and procedures for policing mass demonstrations that employ a continuum of managed tactical resources that are designed to minimize the appearance of a military operation and avoid using provocative tactics and equipment that undermine civilian trust.

115. https://learn.bu.edu/bbcswebdav/pid-365946-dt-content-rid-343009_1/ courses/13sprgmetcj602_ol/course_documents/metcj602_W05_article_ tyler.pdf. 07/15/2017.

8. Community policing should be infused throughout the culture and organizational structure of law enforcement agencies. Community policing emphasizes working with neighborhood residents to co-produce public safety.

9. Law enforcement agencies should work with community residents to identify problems and collaborate on implementing solutions that produce meaningful results for the community.

10. Because offensive or harsh language can escalate a minor situation, law enforcement agencies should underscore the importance of language used and adopt policies directing officers to speak to individuals with respect.

A year later, the Police Executive Research Forum (PERF), whose members are primarily college-educated police chiefs from larger cities, expanded on many of the Task Force's recommendations focusing on the use of force in their report, "30 Guiding Principles on Use of Force."[116] The following guidelines are my choices for the "Top Seven:"

1. The sanctity of human life should be at the heart of everything an agency does.

2. Departments should adopt policies that hold them to a higher standard than the legal requirements of *Graham v. Connor*.

3. Police use of force must meet the test of proportionality.

4. Adopt de-escalation as formal agency policy.

5. Duty to intervene: Officers need to prevent other officers from using excessive force.

6. Respect the sanctity of life by promptly rendering first aid.

7. Shooting at vehicles must be strictly prohibited.

Since the release of these reports, there has been a growing concern

---

116. http://www.policeforum.org/assets/guidingprinciples1.pdf. 07/14/2017.

throughout America about the need to rebuild trust and support of our nation's police since the days of Ferguson. To illustrate this concern, a Gallup Poll during the years 2012-2014 found that overall public confidence in police was at 55%.

This is a high number. The highest level of confidence recorded for police was 64% in 2004. Those polled were adults who were asked whether they had "a great deal" or "quite a lot" of confidence in law enforcement. During 2012-2014, the confidence level did not vary much between Whites, Hispanics, liberals, moderates, or conservatives. As we might expect, Black Americans had a lower (35%) rate of confidence for police during this period.

More recently, as of July 2017, the confidence of Whites, conservatives, and those aged 55 and older are back to the same level of confidence they had for police in 2012-2014 (55%).

However, not so for other groups. It appears that Ferguson changed that. There was a significant drop in confidence since 2014 among Blacks (30%), Hispanics (45%), liberals (39%), and those aged 18-34 (44%). Their level of confidence has not returned to what it was before Ferguson.[117]

Are 1,000 deaths a year at the hands of our police reasonable? When 2017 mid-year data were released indicating police in America had shot and killed almost the same number of citizens they did at this time last year, I was concerned. After all, we have recommendations from a national task force along with a report from leading police chiefs calling for raising the standard of force in *Graham v. Connor*. Additionally, concerns about police use of deadly force among Black Americans continue as many parents of color feel compelled to give their boys "the talk" which is exemplified by Ta-Nehisi Coates' "Letter to My Son."[118] I had hoped the numbers might have gone down, indicating improvements had been made.

But some suggest this is just the way it is in America given our nation's

---

117. http://www.gallup.com/poll/213869/confidence-police-back-historical-average.aspx. 07/24/2017.

118. https://www.theatlantic.com/politics/archive/2015/07/tanehisi-coates-between-the-world-and-me/397619/. July 28; 1735 hrs.

firearms policies, racism, addiction to drugs, failing mental health system, a widening gap between rich and poor, and struggling schools.

Do we really think that we, as a nation with 600,000 police officers working in 18,000 agencies (most of which have fewer than ten officers) that things could be different? So I really don't know if the nearly 500 lives taken in the first six months of this year is good or bad. We only have two years of journalistic data to compare. Police still are not mandated to report their uses of deadly force to the government. While the FBI created the National Use of Force Data Collection in 2015, the most accurate number, name, and circumstances of persons killed by police is through the work of journalists at the *Washington Post* and *The Guardian*.

While it might be the way it is in America, I am compelled to look at what's going on with police use of deadly force in other countries. For example, in Europe, Asia, and Australia they must be doing things a little bit differently because their police use deadly force at a much lower rate. Members of the European Union must endorse the following statement on police use of deadly force.[119]

Article 2: European Convention of Human Rights

"Deprivation of life shall not be regarded as inflicted in contravention of this Article when it results from the use of force which is no more than absolutely necessary." [120]

Between 2013 and 2015, the reported rate of police use of deadly force per million residents was as follows.[121]

---

119. https://www.pri.org/stories/2016-07-12/when-it-comes-police-shootings-us-doesnt-look-developed-nation. 07/14/2017.

120. http://www.europarl.europa.eu/aboutparliament/en/displayFtu.html?ftuId=FTU_5.12.7

121. Data were available for different time ranges in each country. Deaths per capita were calculated by dividing total deaths during those periods by the estimated population in the last year data was available. Sources:

Country	Rate/Million	Deaths
Singapore	0.03	3
England and Wales	0.04	58
Germany	0.10	117
Australia	0.21	105
United States	3.11	3,003

It has been painful to watch how many police leaders fail to respond to the concerns of those whom they have the most contact, namely poor people, members of minority groups, and those suffering from mental illness. For the most part, it is these citizens who receive the most contact, the most "service," from police. Shouldn't these groups be able to expect the same level of police service as wealthier White communities receive?

Early in my career, I saw my job in as a police officer as a "cultural referee" keeping peace among conflicting groups of citizens. When I became a chief, I saw my job as bringing together a city that was often divided. I learned along the way how to do that and those methods that can be learned and used today. Many of them are in this book.

In the late 1960s and early '70s, the dividing issue was the Vietnam War and whether to grant full civil rights to African Americans. Today,

Mapping Police Violence, Australian Institute of Criminology, Danish National Police, Statewatch, Deutsche Welle, *NZ Herald*, Inquest, *The Straits Times*. Population data is from the World Bank. https://www.pri. org/stories/2016-07-12/when-it-comes-police-shootings-us-doesnt-look-developed-nation. 07/14/2017.

the issue is police use of deadly force. The Four Obstacles I overcame in Madison and the Seven Steps I took are actions America's police leaders should consider if they are going to rebuild the trust and support that has been recently lost among younger people and those of color.

Police have always had difficulty incorporating new ideas, alternatives, or just about anything outside of the *status quo*. This is unfortunate and continues to arrest their development, creativity, and effectiveness. This is especially true when it comes to reducing their uses of deadly force. When the deadly force discussion begins, police hunker down, get defensive, and worry that they will violate those strong subcultural norms I addressed in the first chapter of this book.

So what's the answer? Much of the literature available today from the business and corporate world is consistent with what I learned and lived during my police career. For me, it falls into three primary leadership practices:

1. Learning to think in terms of systems,

2. Deeply listening to citizen-customers (recipients of police services and actions), and being able to cast off the vestiges of authoritarian and coercive leadership, and

3. Practicing the new leadership, and teaching and leading others how to do it up and down the chain of command.

To move forward, leaders are going to have to permit their officers to think creatively and partner with them in running the organization; doing this will take a bold and courageous leader, but the positive results will be dramatic.

I must add an important point here: the need for racial reconciliation in among our police and in our nation. I believe it is the role of police to actively seek reconciliation from persons and communities who have been harmed by them. It must be a sincere public apology. It begins with being visibly sorry for the past. Police work in a system today whose actions have tended to work against the poor and people of color. Without apology, trust is impossible.

Any apology must be accompanied with a visible change in behavior. It is not sufficient to apologize for historical abuse. Apology must also be made for present-day practices that do not treat all citizens fairly and justly. For an apology to be accepted, those receiving it must perceive the giver as remorseful and sincere. The giver of the apology must also be willing to do better in the future, to work to improve the present relationship. It is up to the giver of the apology to take the first step. It is difficult to apologize to someone who is angry and does not trust you. But it can be done and done effectively. Collective apologies have worked in South Africa, Rwanda, and Bosnia.

In 2013, Chief Kevin Murphy of Montgomery, Alabama, apologized to Congressman John Lewis for the brutal reception and beating he and other Freedom Riders received at the hands of Montgomery police in 1961.[122] At the time the incident happened, Murphy had not yet been born. He was apologizing for the past to clear a path forward. Chief Murphy knew that without apology, progress is impossible and, without his apology, both police and Black citizens in his city would remain distrustful of one another.

A similar apology was made earlier this year by Chief Lou Dekmar of LaGrange, Georgia. He apologized for a lynching that occurred in his city in 1940.[123] Dekmar knew that unless this historical tragedy was openly acknowledged and dealt with, the future of relations in his city between his police officers and people of color was never going to improve.

Last year, Chief Terry Cunningham, president of the International Chiefs of Police (IACP), apologized at a large gathering of police chiefs. He apologized for the role police had played in the past enforcing Jim Crow laws and conducting slave patrols.[124] [As a side note: I also have

---

122. http://www.pbs.org/newshour/bb/how-one-chief-tried-to-reverse-police-wrongs-of-the-civil-rights-era/. 07/14/2017.

123. https://www.nytimes.com/2017/01/26/us/lagrange-georgia-lynching-apology.html?_r=0. 07/14/2017.

124. http://www.npr.org/sections/thetwo-way/2016/10/18/498380373/head-

apologized for being part of and a leader in a system that did not treat African Americans fairly.[125]]

He said that policing is a "noble profession" that has seen dark periods in its history:

> *"There have been times when law enforcement officers, because of the laws enacted by federal, state and local governments, have been the face of oppression for far too many of our fellow citizens. In the past, the laws adopted by our society have required police officers to perform many unpalatable tasks, such as ensuring legalized discrimination or even denying the basic rights of citizenship to many of our fellow Americans... this dark side of our shared history has created a multi-generational—almost inherited—mistrust between many communities of color and their law enforcement agencies. We must move forward together to build a shared understanding."* [126]

Now back to those three basic leadership practices that can help police better respond to public issues and crises:

1.   THINK SYSTEMS: All work is systematic. Learn the parts. Those who do the work know how to fix things.

Earlier, I addressed the important role Dr. W. Edwards Deming played mid-career in my life. He taught me how to think in systems to improve outputs and services. Accordingly, when things go wrong, it most likely is not the result of an employee error but rather the system in which employees worked. Such thinking helped me see the "big picture"—the

of-police-chiefs-group-apologizes-for-historical-mistreatment-of-minorities. 07/14/2017.

125. https://www.usatoday.com/story/opinion/policing/spotlight/2016/10/20/top-cops-apology-blacks-falls-short-voices/92427284/. 07/14/2017.

126. http://www.npr.org/sections/thetwo-way/2016/10/18/498380373/head-of-police-chiefs-group-apologizes-for-historical-mistreatment-of-minorities. 07/27/2017; 1700 hrs.

system in which I worked and led. But most of all, Dr. Deming helped me to see that such a system is capable of being improved. And he changed the way I saw myself as a leader.

If I wanted to improve things, blaming police officers wasn't the way to go. Instead, ask, listen, and fix the things that are causing the problems. Only a leader has the power to do that. Employees cannot. And the way to do that is ask those who are doing the work as to how it can be done better. That takes humility. When leaders focus on how work is done, and sincerely and honestly ask those doing it how it can be done better, magic happens, that is, a high-quality, just, and respectful outcome between a police officer and citizen.

But who decides what quality is? What is quality to those on the receiving end? Remember, only those on the receiving end can define the quality of any kind of service, that is, customers. Customers of policing are those with whom police have contact, those they caution, advise, and, yes, arrest. These customers will have opinions about the service they received, and they're worth hearing.

Quality is a comprehensive approach to the organization and the design of work processes. It is a way to think about stuff. It is a way to treat each other. It is a way to constantly improve everything we lay our hands on.[127]

In short, if leaders don't provide high-quality training to their employees, and respectful, growth-oriented leadership, how can they expect their employees to do any better, to deliver the high-quality police services to the community for which the leader is responsible?

The crucial question today is whether you believe quality police services include controlling and managing uses of force. Sir Robert Peel thought so in 1829 when he issued his "Nine Principles of Policing."[128] Two of them warn that the important relationship between police and citizens, and their level of support, can be put in jeopardy if police use excessive force.

---

127. Lee Cheaney and Maury Cotter, *Real Work, Real People*, SBAK Productions, 1990.

128. See page 37 above.

2. ASK CUSTOMERS: Those who are impacted by what you do or fail to do.

Asking and listening to employees and citizens are vital police leadership tasks. Sometimes the two groups don't agree. Sometimes they ask leaders to take conflicting actions. Deadly force use is one good example. Citizens may ask the police chief to restrict its use while police officers want the chief not to restrict them but continue to use the *Graham* standard in training and policy. The only way to resolve this is through honest and open discussion between the two groups. Whatever the outcome, if police and citizens can respectfully hear one another, movement is possible.

Has this been done? I would be surprised, because it takes a great amount of courage for police to walk into a community meeting with activists who want them to restrict or restrain their right to use force—including deadly force.

It is much better to have this conversation *before* a questionable use of force occurs. Doing this after an event is extremely difficult and most likely will be ineffective. Tensions and anger at that time will prevent the kind of discussion that is so needed. Unfortunately, most police and community leaders are not engaging directly with one another about this important issue. Instead, social media and local journalists duke it out with police standing resolutely and defensively in the background. This must change if we are to live and work together. Dr. King reminded us that "We must learn to live together as brothers or perish together as fools." Learning to live together is having these difficult conversations.

In addition to public forums on community expectations surrounding uses of force, police leaders must also *directly* and *frequently* ask community members how they feel about a police service they have recently received—and not just after a shooting. Today, on-going, real-time surveys must be conducted on a regular basis. Otherwise, how will leaders know how their men and women are doing and on what particular things they should be working?[129]

---

129. For a unique and creative way to do this visit http://openpolicing.org.

In the business world, customer feedback is absolutely essential; it is the lifeblood of a successful organization and a matter of economic survival. For police, it helps them know what's going on and in what direction they should be working. Feedback helps them improve. It is not about just how citizen-customers evaluate them, but more critically, identifying what specifically needs to be improved. You say your police officers are improving? You believe you are trusted by your community? How do you know that? Where are your data? You might be surprised.

3. IMPLEMENT NEW LEADERSHIP: Lead with integrity. Coach and help your employees grow.

My leadership epiphany occurred when I came to understand deep down in my heart that top-down coercion is not leadership but rather intimidation. I hope I have made my point about this in earlier chapters. Improvements in policing (and control of deadly force) cannot occur under an entrenched defensive leadership style. I became convinced that a new style was needed because the old way was no longer working. I needed to find a style that would attract the mature, educated, and diverse police we needed in our organization and to lead the officers I already had better. The new leadership had to be collaborative, focused on growing and coaching people, and include actively listening to them and members of the community. The new leadership had to be able to bring what we call today "Procedural Justice" into the workplace as well as the community. And the new leadership needed to be practiced not only by me but by every leader in the department. It wasn't going to be voluntary, it was mandatory without being coercive. This is how Prof. Tom Tyler, who developed Procedural Justice, defines it:

> *"One element of procedural justice is giving members of the public an opportunity to explain their situation or tell their side of the story in a given situation. People also feel they are receiving procedural justice if an officer makes decisions in a neutral and fair way, and not based on*

the officer's personal opinions or biases. People also wish to be treated with dignity and politeness. And they make judgments about whether an officer is trustworthy, caring, and trying to do what's best." [130]

When officers practice Procedural Justice, they build their legitimacy among community members. We have found today that the practice of Procedural Justice is not just for the community, but also how police leaders deal with their officers and employees. My wife, also a veteran police leader, joined me in writing this about the new leadership years ago. We called it "Quality Leadership" (Refer to "Step Four: Train and Lead" in Chapter Six). It fits right in with practicing Procedural Justice.

> *"This style of leadership will assure the achievement of quality police services, a more community-oriented policing style, and the use of new approaches to problem-solving because it sets an organizational culture that permits not only movement to these new concepts in policing, but gives us the ability and flexibility to move beyond them. This new style is oriented not only to changing community needs, but also to the changing needs of our employees.*
>
> *"There is flexibility in this style, a built-in survival mechanism that is attuned to the inside as well as the outside of the organization—employees and citizens. We will be able to exist as a viable organization in the future and it will help us achieve quality, a quality defined by keeping the public's peace and closely serving our neighborhoods; all within the rule of law."* [131]

---

130. From: "Legitimacy and Procedural Justice: A New Element of Police Leadership," The Police Executive Research Forum (PERF): http://www.policeforum.org/assets/docs/Free_Online_Documents/Leadership/legitimacy%20and%20procedural%20justice%20-%20a%20new%20element%20of%20police%20leadership.pdf. July 27, 2017; 1430.

131. David C. Couper and Sabine Lobitz. 1987. "Quality Leadership: The First Step Toward Quality Policing." *The Police Chief* magazine. Washington, DC: International Association of Chiefs of Police. April issue.

Two major transformations occurred during my leadership career. The first addressed our training needs as we worked to recruit and hire more educated, diverse, and talented officers, brought women into patrol and supervisory positions, and improved the way in which we responded to protests and demonstrations (frequent events in Madison and on the campus of the University of Wisconsin).

The second transformation focused on developing a work environment and style of leadership that tapped the intelligence and experience of our officers and employees. It was designed to get even closer to those whom we served. The questions I asked of department leaders, from sergeants to deputy chiefs, were these:

1. Tell me how you spend your time?

2. What are the questions you ask your employees?

3. How do you handle critical incidents?

4. What are your officers' work behaviors that you reward and how are they rewarded by you?

Being a police officer is a difficult job, yet one that can be highly and personally rewarding. Policing always has been a calling for those who do it best. But now millions of Americans have watched disturbing images of their police as their actions are placed under a microscope and uploaded into the world of social media and network news. These videos have shown that what was once standard operating procedure can no longer be tolerated or accepted. The old must give way to the new as police must commit themselves to the protection of life as a core operating value. And that may mean slowing things down in the face of conflict and violence, working to de-escalate the situation, and not being so quick to shoot.

To do this is going to take solid, educated, well-trained, respectful, and emotionally-controlled police. Citizens need to demand this and work with their police and community leaders to make sure this happens. They must see that their community's "best and brightest" are selected to serve as police and receive the best training possible from instructors who are wise and mature. Our nation deserves great police—and today's police deserve the chance to be great police officers.

Outsiders are never going to change police. Believe me, I've worked in the field for over 30 years of my life and watched and studied police for another two decades. When I decided to stay in policing after graduate school, I knew this to be true. From the outside, I could never help improve police no matter how highly educated I was or what public office I held. The only way to do this was to become a chief of police.

Chapter 9
George Floyd: Where To From Here?

October 2014: Laquan McDonald.
McDonald was shot 16 times and killed by Chicago police while walking away from police with a small knife is his hand. The dashcam video of this incident was not released by Chicago police until 2018.

November 2014: Tamir Rice.
Rice, a 14-year-old, was killed by Cleveland police in a park while playing with a fake gun. A park CCTV camera recorded the shooting.

April 2015: Walter Scott.
Scott was shot and killed by a North Charleston police officer after they scuffled and he broke away. The officer responded by shooting him in the back. Officers on the scene were slow to summon emergency medical care for Scott who died. A bystander videotaped the event.

July. 2016: Alton Sterling.
Sterling was killed in Baton Rouge, LA after police responded to a disturbance call outside of a local business. He was shot while struggling on the ground with police. The incident was filmed by a bystander and CCTV security cameras.

July 2016: Philando Castile.
Castile was killed by a police officer in Falcon Heights, a suburb of St. Paul, MN after being stopped and telling the officer he was licensed to carry a firearm. He was shot while reaching for his license. His

girlfriend and her daughter were in the car and witnessed the shooting. His girlfriend captured most of the event on her cellphone camera.

March 2018: Stephon Clark.
Clark was shot at least seven times and killed in Sacramento, CA after a foot chase. Officers said they believed the cellphone in his hand was a firearm. The event was recorded by officer's body cameras.

March 2020: Breonna Taylor.
Taylor was shot eight times and killed after Louisville, KY police raided her apartment to arrest her boyfriend.

May 2020: George Floyd.
Floyd died on the ground, handcuffed, after a police officer knelt on his neck for over nine minutes, during which he cried out, "I can't breathe!" A young bystander recorded the event on her cellphone.

April 2021: Daunte Wright.
Wright was shot and killed by police in Brooklyn Center, MN after he struggled, broke away, and attempted to get into his vehicle. A veteran police officer said she thought she had used her Taser (an electronic control weapon) instead of her firearm. Recorded on the officer's bodycam.

I had just about finished writing the first edition of this book over a decade ago when the Occupy Movement surged in our nation's cities. The protest in 2011 was a progressive socio-political movement which primarily engaged young white Americans. Occupy called attention to inequality in our nation and offered new ways to think about democracy here and throughout the world. I had to quickly add a new chapter to my almost-completed manuscript titled "2011: Year of Protest."

I was compelled to do this after observing police around the nation responding violently to those who refused to move. Police in many of our nation's cities were once again unprepared to effectively handle large groups of citizens exercising their First Amendment rights. The violent police response was often done without dialogue or negotiation with those assembled. Historically, police response to public protest in America has continually run into problems with the right of the people to assemble and protest governmental actions.[132]

Then in 2014, Michael Brown was shot and killed by a police officer in Ferguson, MO. His bleeding body remained on the street, uncovered, for hours in broad daylight. As expected, protest, often violent, erupted across the nation. There was no video recording of the shooting either by body camera or bystander. Nevertheless, a second edition needed a chapter entitled, "Stop, Don't Shoot."

Chapter Eight in this book focused on police use of deadly force as a major problem facing our nation, especially when, as we later found out, the actual number of people shot and killed by police each year far exceeded what police were reporting. Further, this number included a disproportionate number of young Black men. In fact, it is one of the leading causes of death for young Black men.[133] When a Black mother states she is fearful that police may kill her son, that is not an unreasonable fear.[134]

Before Ferguson, the number of persons reportedly shot and killed by police appeared to be small in number. But when teams of journalists from the *Washington Post* and *The Guardian* scoured news reports, they found a much larger number. Over the years, police departments had grossly underreported the actual number of citizens killed. Their investigations, which continue to this day, revealed police actually had taken the lives

132. https://www.washingtonpost.com/national/on-leadership/occupy-wall-street-zuccotti-park-and-the-history-of-force/2011/11/15/gIQAalBlON_story.html

133. https://isr.umich.edu/news-events/news-releases/police-sixth-leading-cause-of-death-for-young-black-men-2/

134. https://www.usnews.com/news/healthiest-communities/articles/2019-08-05/police-violence-a-leading-cause-of-death-for-young-men

of citizens in almost four times the numbers reported. Today, there is no central reporting of these deaths save for the work of these journalists.[135]

Further investigation reveals that one-third of the thousand deaths caused by police each year are disproportionately young men of color. Since that time, and despite a constant call by citizens for police to be more restrained in the use of deadly force and to seek alternative control methods, the number of citizens killed by police remains relatively unchanged. I find this shocking as it reinforces my thesis that the development and improvement of our nation's police continues to be "arrested!"

The failure to reduce the number of citizens killed by police each year leads many citizens, especially those of color, to believe that police are either incapable or unwilling to reduce the number of citizens they kill each year. When a Black youth is killed by police under questionable circumstances, it leads to more mistrust of police from those with whom police have the most contact.

When rates of police use of deadly force in America are compared with those in other democratic countries around the world, a striking picture emerges. Police-related deaths of citizens in the United States are reported to be 33 deaths per 10 million population. The illustrated graph reveals that in every other democratic country in the world, the number of citizens killed by police is significantly lower than those killed by police in America.

Why is this? Why haven't the police in our country been able to reduce this number? Is it our low standard for using force?[136] The paucity of police training compared with those countries in which police are more restrained? Our lack of gun control? Or are we simply a more violent nation?

The excuse for our nation's low standard for police use of deadly force is found in the 1989 decision of the U.S. Supreme Court in *Graham v. Connor*. In that decision, the term "reasonable objectiveness" is found. This term has been taken to mean that if a police officer, in his or her own mind, senses a threat, deadly force is justified.

135. https://www.washingtonpost.com/graphics/2019/national/police-shootings-2019/

136. *Graham v. Connor*: https://www.oyez.org/cases/1988/87-6571)

Unfortunately, this doctrine was quickly adopted by police trainers some years later as "If we fear, we can shoot!" (Note: the *Graham* decision came down when I served as Chief of Police in Madison. Our policy on use of force did not change. In later years, this decision, which was NOT a deadly force case, was used to justify police use of deadly force by both police trainers and leaders.)

I argue in Chapter Eight that our nation's standard for police use of deadly force must be that required by the European Union—"absolute necessity."[137] I might add that nothing prohibits a police agency from setting a higher standard than what the law might permit. For example, an officer violating an agency's use of force policy may not be criminally prosecuted for his or her actions, but the officer could suffer discipline, including termination for not following organizational directions.

This was the situation before the United States Supreme Court ruled in *Tennessee v. Garner*. In *Garner*, the court ruled that deadly force could no longer be used by police to stop non-dangerous fleeing felons, specifically, shooting youths who ran away after ditching a stolen car.

Police in Madison, WI, and a few other progressive departments across the nation, already had a work rule (policy) in effect that prohibited deadly force from being used to stop fleeing criminals who did not present an immediate, dangerous threat to the community. Yet at the same time, state law permitted police to use deadly force to arrest any fleeing felon whether the offender was immediately dangerous to others or not.[138] Why can't that occur with the *Graham* decision?

Since the stunning attack on our nation in 2001, we have become a more fearful nation. This collective fear has deeply affected our police. Slowly, a work attitude of helping and serving others was replaced by that of a warrior, armed and ready to confront the many dangers police have come to believe they face.

You can see this on the face of Minneapolis Police Officer Derek

137. See Article Two of the European Convention of Human Rights: https://www.echr.coe.int/Documents/Handbook_European_Convention_Police_ENG.pdf).
138. https://www.oyez.org/cases/1984/83-1035

Chauvin as he restrained George Floyd and ignored his cries and the protest of those who witnessed this event. So the issue of police use of deadly force had, once again, captured headlines around the world. Like the beating of Rodney King three decades ago by Los Angeles police, Floyd's death was captured on a cellphone video. It quickly appeared on network news and social media sites around the world and caused outcry and protest. Chauvin was arrested, convicted, and sent to prison in 2021, but not before protest, including property damage, had occurred in many American cities. Still, the rate of American citizens shot and killed by police remains unabated.

In the meantime, the city of Minneapolis, where I served as a police officer in the 1960s, experienced violent protests for months and suffered millions of dollars in property loss including the torching of the local precinct station. A call went out to "defund," and even eliminate, the police department. Unrest, protest, calls to defund the police, and occupation of the site where Floyd was murdered continue.

The casual observer of police might assume that after Trayvon Martin, a young Black man, was shot and killed in 2013 by a white vigilante in Florida and the nationwide "Black Lives Matter" movement was formed, police would work to modify their policies and training regarding the use of force.

Given the number of events of deadly force use by police across the nation, one would think that governmental leaders would respond by ordering police to tighten up their deadly force policies. After all, each event tends to reduce the trust and support police need to conduct their work effectively and safely.

Even in justified uses, public trust and support of their police erode when victims are shot multiple times. This also happens when police use deadly force to kill a suspect armed with a knife. This often quickly happens because police have been trained and led to believe in the "21-Foot Rule." That is, a person armed with a knife can kill you before you can react if they get within 21 feet of you.

This "rule" was not factual, yet it became a justification for officers to shoot suspects with knives if they got closer than 21 feet to them. Research proved otherwise and demonstrated that different strategies of movement can increase the officer's ability to survive such an attack.[139]

Now let us go back to the death of George Floyd in Minneapolis. It must be realized that in the present time, if the young woman had not videotaped Officer Chauvin kneeling on Floyd's neck for over nine minutes, Chauvin would most likely not be convicted or in prison today. Without the video evidence, Floyd's death would most likely have been justified.

For example, police would report that he was dangerous and out of control. Further, a medical examiner could rule he had drugs in his system and died from "excited delirium," which was used in Chauvin's defense.[140]

Since Michael Brown's death in 2014, I hoped that police leaders would have effectively responded to the problem of deadly force use. In effect, the framework for doing so came about when President Obama created the 21st Century Task Force on Policing. It soon fell by the wayside after the 2016 presidential election.

While some cities and states enacted laws prohibiting police choke holds, requiring body cameras, mandating peer intervention, and prohibiting shooting at fleeing vehicles, the number of killing is yet to be reduced. After all, that must be the measure of effectiveness of these laws. (By the way, all of these "reforms," except for body cameras, were actions taken by most progressive police agencies over three decades ago.) Police misconduct occurs even when officers know they are being recorded on camera; police vehicle dash cameras have been in operation since the 1980s with seemingly little impact on persons killed by police.

Actually, the proposals being considered will do little to improve the nature and practice of policing in our country. What's needed, however, is to address the negative *attitude* many police officers carry with them every day. That's the real problem in policing today—it's about attitude!

When Derek Chauvin knelt on the neck of George Floyd, all America

---

139. Police Practice and Research Volume 22, 2021 –Issue 3

140. https://apnews.com/article/thomas-lane-trials-minneapolis-racial-injustice-death-of-george-floyd-fb1f3a6430da36b8470080c82c385d67

saw it. Despite Floyd's cries and the outcry from bystanders, Officer Chauvin did not appear to consider what he was doing was in any way out of the ordinary. Chauvin was essentially saying through his body posture, "This is the way we do things here." And the cries of Floyd and those who were standing by did not matter.

It is this kind of attitude that I have frequently confronted during my three decades in policing. It is the disdain for other people. It is internalizing and living with the belief "We are the police and you're not. We can do anything we wish to you, and you have no power to stop us!"

It is a developed attitude with echoes from the days of slavery and Jim Crow. No longer can our past be carried into our future, nor can it be ignored or forgotten along the way. This negative attitude towards others must be replaced by another attitude, the positive attitude of duty, honor, fairness, compassion, and accountability. This is the attitude that needs to be demanded of our nation's police. Those who cannot make this adjustment need to find other employment.

I began writing my online blog "Improving Police" in 2011 (improving police.blog). As of this writing, this site contains nearly 1,500 posts, 500,000 views, and 1,800 followers from 30 countries around the world. In it, interested police, students, and citizens can find answers to many of the problems confronting the leadership and management of police: how to select and train, facilitating citizen feedback, and the best-known methods of leading, developing, and fielding competent, sensitive, and effective police officers, in short, the kind of police who can adopt an attitude of "service above self." I do not use the term "serve" lightly.

For the most part, the problem with improving police is the absence of leadership, a void which has permitted a vicious, negative attitude to develop and remain within the ranks, affecting far too many of our nation's police officers.

Due to the present division and acrimony in our local and national politics (those are kind words), I expect little will be done to improve our police until we learn to listen and get along with one another. You know, the practice of basic civility. This includes developing a common understanding of the role of police in our society. For example, after the conviction of Derek Chauvin in Minneapolis, a national poll revealed that half of conservatives surveyed believed the jurors had come to the wrong decision by convicting Chauvin. On the other hand, 90% of liberals believed the opposite. In such a political environment it is difficult to see how we, locally or nationally, can ever come to agreement as to the steps we should take to improve our police.[141]

Permit me to also add, as a tragic and stunning example, what happened in our nation's Capitol building on January 6, 2021. If you have any question or reservation as to what did happen on that day, I invite you to view the 40-minute documentary of a team of journalists who followed the tragic, highly-coordinated, and deadly events of that day.[142] The constant diatribe against our system of government and its electoral system led to thousands of people being encouraged to "stop the steal," referring to the 2020 election, which was about to be ratified in Congress. Somehow, they came to believe it was their patriotic duty to break into our nation's capital building and prevent lawmakers from ratifying the election results.

This "call to arms" resulted in an orchestrated attack and break-in at our nation's capitol building on January 6, 2021. These insurrectionists were not "tourists."[143]

During that tragic day in our history, over a hundred police officers were assaulted and injured, and Capitol police officer Brian Sicknick lost his life. Those who showed up in Washington and came to the Capitol building were ready with walkie-talkies, baseball bats, and bear spray to injure and overcome Capitol and Metropolitan police. So much for the "Back the Blue" slogan many of these rioters no doubt espoused in the past. Can you imagine what would have happened if thousands of Black men had stormed our nation's Capitol during the "Million Man March" in October of 1995?[144]

141. https://thehill.com/homenews/state-watch/550179-almost-half-of-republicans-say-chauvin-jury-reached-wrong-verdict-poll

142. https://www.nytimes.com/video/us/politics/100000007606996/capitol-riot-trump-supporters.html.

143. https://www.vanityfair.com/news/2021/05/capitol-attack-tourist-visit

144. https://www.britannica.com/event/Million-Man-March

So here I am. In the eighth decade of my life, having spent over three decades as a police officer and leader, and now devoting most of my post-retirement life to talking, teaching, and writing about police and their improvement. I find myself struggling to think about the future, how needed reform can ever proceed in our nation with its present political divisions and the negative attitude among many of our nation's officers.

Even with an agreement on what reform measures need to be taken, we are a nation with over 600,000 police serving in 17,000 police agencies. Policing in America is, and always has been, a local endeavor; therefore, reform, even incremental improvement, is necessarily in the hands of local citizens. They are the ones who should be addressing how and by whom policing should be conducted.

As I mentioned earlier in this book, the requirements to be licensed as a barber or beautician in most states are far greater than those for police officers. The number of hours we train our police falls far below that required of police in Europe, Australia and Canada. (See "Chapter Six: The Seven Steps." Step Four addresses the importance of training and leading in police improvement.)

This shocking fact was first revealed over 40 years ago in the report of President Johnson's Commission on Law Enforcement and the Administration of Justice.[145] It remains so today.

While most American police officers today are better educated than those with whom I served, the fact remains that only one percent of our police agencies require a four-year baccalaureate degree for entry. That was true in 1969 when I served as police chief in Burnsville, MN, and it remains true today. Do we not care enough about our police to require them to be educated? In Burnsville, we instituted a four-year degree requirement for all new officers. That was 1969. Today, the city continues to hold this requirement because it makes good sense to have educated police. A college education doesn't assure that our police will be perfect, but they will better understand their job, what they are called to do, and how they are to treat people.

145. https://www.ncjrs.gov/pdffiles1/nij/42.pdf

I find I am ending where I began: how to effectively practice the art of policing in a free and democratic society. We must not forget the Four Obstacles I outline in this book for they continue to arrest the improvement of our nation's police. To begin to travel the road ahead, we must craft and maintain a strong, unyielding vision which encourages fair, equitable, controlled, and community-oriented policing.

But today my vision is greatly narrowed. I see it happening only in individual progressive communities, communities that can come together and craft an effective and lawful way forward with their police. If you are angry about police and their behavior, whether you are a police officer or a citizen, I suggest that instead calling for defunding or eliminating your police, you work together with them. Rethink your approach, in or out of the ranks, and re-imagine policing in your community. What would such an organization look like? How should its officers be selected and prepared? How should its officers and their leaders be evaluated?

Remember, police are our designated functionaries. They do our work (work many of us would not necessarily want to do). They represent us— at night, in heat and snow, with people who are intoxicated, angry, or are experiencing a mental health crisis. When a citizen may want to run away from a danger, police run towards it.

While some people are dangerous, the job of police is to help. Research (and my experience) reveals most police work is not about arresting or fighting with people, it's about helping and serving them.[146] Police work remains the business of helping.

Police are necessarily guardians, not warriors. They are not to be selected because they are the toughest, but because they are the wisest. Simply put, it's a lot easier to train a person with a guardian orientation to be a warrior than to train a warrior to be a guardian.

Therefore, our police should not look or act like paramilitary troops. Change begins by communities selecting college-educated, emotionally intelligent men and women from diverse backgrounds, sufficiently trained, who are *predisposed* to help, serve, and protect others; that is, police

---

146. https://www.nytimes.com/2020/06/19/upshot/unrest-police-time-violent-crime.html

candidates must begin their careers with the right attitude and understanding of what they are called to do: guard, serve, and help, and dress them accordingly. Chapter Three describes the reason for outfitting police in non-military-style uniforms.

Police aspirants must understand that at the present time they are entering a job with a strong historical, and present, system of racial bias. Today, police must be able to see and process their work through the prism of race. This is the basis of Critical Race Theory (CRT); it is understanding race and racism as a social construct and holds that it is unwise to think that a significant population in our nation who has been enslaved and discriminated against for generations will simply "get over it."[147]

The right attitude I call for must be supported, not erased by the initial training experience of police. And when police recruits return to their departments after training, they must be met by wise and experienced leaders (both formal and informal) who support a working attitude of guarding, serving, and helping.

Police can be better trained to de-escalate dangerous situations and control their use of force in handling emotionally disturbed and aggressive people. We all must understand that the authority we grant our police to use deadly force is a responsibility that no one else is accorded in our society. There is a sacred nature to it. Over 150 years ago, Sir Robert Peel and others observed that the more force police used in performing their duties, the less support they had from the community. That is also true today and is why trust must be built. (See "Peel's Principles" in Chapter Two.)

Therefore, police, who serve our democracy and support its values, must be willing to be true community-oriented workers, that is, able to work with citizens to solve their police-related problems. This is the essence of Community-Oriented Policing that I discuss throughout this book. In doing this, police must act as if *all* lives matter, and the protection of lives is their fundamental duty.

If we, however, wish to improve our police, it will not be easy. We must

147. https://www.edweek.org/leadership/what-is-critical-race-theory-and-why-is-it-under-attack/2021/05

create a new way of policing and a new breed of police. There exist few examples across the country. Several years ago, I wrote "How to Rate Your Local Police: A User Guide for Civic, Governmental, and Police Leaders." This booklet is a way to assess the quality of your local police agency. It is something any officer or citizen can do.[148]

In the late 1960s, our nation attempted to become a "Great Society." It was the idea of President Lyndon Johnson, and he sold it to Congress. One of the ideas was to create Model Cities: places in which the ideas and practices of a Great Society were being effectively implemented. As a young graduate student, this seemed to me to be a great idea for policing. If we can develop model cities where leaders from other cities can come and learn, why not create model police agencies which can, for example, implement the recommendations of the 1967 Task Force on Policing as well as those from the 21st Century Task Force and the PERF Guidelines? We did that in Madison in the late 1980s and early '90s when we offered three-day training sessions for other police to learn what we were doing in Madison and how it was working.[149]

But how do we do this? Aren't police resistant to new ideas and change? Won't they resist outsiders? I suggest that proposing police improvement at the local level does not have to be confrontational. It can be seen as helpful for both police and community. Think about taking this approach with your Chief of Police or Sheriff:

> *"Chief/Sheriff, we all know that everyone of us could become more effective. I certainly could. But how do we do that without it appearing that we have been doing a poor job? One way is to think about and adopt the idea of "continuous improvement" as both a personal and organizational goal. I would be willing to help you and your department do this. After all, an effective police organization is one that is trusted,*

---

148. https://www.amazon.com/How-Rate-Your-Local-Police/dp/1505943221

149. (See The Task Force on 21st Century Policing https://cops.usdoj.gov/pdf/taskforce/taskforce_finalreport.pdf and the Police Executive Research Forum's report "Guiding Principles On Use of Force:" https://www.policeforum.org/assets/30%20guiding%20principles.pdf).

supported, and respected by the community. It is possible. You and your officers will be able to strengthen your community's trust, support, and respect by working with us and finding way to build that trust and support and get closer to the community. We can do this by working together. Would you be willing to give it a try?"

Unless citizens at the local level are willing to take this bold step, little will ever be accomplished regarding improving their police. There are simply too many police and agencies to do anything significant at the state or federal levels of government. We must realize that improving police begins at home, in your neighborhood. It begins with you, whether you are a police officer or a member of the community.

I have argued over the years since Ferguson that our police have failed to either hear or understand what is being asked of them by Black citizens. I hear, "Stop killing us. Be who you say you are. Treat us as you treat white people." This cry can be heard through American history, from the days of slavery to those of Jim Crow. I hear it today.

Yet I am reminded what my dear friend and mentor Herman Goldstein often told me during our decades-long discussions about police and their improvement. Herman would say, "Remember, David, there are police and there are police!" He was reminding me of the variety of police and their behavior throughout the country. Among those agencies exists a wide range of capacity and ability. Among 17,000 police agencies are tremendous differences.

New York City, for example, has a police department of over 30,000 members; it is larger than the armies of many nations. Yet 90 percent of police agencies across the country have fewer than ten officers. It is impossible, therefore, to make a sweeping generalization about police in America. Instead, we must realize the only effective way police are going to be improved is locally, a department at a time, and it can begin in your town or city.

The communities which will be successful in doing this will do so through continuous action and pressure from citizens who are clear about what they are trying to achieve, citizens who are able to bring police into the discussion and build coalitions and goals.

Will your town or city be one of them? Unless you act, the development and improvement of your police in your town or city will continue to be arrested, and we all will suffer as a nation.

Good luck and Godspeed.

Epilogue

IT IS POSSIBLE TO BRING sound and lasting change to the police so they reinforce and uphold the traditions and values of our society. It isn't only possible but essential to change the direction that many are headed today.

There are essentially two critical functions a free and democratic society ought to expect from its police. First, that they be well-organized and restrained in their response to public protest. Secondly, they must be judicious about when and how force is used in carrying out their duties. These are not easy tasks. They demand that the best people among us be charged with these duties, that we train and lead them well, and make sure they are adequately compensated for what we ask of them. How to go about accomplishing this has been one of the primary focuses of this book.

This means we need to create moral police organizations; staffed by men and women who reflect the community they serve and see their function as community leaders. They should be not only the police we want but also the police we deserve as we work with them to overcome the historical obstacles I mentioned earlier that have tended to "arrest" police progress: anti-intellectualism, violence, corruption, and discourtesy.

The Madison experience makes me confident that the Four Obstacles can be overcome, and improvements can be sustained beyond the tenure of an individual reform-minded police chief. By making a solid commitment to higher education and collaboration with academia, police will no longer become narrow-minded and bigoted technicians. When police are trained in the proper use of physical force and the practice of Procedural Justice, the community will come to trust and support them as thoughtful, knowledgeable, and restrained professionals.

Corruption and other illegal behavior by police have, as I documented

236

earlier, been with us throughout our nation's history. Yes, power can lead to corruption.[150] Whether real or perceived, this is the albatross that will forever be around the neck of our nation's police. That said, when the overwhelming majority of officers in our nation are stalwartly committed to obeying the law while they enforce it and sanctioning those who don't, a culture of honesty and candor will begin to prevail.

Finally, courtesy and civility can be trained and maintained even in a police organization in which the core of its role is the capacity to use force. Force can be used in a civil manner if it becomes a professional tenet and officers believe everyone is worthy of being treated with dignity and respect.

Throughout this book, I have also attempted to argue the vital role that Quality Leadership plays in a police agency. The top leader must have vision, passion, education, and tenacity; and those on the front line, the same. Developing accountable leaders in all ranks, from the top to the bottom of the organization, will assure that all this will be sustainable.

It was my life-long passion for what I will call the "art of policing" that moved me to write this book and then to create a second edition. However, with that passion came many mistakes and bad decisions. Is there anything I wished I had done differently along the way? Of course—who doesn't wish their life had a rewind button? I literally grew up and into this job. I had my share of struggles. But I believe I learned from my mistakes.

My life as a chief would have been easier if I had learned and practiced the following earlier in my career: listening more, speaking less, managing by walking around, working more closely with the police union, and knowing more about the personal lives of my employees (there is no way police officers can leave their personal lives in their lockers when they come to work and strap on a gun). I wish I had more understanding and empathy when my officers were suffering from depression, a divorce, or a death in the family.

---

150. This popular saying is attributed to John Acton (1834–1902), a historian and moralist who was known as Lord Acton. He expressed this opinion in a letter he wrote to Bishop Creighton in 1887: *"Power tends to corrupt, and absolute power corrupts absolutely. Great men are almost always bad men."*

This book, therefore, has been both practical and personal. Every transformational police leader pays a personal cost trying to make a bold vision become a reality. Whether this can be avoided by a future generation of leaders remains to be seen. Perhaps what I have suggested about paying attention to not only the interior lives of my officers, but my own as well, may help. In my own case, my survival depended on maintaining my physical health, exercise, balancing work and family, and having social, recreational, and intellectual interests outside the police. This is because the subculture of police is very powerful and can easily subvert the finest intentions—even the moral structure—of its practitioners if it isn't recognized and controlled.

It is my hope that the Seven Steps I describe in this book will be discussed, shared, and put into practice, not only by the police but in their communities as well. I'm not suggesting here anything that police are not able to accomplish. Transformation isn't an exercise in capital but in brainpower. It doesn't cost money to cast a bold vision or to raise the hiring standards, or to train officers and their leaders internally with existing resources. It doesn't cost money to listen, and it doesn't cost money to continuously upgrade the systems in which we work. It may cost some dollars to do outside research, but in the meantime, police chiefs can do their own surveying just like we did. And it doesn't cost money to sustain an outstanding, community-oriented police department because with the changes I am suggesting comes trust, cooperation, and community support—things no money can buy.

But it will take time. It will require bold leadership from the police themselves. It can't begin in the squad room; it must begin with the chief. A mayor cannot do it, nor can a city council. Citizen committees cannot do it (just look at the miserable track record of police review boards around America). If police are to realize their potential as Constitutional officers, their leaders will have to take and be the first step. Perhaps one is reading .this book.

Every time I visit Madison I see the results. I see a police department that is highly educated, many officers with graduate and law degrees. I see a police department that is extremely representative of and responsive to the community it serves—nearly 30 percent of the officers are women, and over 10 percent are men and women of color. But most of all, I see a police department which is respected, effective, fair, supported, and appreciated by the community.

Since I first wrote this book, much has occurred in Madison since Michael Brown, Jr. died at the hands of police in Ferguson. Madison has experienced its own questionable uses of force as a young, intoxicated white man, an African American teenager, and a suicidal veteran were shot and killed by officers. These three shootings, all absolved by the district attorney and, according to police, consistent with department policy and training, have cost the City of Madison over $10 million settlement monies. This has caused unrest in the Madison community, and the city council to authorize $400,000 for an outside study to review the practices of the police department. That study is now complete[151].

With a more observant community at large, Madison has had to account for these deaths of citizens which many community members, including myself, have questioned.

This has not been easy for the department and its leaders. The use of deadly force by police in our country will continue to come under scrutiny. Wise police leaders will listen, talk with their officers and community leaders, and work together to reduce the number of times and amount of force they believe is necessary to carry out their duties. Police are not soldiers; they are the community's protectors and guardians. They are the men and women among us who are expected to be more respectful, reasonable, and self-controlled than the average citizen. It is right that we expect them to model our collective values.

My life has goes on. I retired into a second and, I might say, equally challenging and fulfilling career as a member of the clergy. The shift was relatively easy as both pursuits are about caring for and helping people. And what I learned serving with the police applies there as well—including the Seven Steps.

---

151. https://madison.com/ct/news/local/govt-and-politics/city-council-accepts-report-from-committee-studying-madison-police-department/article_94a1869f-a185-55c0-a0cf-ad7de4d5260b.html

Since I first wrote this book, I have gone back into teaching at the university after many years being away. I take great joy in teaching an introductory course in criminal justice to new students, many of whom wish to pursue a career in policing. I also teach a senior-level course called "Leadership in Changing Times." This has been a special delight as I get to have a hands-on experience teaching students who are about to enter police work in the coming year. They are our future.

For many years, I thought I had left the police behind me. But I was wrong. I kept coming back to them. I kept thinking about them, and I soon found that my concern was as enormous as it ever was. They are the men and women who now protect me, my rights, and the rights of my children and grandchildren.

Again, our nation faces an epic challenge in how its police are responding to political protest and how they are going to manage the problem of deadly force, especially against persons not possessing a firearm. As we have seen from Cairo to Moscow, protest among people isn't a thing of the past nor something only democracies face. In every nation across the world, police are being tested.

I hope and pray that this book will be read, and those who read it will learn from my experience and my mistakes. I hope everyone will find inspiration and direction here no matter where they work. I also hope that young men and women will continue to have the desire to contribute to their society as I did and join the police. Join your police to improve them and be the kind of police officer I have described in this book—smart, restrained, honest, and courteous.

To learn more about contemporary police issues and how to improve our nation's police, I urge you to follow me on my weblog.[152]

—Soli Deo gloria—

---

152. http://www.improvingpolice.blog.

Acknowledgements

LET ME START FROM THE beginning. Wayne Bennett was chief of police when I joined the Edina Department a few months after I was discharged from the Marines in 1960. I quickly learned that education mattered in Edina and professional ethical values were central to them. Chief Bennett set the standard. It was a good beginning.

When I left Edina for Minneapolis, I met Deputy Inspector Ed Farrell, who was an educated cop and director of the training academy. He, too, left a positive impression on me of the necessity of an educated police. Later on in Minneapolis, Inspector Don Dwyer (later chief) was one of the few college-educated officers on the department and someone I respected and tried to emulate.

When I joined the police, I also began my studies at the University of Minnesota. My two mentors were Professors David A. Ward and John Clark. They inspired me as I saw the valuable link between social research and practice in policing.

It was Patrick McInnis, the Burnsville City Manager who gave me my first chief's job. We both were young. As a city leader, he was creative and innovative. He took a chance with me and let me build Burnsville into a highly professional police organization and require a college degree for all police officers. To this day, Burnsville is among the one percent of the police departments in our country that require a baccalaureate degree as an entrance standard.

Three close personal friends and colleagues shared my dream for policing: David Gorski, Bill Mavity and Jack Morse. David and I were both Marines. He worked with me in Minneapolis and Burnsville and went on to head police departments in Golden Valley, MN, Harvard University, and then Appleton, WI from 1977 to 1995. Sadly, he died of cancer in 2000. To this day, I miss his wit and counsel.

Bill Mavity and I attended Minneapolis recruit school together. He was a great cop. After several years, he left the department and headed up the criminal justice section of the Metropolitan Council. While he was there, he stood for election for Hennepin County Sheriff. He then went on to law school at the University of Minnesota, graduated, and was admitted to the bar. The rest of his career was spent as a working lawyer representing many police clients. He and I remain in close contact to this day.

Jack Morse was the chief of police in New Hope, MN, when we began our professional law enforcement fraternity in Minneapolis. He was an educated chief and one of our first members. He served as assistant chief to David Gorski during his Harvard years and eventually retired from there as second-in-command. Jack lives in Hull, just across the bay from Boston. He and I also remain close friends.

I must also mention the national effort to improve police. There was Gary Hayes at the Police Executive Research Forum, Hubert Williams with the Police Foundation, and other like-minded colleagues, such as Chiefs Lee Brown who served in New York, Atlanta, and Houston, and Joe McNamara, who served in Kansas City and San Jose.

In Madison, there is much to be acknowledged. Assistant Chief Edward Daley and Policewoman Morlynn Frankey were the first officers to support my ideas and welcomed me to the department. They were soon followed by many others who, along with them, soon became members of my top command staff: Ted Balistreri, Jeff Frye, Jack Heibel, Tom Hischke, and Rick Wallden.

I must also mention the three outstanding administrative assistants over the two decades I was in Madison that I was blessed to work with: Eileen Scrivner, Luisa Prey, and Sharon Kittle.

Three months after my appointment, a young student-councilman, Paul Soglin, was elected mayor of Madison defeating incumbent mayor Bill Dyke. Dyke never was in my corner. Paul's support was vital to my tenure in Madison. I also want to thank Mayor Joel Skornicka, who had the insight to grant me my leave of absence in 1980.

On the nearby University of Wisconsin campus, two professors from the Law School stand out: Frank Remington and Herman Goldstein. They both became close friends and mentors of mine. Herman continues to serve in that capacity. Sadly, Frank died in 1996. The Frank J. Remington Center continues his legacy of restorative justice and law-in-action.

A decade later, a newer breed of officers emerged to share my second effort in the transformation of the department—Deming-oriented quality improvement and a collaborative form of leadership. Of significant help and encouragement then was our forward-thinking mayor, Joe Sensenbrenner, along with other quality champions in city government: Tom Mosgaller, Pat Natzke, and Dorothy Conniff. In the police department, Cheri Maples, Noble Wray (now chief of police), Mike Masterson (now chief in Boise, Idaho), Joe Balles, and others became instrumental in continuing to help me move the department during this significant period in the department's history.

It was also when I met my wife, Sabine Lobitz. She continued to be the light of my life during the 40 years we were married. She sadly died in 2020. As a police commander herself with the State Capitol Police Department, she wasn't only an unsurpassed friend and confidant, but also a noteworthy sounding board, and a loving, confidential critic. Together, we wrote books and articles and shared a common vision for policing a democracy.

Finally, I'll never forget the many Madison police officers who, without their sturdy support, my years in Madison would have been difficult, if not impossible. I chose to hire these men and women because I was impressed by not only their education and intelligence, but also by their compassion and commitment to serve others.

Gratefully looking back, most of what I did in Madison has been sustained. Some has not. As we all should know by now, change does not come easy to the police—but sustaining those changes beyond the tenure of a change-oriented chief is almost unheard of. Some would say it is a miracle.

I also want to thank my first editor, Josh Wimmer, my final editor, Rob Zaleski, and my youngest son, Ezekiel Couper, who helped with the final manuscript review. Gwen Walker from the University of Wisconsin

Press also gave me prodigious help, advice, and encouragement during this project. Recently remarried, I thank Christine for coming alongside me and encouraging my involvement in policing matters. Police matter greatly in our nation's experiment with democracy.

Thank you, every one of you.

Appendices

Appendix A
Major Recommendations National Commission on Law Enforcement and the Administration of Justice

Appendix B
Madison's Improvement Plan

Appendix C
Madison's Improvement Timeline

Appendix D
The Twelve Principles of Quality Leadership

Appendix E
Outline: How to Rate Your Local Police

Appendix F
Professional Leadership Expectations

Appendix G
The Law Enforcement Code of Ethics

Appendix H
Twelve Qualities of Police

Appendix I
Report of the President's Task Force on 21st Century Policing

Appendix J
Guiding Principles on Use of Force

Appendix A
Major Recommendations:
National Commission on Law Enforcement and
the Administration of Justice (1967)

1. *Citizen advice:* In each police district that has a minority-group neighborhood, there should be a citizens' advisory committee that meets regularly with police officials to work out solutions to conflict problems that arise; it should include those who are critical or aggrieved.

2. *Community relations:* Police departments should have community relations machinery that plans and supervises the department's community relations programs. Such machinery is a matter of the greatest importance in communities with a substantial minority population.

3. *Minority recruitment:* It should be a high-priority objective of all departments with a substantial minority population to recruit, deploy, and promote them fairly.

4. *Citizen complaints:* Every jurisdiction should provide adequate procedures for full and fair processing of all citizen grievances and complaints.

5. *Written policies:* Police departments should develop and enunciate policies that give police personnel specific guidance for the common situations requiring exercise of police discretion.

6. *Three-tiered entry:* Basic police functions should be divided among three kinds of officers, here termed the community service officer,

the police officer, and the police agent. The ultimate aim of all police departments should be that all personnel with general enforcement powers have baccalaureate degrees.

7. *Recruitment:* Police departments should recruit far more actively than they now do, with special attention to college campuses and inner-city neighborhoods.

8. *College degree:* Police departments should take immediate steps to establish a minimum requirement of a baccalaureate degree for all supervisory and executive positions.

9. *Selection:* Until reliable tests are devised for identifying and measuring the personal characteristics that contribute to good police work, intelligence tests, thorough background investigations, and personal interviews should be used by all departments as absolute minimum techniques to determine the moral character and the intellectual and emotional fitness of police candidates.

10. *Criteria:* The appointing authority should place primary emphasis on the education, background, character, and personality of a candidate and less on present employment standards of age, height, weight, visual acuity, and prior residence.

11. *Compensation:* Police salaries must be competitive with other professions and occupations that seek the same graduates.

12. *Promotion:* Promotion eligibility should stress ability above seniority.

13. *Lateral movement/pension transfer:* To encourage lateral movement of police personnel, a nationwide retirement system should be devised that permits the transferring of retirement credits.

14. *Probationary period:* Entering officers should serve probation periods of, preferably, eighteen months and certainly no less than one year. The probationary officer should be systematically observed and rated. Chief administrators should have the sole authority of dismissal

during the probationary period and should willingly exercise it against unsatisfactory officers.

15. *In-service training*: Every general enforcement officer should have at least one week of intensive in-service training a year. Officers should be given incentives to continue their general education or acquire special skills outside their department.

16. *Improvement*: Each state should provide financial and technical assistance to departments to conduct surveys and make recommendations for improvement and modernization of their organization, management, and operations.

17. *Police legal advisor*: Every medium- and large-sized department should employ a skilled lawyer full time as its legal advisor. Smaller departments should arrange for legal advice on a part-time basis.

18. *Management team*: Every department in a big or medium-sized city should organize key ranking staff and line personnel into an administrative board similar in function to a corporation's board of directors, whose duty should be to assists the chief and his staff units in developing, enunciating, and enforcing departmental policies and guidelines for the day-to-day activities of line personnel.

19. *Maintaining integrity*: Every department, regardless of size, should have a comprehensive program for maintaining police integrity.

20. *Team policing*: Police departments should commence experimentation with a team policing concept that envisions those with patrol and investigative duties combining under unified command with flexible assignments to deal with the crime problems in a defined sector.

21. *Deadly force*: A comprehensive regulation should be formulated by every chief administrator to reflect the basic policy that firearms may be used only when the officer believes his life or the life of another is in imminent danger, or when other reasonable means of

apprehension have failed to prevent the escape of a felony suspect whom the officer believes presents a serious danger to others.

22. *Records and communications*: States should assume responsibility for assuring that area-wide records and communications needs are provided. In every metropolitan area, there should be laboratory facilities for all the communities in the area. Specialized personnel from state or metropolitan departments should assist smaller departments on major investigations and in specialized law enforcement functions. Each metropolitan area and each county should take action directed toward the pooling or consolidation of police services…that will provide the most satisfactory law enforcement service and protection at the lowest possible cost.

23. *Police standards*: Police standards commissions should be established in every state and empowered to set mandatory requirements and to give financial aid to governmental units for the implementation of standards.

Appendix B
Madison's Improvement Plan

Step 1: Educate and inform employees about our vision, our goal, and the quality improvement method.

- Begin discussion with top management team and train them.

- Discuss with and ask employees; get feedback from them.

- Share feedback with the chief and his management team.

- Get buy-in from top department managers.

- Survey external customers—our citizens.

- Ask, inform, and keep the Officer's Advisory Council up to date on all this.

- Tell, sell, and persuade through the department newsletter and during employee meetings.

Step 2: Prepare for the transformation.

- Appoint an internal Quality Coordinator to help with the transformation.

- Form an internal Quality Leadership Council to work through problems and barriers encountered during implementation of the new leadership.

- Require all who seek to be promoted to leadership positions to have both the knowledge and ability to practice the new leadership.

- Actively and strongly tie our quality improvement efforts in with the city's efforts in this area.

Step 3: Teach quality improvement and the new leadership skills.

- Train all supervisors and managers in the new leadership and methods of quality improvement.

- Train all employees in the new leadership and methods of quality improvement.

Step 4: Start practicing the new leadership.

- Require department leaders to begin to implement the new leadership, principle by principle.

- Begin a system of employee feedback to all department leaders.

- Top leaders are required to identify three to five things that need improving, work on them, and take responsibility for them.

- Top leaders are to develop a plan to demonstrate their advocacy for quality improvement methods and start practicing the new leadership.

- Top leaders start identifying and sharing with each other and their employees each week the improvements they are working on and those they have accomplished together with their employees.

Step 5: Check progress and make corrections.

- During monthly meetings for sergeants and lieutenants, the chief asks them how they are doing and they report in.

- Make changes, if necessary, to make the department more responsive to the new leadership; use quality improvement methods to do so.

- Add an elected police officer to the chief's management team.

Step 6: Make continual organizational improvements.

- This step is to be an ongoing process—it is continuous improvement within the organization. It is understood that if an organization stays as it is, it is, in reality, falling behind the rest of the world.

- To get a snapshot of what went on within the Madison department during this time of intense organizational transformation and change, Appendix C captures ten years of organizational effort (1981 to 1990) and indicates the various steps we took, and when we took them.

Appendix C
Madison's Improvement Timeline

1981

- An elected Officer's Advisory Council created

1984

- Committee on the Future of the Department created

1985

- Committee on the Future of the Department issues its report

1986

- Neighborhood Service Officers created in six city districts

- Mission statement developed by management team

- Experimental Police District (EPD) planning team created

- EPD begins to survey internal and external customers

- City of Madison under Mayor Sensenbrenner begins Quality and Productivity (QP) program.

- Principles of Quality Leadership (QL) developed within the police department.

- Employee information sessions held on QL—everyone attends; chief teaches.

- Team leader/facilitator training begins.

1987

- Top management, lieutenants, and sergeants trained in QL (five sessions of six days each).

- Customer survey form developed, pretested, and sent out to randomly-selected. citizen-customers who have had police contact.

- First department Quality Coordinator appointed.

- Quality Leadership Council (QLC) formed champions throughout the department to help the chief keep improvements going and support the change in leadership style.

- QLC begins work on number-one problem identified by police officers: the promotional system.

- OAC given final decision-making authority—patrol vehicles and weapons.

1988

- Experimental Police District established in South Madison.

- Three-day quality training for all employees.

- Reorganization—top staff and bureaus of the department organized into working teams instead of bureaus and sections.

- Chief holds progress checks with lieutenants and sergeants during one-day quality training sessions.

1989

- Four-way check expanded requiring leaders to solicit input from subordinates, peers, the chief, and to do a self-assessment as to how they are doing.

- Chief's check-ins continue with lieutenants and sergeants.

- Planning for the skills portion of the Quality Leadership Academy begins.

- Emphasis on practicing what we have learned so far.

- Police union president joins the chief's management team as a full voting member.

1990

- Quality Leadership Academy begins for all promotional aspirants and is one of the recommendations of the QLC.

- Field operations decentralized.

- Stressing teamwork and use of quality improvement methods.

1991

- Focusing more intently on who our customers are.

- City-wide customer surveying.

- Detective check-ins with the chief and begin to discuss how their work can be improved.

- Neighborhood foot patrol officers increased.

1992

- Revised Quality Leadership workbook published based on what we have learned. Other departments purchase the workbook and send their members to look at what we are doing.

- More neighborhood foot patrol officers added, increasing to thirteen the number of independent, district foot patrol assignments in key city areas.

- A citywide cross-functional team with other city departments established the way various city departments can begin to learn from one another. Facilitators are shared between city agencies.

- Neighborhood Intervention Task Force created to address growing gang and drug problems.

- Customer surveys analyzed by neighborhood.

1993

- Reorganization of the detective team into four districts with a central support team.

- National Institute of Justice Report Community Policing in Madison: Quality from the Inside, Out: An Evaluation of Implementation and Impact is released.

Appendix D
The Twelve Principles of Quality Leadership

1. Believe in, foster, and support teamwork.

Teamwork is working together—working to solve crimes and conduct investigations as well as to resolve problems that arise at work or in the community. It is helping each other, being one team. It is taking pride in our collective achievements. It is belief in the ability of the group over anyone's individual effort—that is called synergy. We should try to do our work with teams whenever possible.

2. Be committed to the problem-solving process; use it and let data, not emotions, drive decisions.

Use the problem-solving process: Identify the nature and scope of the problem, seek several alternatives that will solve the problem, choose the most effective alternative, implement the chosen alternative, follow up on its implementation (correct, if necessary, to make it better). Too often we use our emotions or feelings to choose a course of action. This principle encourages the use of data, figures, information, and facts to drive that decision-making. Soliciting input isn't data—it is necessary, but let's not call it data. You should know the data tools: how to gather data, how to show it graphically, and how to look at variation of data. Let data do the talking. When employees ask for new things or new ways of doing things, encourage them to use data to support their recommendations—not use of power (We have all decided that…) or use of feelings (You know this is the better way of doing that…). Collecting data is using statistical tools to understand, bring into control, and correct a process. Using data will help our decision-making because we will be able to answer that extremely crucial question: How do we know this is true?

3. Seek employees' input before you make key decisions.

This is a commitment to ask your employees about what the key decisions are in the workplace. They may be staffing levels, assignments, transfers, or taking time off. Whatever they may be, they are things that the employees feel are decisions on key matters—not things you or I think. The commitment is to ask before these decisions are made. It does not mean that you must do what your employees believe you should do. (This is a very fundamental point in the principles: Our commitment is to input. We may, in fact, do what our employees want; or we may choose to delegate to them our authority to make the decision; or we may simply take their input under advisement; but we promise to ask them before we make the key decisions.) Key decisions are those that affect the three to five things that are essential to workplace satisfaction *as defined by employees*. They may be determined either by individuals or by groups of employees. Key decisions should be discussed and an agreement reached as to what constitutes these key decision areas. Leaders should then agree to ask for employee input on these key decision areas before they make any decisions regarding them. Employee input does not mean decision-making by taking a vote without group discussion. It is the power of group discussion, hearing everyone's point of view, understanding and deliberating on what has been discussed, that makes group decision-making far more effective than one person's decision or a group of individuals voting on solutions without discussion. When employee input is requested, it should be clear at the beginning of the process how the decision will be made and who will make it.

4. Believe that the best way to improve the quality of work or service is to ask and listen to employees who are doing the work.

As supervisors and managers we don't do the front-line work. We depend on others to do the job of responding directly to the customers, the citizens of our city. It has been a long time since most of us have performed this job. Therefore, we depend on the men and women who do this job to tell us what they need to do get the job done. As bosses, one of the most fundamental things we can do for our employees is to ask them what they need and listen to what they say. Listening is the difficult part for those of us who have spent years learning how to tell people what to do. Active listening is a skill that can be learned and developed. Using the inquiry process, which is about asking the right questions, is also a skill that can be learned. Quality leaders refrain from telling; they ask the right questions: How do you know that? What have you learned through this effort? What kind of help do you need from me? The power of this is that an individual comes to his or her own solution with the help—not the direction—of the leader. Listening and questioning are crucial skills to develop as a supervisor or manager. Employees want bosses who are willing to listen, and we need employees who will honestly tell us about what's going on.

5. Strive to develop mutual respect and trust among employees.

How do we develop respect and trust in the workplace? One of the keys is to do unto others as you would have them do unto you. People want to be respected and trusted. Bosses who show respect and trust have respected and trusted employees. We must come to the workplace with the basic belief that our employees deserve respect and can be trusted—that's why we hired them in the first place. For example, when checking out a complaint regarding an employee, there are ways to do it that may not compromise the respect and trust of the individual involved. In many cases, our attitudes have a more lasting impact than our words or the processes we use. Our employees have a right to know what's going on, when the process has been completed, and what our findings are. In every case, except those in which a serious offense has occurred, we want to correct and rehabilitate employees and get them back to duty. We must all be committed to driving fear out of our workplace.

6. Have a customer orientation and focus toward employees and citizens.

A customer orientation and focus mean that we listen to our customers. Customers may be citizens, elected officials, employees, or interest groups. As supervisors and managers, we have as direct customers our employees, who provide service to their customers, the citizens and taxpayers. Listening and being responsive to citizens is our goal. There are, of course, several parameters—the law, ethics, and budgetary constraints. In this new era of community policing, listening to the customer is a vital part of the job. It is a change. Professionals today don't have the exclusive market anymore of knowing what is best for their patients, clients, or customers. Today, people want to be heard and participate.

7. Manage the behavior of 95 percent of employees and not the 5 percent who cause problems. Deal with the 5 percent promptly and fairly.

This is a fundamental principle regarding people. It should help us to look at how we view our employees. Do we believe that they can be trusted, are mature adults, and want to do a good job? Or do we believe that they are untrustworthy, immature, and want to avoid work? This principle causes some supervisors and managers a great deal of difficulty. They have trouble accepting the notion that they should trust their employees. Let's look at how many of your employees are in the first group and how many are in the second. We believe 95 percent of our employees fall into the first group and 5 percent or fewer falls into the second group. For too long, the actions of the 5 percent have dictated the rules and policies and how the organization is run. We believe that the actions of the 5 percent shouldn't dictate how the rest of the employees are treated in the workplace. Five-percenters should be responded to in a prompt and fair way. Rules shouldn't be written based on the behavior of the 5 percent, nor should the department be run as if all employees were in the 5 percent group. The 5 percent must, however, be dealt with and not ignored. We have all heard a great deal about the need for consistency and fairness in the disciplinary process. Being fair is more important.

8. Improve systems and examine processes before placing blame on people.

Continually monitor the systems you are responsible for to enhance them and, ultimately, the quality of the output. Leaders have responsibility for the performance of systems—this is creative and valuable work. In the past, we have emphasized that the job of a manager was to watch over, maintain, and inspect systems. No more. Our job today is to enrich these systems—continually, incessantly, and forever. If we see our job as inspecting systems, a machine—a computer can replace us. Our employees also see that kind of work as being not essential or necessary. If we see our job as the improvement of systems, a machine cannot replace us—only creative and caring people can do this kind of work, and our employees know it. This is also a good human behavior rule. People don't like to fail. When they do, it is wise to look at systems first. Only after systems are examined is it fair and safe to examine how people may have failed. We should be trying to get at the root of the problem, not attempting to fix blame on an individual. If a system is out of control, it is only a matter of time before the next employee gets in trouble. The solution is to fix the system. Leaders work on the system; employees work in the system. Standards need to be set, feedback given, and control limits established. There will be variation in performance, but it should be within the established upper and lower control limits. Variation is a fact of life and to be expected. Those who fall below acceptable performance shouldn't be punished. Our job is to ascertain what they need from us—training, encouragement, support, and feedback—to get them into the range of acceptable work performance.

9. Avoid top-down, power-oriented decision-making whenever possible.

We should avoid the use of coercive power whenever possible. When we use it we should remember that we all pay a cost in its exercise—giver and receiver. The finest decisions are those in which we all participate and concur. The next are those decisions in which everyone is asked for their input before something is decided. Of course, we will have occasional no-discussion decisions in our work. When we do, we should make a commitment to our employees that we agree to critique those decisions whenever possible. Tom Gordon, in his book *Leader Effectiveness Training*, illustrates the costs to leaders who use coercive power to get the job done: costs of time, enforcement, alienation, stress, and diminishing influence. There is also the cost of making a less-than-quality decision, because communication between employees and leaders who use coercive power is greatly reduced.

10. Encourage creativity through risk-taking, and be tolerant of honest mistakes.

We will never get creativity and innovation from our employees when we tell them they cannot make mistakes. All that we know about people tells us that creativity is chilled and repressed in such an environment. It isn't easy to accept honest mistakes. The price we pay for zero defects, however, is zero creativity. Many of us have been working together for many years. We all remember each other's mistakes and failures. Without forgiving and forgetting, we will never be comfortable in the workplace. If we don't permit honest mistakes, new ways and ideas will never be tried. It's simply too risky in an authoritarian organization. Quality and creativity are the results of a constant process of trying and improving.

11. Be a facilitator and coach. Develop an open atmosphere that encourages providing and accepting feedback.

A leader's job today is different. It is challenging and gives us opportunities for personal growth because it offers so many new options. Being an effective quality leader means being a coach, teacher, student, role model, and, most significant, a champion of the new philosophy. We are in the business of helping people develop and experience personal growth. Our employees' goal is to deliver a quality service to our citizens by being responsive and sensitive to those citizens' needs. We can model this behavior by being responsive and sensitive to our employees' needs. All this can only be accomplished in an atmosphere of trust, honesty, and openness. Part of this process is honest feedback. An honest feedback system is essential for the creation of a quality organization. Feedback is for the receiver. It isn't designed to make the giver feel better by venting. Venting is sometimes necessary, but don't mistake it for feedback. Leaders have consistency of purpose—a vision as to where they are going. Leaders develop the competence of their people. They are committed. Their employees know where they stand.

12. Use teamwork to develop agreed-upon goals with employees and a plan to achieve them.

This principle tries to capture the importance of progress and moving forward as a team. We plan where we are going and establish agreed-upon ways to achieve that goal with input from and discussion with our employees. We help create a vision. Our job is then to align that vision with our practices. We can do that by coaching our employees toward excellence—not by trying to control them. Long-term goals are essential to the performance of a quality organization. Once goals are set, it is critical for leaders to follow up and—at least weekly, if not daily—to coach employees to success. There is a technique used to achieve maximum performance from individuals, frequently adopted by athletes who want to capture world records. It is called visioning—mentally picturing you, yourself, achieving something. For example: jumping higher or running faster or farther than you ever have before. Organizations need to create similar visions and plan accordingly (1992).[153]

---

153. *Quality Leadership Workbook.* Madison Police Department. 1992. An updated and revised *New Quality Leadership Workbook for Police: Improvement and Leadership Methods* (2014) by the author and Sabine Lobitz is available at Amazon.com

Appendix E
Outline and Key Questions:
How to Rate Your Local Police

Leadership Characteristics

1. What kind of person is the chief?

- Clear vision

- Willingness to challenge the status quo

- Take risks, be innovative, and build a coalition of support for change

- Self confidence

- Personal integrity

- Respect of community and elected officials

- Ability to inspire and motivate

2. What tone does the chief set for the agency?

- Coherent crime control strategy

- Concrete crime prevention strategy

- Defend rights of unpopular groups

- Equal delivery of community police services

3. Does the chief articulate the policies of the agency clearly and understandably?

- Speaking out and taking a stand

- Spokesperson on crime control and public safety

- Advisor on personal security

- Preserver of due process guarantees

- Defender of minority rights

- Protector of the weak and injured

- Manager of a complex bureaucracy

- Guardian of the rule of law

Policy Characteristics

4. Does the police agency have a clear sense of its objectives?

- American Bar Association: Standards Relating to the Urban Police Function

- Are there written policies for all operational practices?

- Does the police agency select the finest individuals to be police officers?

- Does the police agency provide high quality training for its officers?

- Does the police agency reinforce the minimum requirements for a good police officer?

- Effectiveness

- Integrity

- Civility and courtesy

- Health and physical fitness

5. Does the police agency guide, train, and supervise police officers in the restraint of the use of force?

6. Is the police agency willing to investigate and discipline officers engaging in misconduct?

Organizational Characteristics

- Do police officers respect individual rights?

- Does the police agency address crime and order problems by using all community resources?

- Does the police agency cooperate and coordinate with neighboring law enforcement agencies and with other agencies in the criminal justice system?

- Does the police agency communicate well with the public?

- How does the police agency approach the media?[154]

154. David C. Couper. *How to Rate Your Local Police*. Washington, DC: Police Executive Research Forum, 1983.

Appendix F
Professional Leadership Expectations:
Chief of Police

Tenure. A binding employment contract of at least seven years. A police department that needs improvement must be assured that there will be a continuity of top leadership. To think about transforming a police department in less than seven to ten years is foolhardy.

Leadership. The department leadership style must ensure the growth and development of its members. Not only must the chief officer be assured of an appropriate amount of time necessary to do the job he or she was hired to do, but the style of the chief's leadership (and that of his or her subordinate officers) is critical. To permit a chief officer to lead the department coercively and instill an atmosphere of fear within it is to shut down the kind of open and collaborative communication that is necessary for any organization seeking continuous improvement of its operations and functions.

Training. Even if the chief officer has tenure and is committed to an open, participative leadership style, the department must also be committed to providing high-quality training for everyone and have the same commitment to providing on-going training through an officer's career. Training is what develops and maintains the skills expected of a professional police officer.

Experimentation. Police in a democratic society must be willing to experiment with new ideas and concepts. This means that a police organization must develop a culture that encourages innovative thinking and challenges current practices. This is a rapidly changing, technologically-oriented world and those who serve as police must be aware of social and cultural trends and understand the diverse thinking that holds a free society together. In today's world, to remain in place is to fall behind.

Evaluation. A commitment to experimentation must be concurrent with a commitment to evaluation. A department must be willing undergo constant self-evaluation and open itself to outside research and evaluation as well. It must have a way to evaluate the results of well-thought experimentation and be open to new ideas and practices that this kind of evaluation will suggest.

Appendix G
The Law Enforcement Code of Ethics

As a law enforcement officer, my fundamental duty is:

- To serve mankind *[sic]*.

- To safeguard lives and property.

- To protect the innocent against deception, the weak against oppression or intimidation, and the peaceful against violence or disorder.

- To respect the constitutional rights of all men to liberty, equality, and justice.

I will keep my private life unsullied as an example to all.

I will maintain courageous calm in the face of danger, scorn or ridicule.

I will develop self-restraint and be constantly mindful of the welfare of others.

I will be honest in both thought and deed in both my personal and professional life.

I will be exemplary in obeying the laws of the land and the regulations of my department.

Whatever I see or hear of a confidential nature that is confided to me in my official capacity will be ever kept secret, unless revelation is necessary in the performance of my duty.

I will never act officiously or permit personal feelings, prejudices, animosities, or friendships to influence my decisions.

With no compromise for crime and with relentless prosecution of criminals, I will enforce the law courteously and appropriately without fear or favor, malice or ill will, never employing unnecessary force or violence, and never accepting gratuities.

I recognize the badge of my office as a symbol of public faith and I accept it as a public trust to be held so long as I am true to the ethics of the police service.

I will constantly strive to achieve these objectives and ideals, dedicating myself before God to my chosen profession...law enforcement.

(Adopted by the International Association of Chiefs of Police, 1957)

Appendix H
Twelve Qualities of Police

Michael Scott and I developed the following document in mid-2012. We felt there was a need to clearly build on earlier works defining the police function and develop what we believed to be the essential qualities of police in a free and democratic society. This document was put on the Internet site GoPetition.com.

We know that policing a democracy is a difficult business. It is mainly so because the government assures its citizens certain rights that limit, and even challenge, the power of the state. This is especially evident in assuring those who live in a free society the right to protest, to be secure in their persons and homes, and the right of due process.

In establishing our nation's Constitution, the founders wrote they were doing so "to form a more perfect union, establish justice, insure domestic tranquility, provide for the common defense, promote the general welfare, and secure the blessings of liberty." Although set forth nearly four score years before the establishment of the first American police agency, these aims could well be understood as the foundational statements of our system of policing. To a large extent, the American police institution exists to advance these goals and help society honor its social contract. Therefore, the quality of a democracy is heavily dependent upon the quality of its police.

Since 1829 when Richard Mayne, Charles Rowan and Robert Peel first proposed principles of policing for mid-19th century London, principles that continue to shape American policing, we believe there is ever a need to revisit these first principles and to reaffirm or adapt them, as appropriate, for the present times. Those original principles are paraphrased as follows:

1. Police exist to prevent crime and disorder.

2. Police ability to perform their duties is dependent upon public approval of police actions.

3. Police must secure the willing co-operation of the public in obeying the law to be able to secure and maintain the public's respect.

4. Police ability to secure public co-operation diminishes the need to use physical force.

5. Police preserve public support not by catering to public opinion but by demonstrating impartial service to the law.

6. Police use physical force to enforce the law or restore order only when persuasion, advice and warning is insufficient.

7. Police and the public share policing responsibilities.

8. Police should never appear to take on the powers of the judiciary.

9. Police effectiveness is to be measured by the absence of crime and disorder, not the visible evidence of police action in dealing with it.

In our own country, several major efforts sought to clarify the police function and to set broad standards for our nation's police. Each effort responded to widespread public concern about crime in America and the police role in addressing it.

The 1967 President's Commission on Law Enforcement and Administration of Justice described the complexity of the police function, the need for police to improve their relationship with the public, the need to improve the quality of police personnel and training, and the need for police to operate with greater restraint under the law. The 1973 National Advisory Commission on Criminal Justice Standards and Goals Report on Police extended the President's Commission's work by publishing more specific police organizational standards.

The 1971 American Bar Association's Standards Relating to the Police Function jointly developed and endorsed by the International Association of Chiefs of Police, were especially helpful in articulating the broad and sometimes conflicting policing objectives. In summary, they are to:

- Prevent and control conduct threatening to life and property, including serious crime.

- Aid crime victims and protect people in danger of physical harm.

- Protect constitutional guarantees, such as the right of free speech and assembly.

- Facilitate the movement of people and vehicles.

- Help those who cannot care for themselves, including the intoxicated, the addicted, the mentally ill, the physically disabled, the old, and the young.

- Resolve conflict between individuals, between groups, or between citizens and their government.

- Identify problems that have the potential for becoming more serious for individuals, the police, or the government.

- Create and maintain a feeling of community security.

Since police- and victim-reported crime rates peaked in about 1980, they have fluctuated and then, beginning in about 1990, steadily and dramatically declined to their present historically low levels. History tells us that unless fear of crime becomes a major public concern, little attention is paid to our nation's police and to what they are or are not doing, and little effort is put forth to improve the institution. But we believe that discussing our core policing principles is best done in an atmosphere that is not clouded by a national sense of alarm or panic about crime.

While our country's police are presently challenged on one hand by increasing demands upon them to address such issues as terrorism and illegal immigration, and on the other by declining fiscal resources, the relatively low crime rates allow some greater space for public discourse about the police role in society. Equally compelling is the need to reconcile core principles of democratic policing with the fast-evolving nature of information, forensic, and surveillance technology. Out of concern that some of our nation's police are undergoing a slow and persistent erosion of trust, fairness and accountability, we believe it is time to state clearly what it is police should do and be in our society.

We believe the following 12 qualities of democratic policing set forth a template that police as well as citizens and their elected representatives can use to evaluate the police institution and, if found wanting, use to guide the quest for continuous improvement.

This statement of principles is not intended to be critical of our nation's police but rather to help all of us clarify the nature of our function, public expectations, and the central importance of the police role in a society that professes to pursue justice fairly, equally, and without bias.

Qualities of Police in a Free and Democratic Society

1. Accountable
Police recognize the nature and extent of their discretionary authority and must always be accountable to the people, their elected representatives, and the law for their actions, and be as transparent as possible in their decision-making.

2. Collaborative
Police must be able to collaborate, as appropriate, with community members and other organizations in settling disagreements, choosing policing strategies, and solving policing problems. This collaborative style must also apply to the way police departments are led and managed. This means police leaders must actively listen to their officers and work with them in identifying and resolving department and community problems.

3. Educated and Trained
All police officers with arrest powers should begin their career with a broad and advanced education in the sciences and humanities. Training should consist of rigorous and extensive training courses in an adult-learning climate that teaches both the ethics and skills of democratic policing.

4. Effective and Preventive
The mark of a good police department and the officers who work within it is that they continuously seek to handle their business more effectively and fairly, emphasizing preventing crime and disorder and not merely responding to it, and applying research and practical knowledge, using problem-solving methods, toward that end.

5. Honest
Honesty and good ethical practice are essential. The search for and cultivation of these traits begin with the selection process and continue

throughout an officer's career. Only those police candidates who have demonstrated good decision-making so far in their lives should be selected.

6. Model citizen

Police officers must not only be good police officers, but good citizens as well, modeling the values and virtues of good citizenship in their professional and personal lives.

7. Peacekeeper and Protector

The police role is, above all else, that of community peacekeepers, and not merely law enforcers or crime fighters. Their training, work, and values all point towards the keeping of peace in the community. As gatekeepers to the criminal justice system, police must see themselves as defenders and protectors of Constitutional and human rights, especially for those who cannot defend or care for themselves in our society.

8. Representative

The members of police organizations must be demographically representative of the communities they serve, both because it reflects fair employment opportunities and because it enables the police to be more effective in achieving their objectives.

9. Respectful

Police officers should treat all persons with unconditional courtesy and respect, and be willing to listen to others, especially to those without social power or status. Likewise, police leaders should treat their workers with courtesy and respect their employment rights.

10. Restrained

The preservation of life should be the foundation for all police use of force. Police officers should continually prepare themselves to use physical force in a restrained and proper manner, with special training in its application to those who are mentally ill. Deadly force should be used only as a last resort and only when death or serious injury of the officer or another person is imminent. Less-than-lethal force should be preferred where possible.

11. Servant Leader

Every police officer, regardless of rank, must simultaneously be a good leader and a good servant, to the public and to the police organization. Servant leaders use their authority and influence to improve others' welfare.

12. Unbiased

Although some bias is inherent in human nature, police officers recognize that they can and should train themselves to reduce their biases and deal with all people fairly and without regard to their race, ethnicity, gender, socio-economic condition, national origin, citizenship status, or sexual orientation.

On this we stand, we who are present and former leaders of police in America. If you agree, we ask you, as a police officer, to go to http://www.gopetition.com/petitions/policing-our-nation.html and join us in signing this important statement.

Appendix I
President's Task Force on 21st Century Policing

TWELVE MAJOR RECOMMENDATIONS

BUILDING TRUST AND LEGITIMACY

1. *Law enforcement culture should embrace a guardian mindset to build public trust and legitimacy. Toward that end, police and sheriffs' departments should adopt procedural justice as the guiding principle for internal and external policies and practices to guide their interactions with the citizens they serve. (1.1)*

2. *Use of physical control equipment and techniques against vulnerable populations—including children, elderly persons, pregnant women, people with physical and mental disabilities, limited English proficiency, and others—can undermine public trust and should be used as a last resort. Law enforcement agencies should carefully consider and review their policies towards these populations and adopt policies if none are in place. (1.5.4)*

3. *Law enforcement agencies should track the level of trust in police by their communities just as they measure changes in crime. Annual community surveys, ideally standardized across jurisdictions and with accepted sampling protocols, can measure how policing in that community affects public trust. (1.7)*

4. *Law enforcement agencies should strive to create a workforce that contains a broad range of diversity including race, gender, language, life experience, and cultural background to improve understanding and effectiveness in dealing with all communities. (1.8)*

POLICY AND OVERSIGHT

5. *Law enforcement agencies should have comprehensive policies on the use of force that include training, investigations, prosecutions, data collection, and information sharing. These policies must be clear, concise, and openly available for public inspection. (2.2)*
6. *Law enforcement agency policies for training on use of force should empha-size de-escalation and alternatives to arrest or summons in situations where appropriate. (2.2.1)*
7. *Law enforcement agency policies should address procedures for implementing a layered response to mass demonstrations that prioritize de-escalation and a guardian mindset. (2.7.1)*

COMMUNITY POLICING AND CRIME REDUCTION

8. *Community policing should be infused throughout the culture and organi-zational structure of law enforcement agencies. (4.2)*
9. *Communities should support a culture and practice of policing that reflects the values of protection and promotion of the dignity of all, especially the most vulnerable. (4.4)*
10. *Because offensive or harsh language can escalate a minor situation, law enforcement agencies should underscore the importance of language used and adopt policies directing officers to speak to individuals with respect. (4.4.1)*

TRAINING AND EDUCATION

11. *Law enforcement agencies should implement ongoing, top down training for all officers in cultural diversity and related topics that can build trust and legitimacy in diverse communities. This should be accomplished with the assistance of advocacy groups that represent the viewpoints of communities that have traditionally had adversarial relationships with law enforcement. (5.9.1)*

OFFICER WELLNESS AND SAFETY

12. [Implement] an annual mental health check for officers, as well as fitness, resilience, and nutrition. (6.1.3)

Read the final report at
https://cops.usdoj.gov/RIC/Publications/cops-p341-pub.pdf

Appendix J
Guiding Principles on Police Use of Force

GUIDING PRINCIPLES ON USE OF FORCE
Police Executive Research Forum, Washington, D.C., March, 2016.

1. The sanctity of human life should be at the heart of everything an agency does.

2. Agencies should continue to develop best policies, practices, and training on use-of-force issues that go beyond the minimum requirements of *Graham v. Connor*.

3. Police use of force must meet the test of proportionality.

4. Adopt de-escalation as formal agency policy.

5. Duty to intervene: Officers need to prevent other officers from using excessive force.

6. Training academy content and culture must reflect agency values.

7. De-escalation should be a core theme of an agency's training program.

8. Mental Illness: Implement a comprehensive agency training program on dealing with people with mental health issues.

9. Tactical training and mental health training need to be interwoven to improve response to critical incidents.

10. Scenario-based training should be prevalent, challenging, and realistic.

11. Officers need access to and training in less-lethal options.

12. Personal protection shields enhance officer safety and may support de-escalation efforts during critical incidents, including situations involving persons with knives, baseball bats, or other improvised weapons that are not firearms.

Read the full report at
http://www.policeforum.org/assets/30%20guiding%20principles.pdf.

Photo Journal Through the Years

My early days in the Marines.

With Mayor Paul Soglin after the first peaceful
Mifflin Street Block Party (1973)

*Under fire as a new police chief from outside
the Madison Police Department.*

Friend and Mentor: Prof. Herman Goldstein

Teaching Quality Policing to Police Outside of Madison

Management Team Building on the Ropes Course

Working with Dr. W. Edwards Deming on Quality Policing.

*Receiving the National Police Leadership award
from my colleagues in PERF (1993).*

Parade Magazine feature in the 1980s with (clockwise)
Chief Lee Brown (Atlanta) and the late Chiefs Joe McNamara
(San Jose) and Hubert Williams (Newark).

*Graduation from seminary and off to leading
churches instead of police departments.*

Off to pastoral ministry as an Episcopal priest with a commitment to continue to work to improve police as a matter of justice, fairness and equity.

Bibliography

Albrecht, Karl and Ron Zemke. 1985. *Service America: Doing Business in the New Economy*. New York: Dow Publishing.

Bayley, David, H. 1988. "Community Policing: A Report from the Devil's Advocate." In Jack R. Green and Stephen D. Mastrofski (eds.) *Community Policing: Rhetoric or Reality?* New York: Praeger.

Bennis, Warren and Burt Nanus. 1985. *Leaders: The Strategies for Taking Charge*. New York: Harper & Row.

Bittner, Egon. 1970. *The Functions of Police in Modern Society*. Chevy Chase, MD: National Institute of Mental Health.

Bolman, Lee and Terrance Deal. 2002. *Reframing Organizations: Artistry, Choice, and Leadership*. San Francisco: Jossey-Bass.

Braiden, C. 1987. "Community Policing Nothing New Under the Sun." Unpublished manuscript. Edmonton Police Department.

Brassard, Michael and Diane Ritter. 1987. *The Memory Jogger: A Pocket Guide of Tools for Continuous Improvement and Effective Planning*, Methuen, MA: Goal/QPC.

The Challenge of Crime in a Free Society: A Report by the President's Commission on Law Enforcement and the Administration of Justice. 1967. Washington, D.C: U.S. Government Printing Office.

Chappell, Allison T. and Lonn Lanza-Kaduce. 2009. "Police Academy Socialization: Understanding the Lessons Learned in a Paramilitary-Bureaucratic Organization." *Journal of Contemporary Ethnography*. Sage Publications.

Coens, Tom and Mary Jenkins. 2000. *Abolishing Performance Appraisals: Why They Backfire and What to Do Instead*. San Francisco: Berrett-Koehler.

Collins, Jim. 2001. *Good to Great: Why Some Companies Make the Leap… and Others Don't*. New York: HarperCollins Publishers.

Couper, David C. 1971. "The Need for Excellence in Campus Policing." *The Police Chief* magazine. Washington, DC: The International Association of Chiefs of Police. January issue.

___. 1972. "The Delivery of Neighborhood Police Services." *The Police Chief* magazine. Washington, DC: The International Association of Chiefs of Police. March issue

___. 1974. "Remarks of David Couper as Director of Public Safety, Burnsville, Minnesota." Changing Police Organizations: Four Readings. United States Conference of Mayors. Washington DC: National League of Cities.

___. 1990. "Police Department Learns Ten Hard Lessons," *Quality Progress* magazine, Milwaukee, October.

___. 1994. "Seven Seeds for Policing," *FBI Law Enforcement Bulletin*, March.

___. 2015. *How to Rate Your Local Police*. Amazon.com.

___. 2017. *It's Just the Way It Is: Couper on Cops*. Amazon.com.

Couper, David C. and Sabine Lobitz. 1987. "Quality Leadership: The First Step Toward Quality Policing." *The Police Chief* magazine. Washington, DC: International Association of Chiefs of Police. April issue.

___. 1991. *Quality Policing: The Madison Experience*. Washington, D.C.: Police Executive Research Forum.

___. 1993. "Leadership for Change: A National Agenda." *The Police Chief* magazine. Washington, DC: The International Association of Chiefs of Police. December issue.

___. 2017. *The Quality Leadership Workbook*. Amazon.com.

Covey, Stephen. 1992. *Principle Centered Leadership*. New York: Simon and Schuster.

___. 1990. *Seven Habits of Highly Effective People*. New York: Simon and Schuster.

Crosby, Philip B. 1979. *Quality is Free: The Art of Making Quality Certain*. New York: Mentor Books.

Deming, W. Edwards. 1986. *Out of the Crisis*. Cambridge: MIT Center for Advanced Engineering Studies.

Eck, John and William Spelman. 1987. *Problem-solving: Problem-Oriented Policing in Newport News.* Washington, DC: Police Executive Research Forum.

Fullan, Michael. 2005. *Leadership and Sustainability: System Thinkers in Action.* Thousand Oaks, CA: Sage Publications.

Goldstein, Herman. 1990. *Problem-Oriented Policing,* New York: McGraw-Hill Publishing Company.

___. 1987. "Toward Community-Oriented Policing: Potential, Basic Requirements, and Threshold Questions." *Crime and Delinquency,* 33, 1:6-30.

___. 1979. "Improving Policing: A Problem-Oriented Approach." *Crime and Delinquency,* 23, 2:236-258

Goldstein, Herman and Charles E. Susmilch. 1982. "Experimenting with the Problem-Oriented Approach to Improving Police Service: A Report and Some Reflections on Two Case Studies." Madison, WI: University of Wisconsin Law School.

Gordon, Tom. 1978. *Leader Effectiveness Training.* New York: Bantam Books.

Guyot, Dorothy. 1979. "Bending Granite: Attempts to Change the Rank Structure of American Police Departments." *Journal of Police Science and Administration* 7 (3)

Heifetz, Ronald. 2004. *Leadership Without Easy Answers.* Cambridge: Harvard University.

Hickman, Craig R. and Michael A. Silva. 1986. *Creating Excellence: Managing Corporate Culture, Strategy, and Change in the New Age.* New York: Plume.

Imai, Masaki. 1986. *The Key to Japan's Competitive Success.* New York: Random House.

Isenberg, Jim. *Police Leadership in a Democracy: Conversations with America's Police Chiefs.* New York: CRC Press. 2010.

Johnson, David R. and Frank P. Johnson. 1987. *Joining Together: Group Theory and Group Skills,* 3rd Ed. New York: Wadsworth Publishing.

Kanter, Rosabeth Moss. 1983. *The Change Masters: Innovation and Entrepreneurship in the American Corporation.* New York: Simon & Schuster.

Manning, Peter and John Van Maanen, eds. 1978. *Policing: A View from the Street.* New York: Random House.

Naisbitt, John and Patricia Aburdene. 1985. *Re-inventing the Corporation.* New York: Warner Books.

National Advisory Commission on Civil Disorders. 1968. Supplemental Studies for the National Advisory Commission on Civil Disorders. Washington, DC: U.S. Government Printing Office.

National Research Council. 2004. *Fairness and Effectiveness in Policing: The Evidence.* Committee to Review Research on Police Policy and Practices. Wesley Skogan and Kathleen Frydl (eds.), Committee on Law and Justice, Division of Behavioral and Social Sciences and Education. Washington, D.C.: The National Academies Press.

Neiderhoffer, Arthur. 1969. *Behind the Shield.* Garden City, NY: Doubleday.

Peters, Tom. 1987. *Thriving on Chaos: Handbook for a Management Revolution.* New York: Knopf Books.

Peters, Tom and Robert H. Waterman. 1984. *In Search of Excellence.* USA: Warner Books.

Peters, Tom and Nancy Austin. 1985. *A Passion for Excellence.* New York: Warner Books.

Prenzler, Timothy. 1997. "Is There a Police Culture?" *Australian Journal of Public Administration*, 56.

Reiss, Albert. 1971. *Police and the Public.* New Haven, CT: Yale University Press.

Roberg, Roy, Kenneth Novak, and Gary Cordner. 2009. *Police and Society*, 4th edition. New York: Oxford University Press.

Rubinstein, Jonathan. 1973. *City Police.* New York: Farrar, Straus, and Giroux.

Scholtes, Peter. 1998. *The Leader's Handbook: Making Things Happen, Getting Things Done.* New York: McGraw-Hill.

Scholtes, Peter, Brian Joiner, and Barbara Streibel. 1988. *The Team Handbook*. Madison: Oriel Inc.

Scott, Michael. 2000. *Problem-Oriented Policing: Reflections on the First 20 Years*. Washington, DC: Office of Community Oriented Policing Services, U.S. Department of Justice.

___. 2006. "Implementing Crime Prevention: Lessons Learned from Problem-oriented Policing Projects." *Crime Prevention Studies*, vol. 20.

___. 2008. "Progress in American Policing?: Reviewing the National Reviews." *Law and Social Inquiry*, vol. 34, issue 1, Winter.

Sensenbrenner, Joseph. 1991. "Quality Comes to City Hall." *Harvard Business Review* (March-April), 64-75.

Sergiovanni, Thomas. 2007. *Rethinking Leadership: A Collection of Articles*, 2nd ed. Thousand Oaks, CA: Sage Publications.

Skolnick, Jerome H. and David H. Bayley. 1986. *The New Blue Line: Police Innovation in Six American Cities*. New York: The Free Press.

___. 1988. *Community Policing: Issues and Practices Around the World*. Washington, D.C.: National Institute of Justice.

Skolnick, Jerome. 1966. *Justice Without Trial: Law Enforcement in a Democratic Society*. New York: John Wiley and Sons.

Sparrow, Malcolm K., Mark H. Moore and David M. Kennedy. 1990. *Beyond 911: A New Era for Policing*. USA: Basic Books.

Tichy, Noel M. and Mary Anne DeVanna. 1986. *The Transformational Leader*. New Jersey: John Wiley and Sons.

Toch, Hans and J. Douglas Grant. 1991. *Police as Problem Solvers*. New York: Plenum Press.

Trojanowicz, Robert C. 1982. "An Evaluation of the Neighborhood Foot Patrol Program in Flint, Michigan." East Lansing: Neighborhood Foot Patrol Center, Michigan State University.

Walton, Mary. 1986. *The Deming Management Method*. New York: Dodd-Mead.

Walker, Samuel. 2005. *The New World of Police Accountability*. Thousand Oaks, CA: Sage Publications.

Wycoff, Mary Ann and Wesley G. Skogan. 1993. *Community Policing in Madison: Quality From the Inside, Out.* An Evaluation of Implementation and Impact. Technical Report. Washington, D.C.: Police Foundation.

Wycoff, Mary Ann. 1982. *The Role of Municipal Police: Research as Prelude to Changing It.* Washington, D.C.: Police Foundation.

____. 1988. "The Benefits of Community Policing: Evidence and Conjecture." In Jack R. Greene and Stephen D. Mastrofski (eds.) *Community Policing: Rhetoric or Reality?* New York: Praeger.

Weisburd, David, and Anthony A. Braga, eds. 2006. *Police Innovation: Contrasting Perspectives.* Cambridge, U.K.: Cambridge University Press.

Index

Symbols

A

B

H

I

N

O

P

Q

R

S

Made in the USA
Monee, IL
23 January 2022

89594483R00184